D1594375

THE CLASSICS
OF **WESTERN**
SPIRITUALITY

THE CLASSICS OF WESTERN SPIRITUALITY
A Library of the Great Spiritual Masters

President and Publisher
Mark-David Janus, CSP

EDITORIAL BOARD

THE NINETEENTH-CENTURY SALESIAN PENTECOST

*THE SALESIAN FAMILY OF DON BOSCO,
THE OBLATES AND OBLATE SISTERS OF
ST. FRANCIS DE SALES, THE DAUGHTERS
OF ST. FRANCIS DE SALES, AND
THE FRANSALIANS*

Introduction, Editing, Translations,
and Commentaries by
Joseph Boenzi, SDB,
Joseph F. Chorpenning, OSFS,
Suzanne C. Toczyski, and Wendy M. Wright

Foreword by
John W. O'Malley, SJ

Paulist Press
New York / Mahwah, NJ

Copyright © 2022 by Wendy M. Wright, Joseph F. Chorpenning, Suzanne C. Toczyski, and the Salesian Society of California

All rights reserved. No part of this publication may be reproduced, stored in a retrieval system, or transmitted in any form or by any means, electronic, mechanical, photocopying, recording, scanning, or otherwise without either the prior written permission of the Publisher, or authorization through payment of the appropriate per-copy fee to the Copyright Clearance Center, Inc., 222 Rosewood Drive, Danvers, MA 01923, (978) 750-8400, fax (978) 646-8600, or on the Web at www .copyright.com. Requests to the Publisher for permission should be addressed to the Permissions Department, Paulist Press, 997 Macarthur Boulevard, Mahwah, NJ 07430, (201) 825-7300, fax (201) 825-8345, or online at www.paulistpress.com.

Library of Congress Cataloging-in-Publication Data
Names: Boenzi, Joseph, author. | Chorpenning, Joseph F, author. | Toczyski, Suzanne, author. | Wright, Wendy M, author.
Title: The nineteenth-century Salesian Pentecost : the Salesian family of Don Bosco, the Oblates and Oblate Sisters of St. Francis de Sales, the Daughters of St. Francis de Sales, and the Fransalians / introduction, editing, translations, and commentaries by Joseph Boenzi, SDB, Joseph F. Chorpenning, OSFS, Suzanne Toczyski, and Wendy M. Wright ; foreword by John W. O'Malley, SJ. Description: New York / Mahwah, NJ : Paulist Press, [2022] | Series: The classics of Western spirituality | Includes bibliographical references and index. | Summary: "Translations of and commentaries on the little-known spiritual writings of Don Bosco, his collaborators, and his contemporaries involved in the Salesian Pentecost. These diverse persons, fully engaged in apostolic ministry or occupied with the demands of ordinary life as lay women and men, were at the same time engaged in conscious spiritual practices that sought the interior exchange of the heart of Jesus for the human heart"—Provided by publisher.
Identifiers: LCCN 2021038363 (print) | LCCN 2021038364 (ebook) | ISBN 9780809106301 (hardcover) | ISBN 9781587685767 (ebook)
Subjects: LCSH: Salesians—History—19th century. | Bosco, Giovanni, Saint,1815–1888.
Classification: LCC BX4045 .B64 2022 (print) | LCC BX4045 (ebook) | DDC 255/.79—dc23
LC record available at https://lccn.loc.gov/2021038363
LC ebook record available at https://lccn.loc.gov/2021038364

ISBN 978-0-8091-0630-1 (hardcover)
ISBN 978-1-58768-576-7 (e-book)

Published by Paulist Press
997 Macarthur Boulevard
Mahwah, New Jersey 07430
www.paulistpress.com

Printed and bound in Colombia

CONTENTS

CONTENTS

FOREWORD

John W. O'Malley, SJ

I grew up in a town in Ohio so small that it could not afford a Catholic school. During the winter, two or three nuns came from a larger town on Sunday mornings to teach us basic catechism for a half hour between the two masses. This meant that I received my real understanding of Catholicism from my parents, especially my mother.

When she was about eleven years old, my grandfather sent her as a boarding student to a Young Ladies' Academy, Mount de Chantal, in nearby Wheeling, West Virginia. As the school's name suggests, it was run by the Sisters of the Visitation of Holy Mary, the order founded by Sts. Jane Frances de Chantal and Francis de Sales.

My mother received an excellent education at Mount de Chantal—six years of French, four of Latin, foundational courses in literature and the sciences, as well as a fine training in both piano and voice. She at the same time appropriated an appreciation of Catholicism that was gentle and inclusive and that was based on the lived assumption that she was beloved of God. Catholicism was a positive, comforting, and even exciting religion.

That was the appreciation of Catholicism that she imparted to me and that has stayed with me all my life. I could not name it, but I noted the contrast with some of my Catholic cousins whose religion seemed to me rigid and rules driven. When after high school, I entered the Jesuits and made the thirty-day retreat using the *Spiritual Exercises* of St. Ignatius, the part I most relished was the "Contemplation for Obtaining the Love of God." Nothing was more consonant with what my mother had taught me about our faith.

Only decades later when I finally read *The Introduction to the Devout Life* did I fully understand my upbringing and the spirituality with which it was imbued. I cannot adequately express how grateful I feel toward the nuns of Mount de Chantal for the influence they had on my mother's spirituality and through her on me. I often say, only half in jest, that the school that most profoundly influenced me was a school I never attended. It was in fact a school I never could have attended because I was a boy.

Once I began to look at the *Introduction* as a professional historian, I came to an appreciation of it that went beyond how deeply it has affected me personally even before I read it. As is often said, it is part of a great revival of Catholic spirituality that marked the sixteenth and early seventeenth centuries, a period of spiritual luminaries such as Teresa of Ávila, Ignatius Loyola, Louise de Marillac, and Vincent de Paul, to name only a few. More to the point, it was a period that produced an outburst of spiritual writings that have become classics.

In that context, the *Introduction* has a number of noteworthy characteristics, which includes being free of any trace of religious controversy or preoccupation with orthodoxy at a time when few authors could abstain from such topics. This is all the more remarkable because St. Francis directly felt the impact of the fierce religious controversies by not being able as bishop of Geneva to reside in his own proper see because it was radically Protestant.

But among all the *Introduction*'s noteworthy traits, I want to call attention to three. The first is its literary genre. It may come as a surprise to learn that treatises on the spiritual life were a relatively new genre in religious literature until the early sixteenth century. What was available until then were lives of saints, miracle stories, accounts of special revelations, collections of spiritual aphorisms such as *The Imitation of Christ*, and similar works. Missing were treatises outlining steps in a program to help persons get in touch with themselves and with God acting within them.

The first real breakthrough came with Erasmus's *Handbook of the Christian Soldier*, first published in 1501. Although a program of moral improvement, it helped solidify the model of a book with an organized program of how to live the Christian life. Other authors began to follow Erasmus's lead. Among the more important was *The Spiritual Combat* published in 1589 by the Italian Lorenzo Scupoli.

Then came in 1609 *The Introduction to the Devout Life*, with which the genre achieved maturity. Published in the early years of the seventeenth century, it moreover marked the shift in religious leadership from Spain to France and was thus one of the first glories of France's "great century," *le Grand Siècle.*

The second feature to which I will call attention is its positive message about human nature's orientation to goodness and its deep and innate openness to divine love. This stands in striking contrast to the contempt of the world and obsession with human sinfulness that was almost axiomatic in the lived experience of the spiritual life that gained force in the Middle Ages. The assumption prevailed that the harsher one treated one's body and neutralized its impulses the closer one came to God.

That tradition began to weaken with the enterprise of St. Thomas Aquinas and other Scholastics to show the compatibility between nature and grace and continued two centuries later with the Christian anthropology of the Italian humanists. With the Jesuits' *Constitutions* in the mid-sixteenth century, the positive anthropology received an institutional form. Even so, Scupoli's *Spiritual Combat*, a best seller in its day, presented the spiritual life as an ongoing battle against one's lower impulses.

Relatively close on its heels, however, came the *Introduction*, a book that utterly transcended the earlier tradition dominated by unrelenting asceticism. It turned spirituality into a loving exchange between God and the soul.

St. Francis wrote the *Introduction* for the benefit of people living "in the world," which means that what he proposed is doable for everybody and does not need special circumstance such as a monastery to be practiced. That is the third trait to which I will call attention. Although other works such as the *Spiritual Exercises* of St. Ignatius were written for a wide public, none before the *Introduction* was as explicitly and specifically tailored for that public.

Nonetheless, despite the *Introduction*'s groundbreaking qualities, it made effective use of time-honored practices of meditation and gave similarly time-honored advice on how persons living in the world might deal with situations challenging to their relationship to God. In terms of the major theme of the *Introduction to the Devout*

Life, the *Homilies on the Song of Songs*, which as abbot St. Bernard had preached to his monks in the first half of the twelfth century, delivered the powerful message of the human heart's yearning for God and of God's yearning to abide in such hearts. St. Francis had studied the Song of Songs under a Benedictine monk when he was still a student in Paris, and he was certainly familiar with Bernard's *Homilies*. That work, deeply imbedded in the earlier tradition, clearly influenced the *Introduction*.

Thus, Francis was able to bring both new and old elements together in a groundbreaking synthesis that was at the same time solidly traditional. That was the momentous achievement of the *Introduction to the Devout Life* and of St. Francis de Sales.

The core message of St. Francis de Sales and the Salesian tradition that spoke so powerfully to me and helped shape my life—human nature is oriented to goodness and the human heart has an innate yearning for God, who yearns to abide there—also struck a responsive chord in and captured the imaginations of men and women across nineteenth-century Catholic Europe who were working to rebuild and renew the Church in the aftermath of the devastating consequences of the French Revolution. What linked these individuals was not a common apostolic activity, but the retrieval of the heart-to-heart quality and communication of Salesian spirituality, which was at once attractive, accessible, and able to be practiced by everybody. They found in Francis de Sales and the Salesian spiritual tradition the resources they needed to reinvigorate the Church of their day. This phenomenon, known as the nineteenth-century Salesian Pentecost, is the focus of this volume in the Classics of Western Spirituality series that is a major contribution to making this important chapter in church history more widely known and understood.

ABOUT THE CONTRIBUTORS

Joseph Boenzi, SDB is professor of theology and director of the Institute of Salesian Studies at the Dominican School of Theology and Philosophy, GTU, Berkeley, California, and Università Pontificia Salesiana, Rome. Fr. Boenzi's research and teaching have focused on Salesian studies, the spirituality of daily life, new ecclesial movements, charisms (Holy Spirit, charismatic gifts, consecrated life), spiritual accompaniment (evangelization and education, Salesian tradition of spiritual direction), and Western traditions in spirituality. An internationally sought-after speaker and retreat leader, he is the author of *Saint Francis de Sales, Life and Spirit* (2013) and *San Francisco de Sales: su espíritu e influencia* (2000). His translations include Joseph Aubry's *Savio, A Study Guide to Accompany "Saint Dominic Savio" by Saint John Bosco* (2002). Among his many Salesian-related articles are studies on "Don Bosco and the Conditions of Pre-industrial Youth in His Times" in *Seminare* 38 (July–December 2014), "Reconstructing Don Albera's Reading List" in *Ricerche Storiche Salesiane* 63, 33, no. 2 (2014), "Spreading the Name and Work of Francis de Sales during the 1600s through the 1800s" in *Sviluppo del carisma di don Bosco fino alla metà del secolo XX: Atti del Congresso Internazionale di Storia Salesiana* (Rome 2014), and "I tempi e le circostanze che indussero Francesco di Sales a comporre e pubblicare l'Introduzione alla vita devota," in *Salesianum* 74, no. 4 (2013). Presently he is Superior of the Salesian House of Studies in Berkeley, California.

Joseph F. Chorpenning, OSFS is editorial director of Saint Joseph's University Press in Philadelphia, president of the International Commission for Salesian Studies (ICSS), and cochair of the International Salesian Scholars Seminar. His publications in the area of Salesian Studies include translations and critical editions of Francis de Sales's *Spiritual Exercises* (1993) and *Sermons on Saint Joseph* (2000), edited books (i.e., *Encountering Anew the Familiar: The "Introduction to the Devout Life" at 400 Years* [2012] and *Human Encounter in the Salesian Tradition: Collected Essays Commemorating the 4th Centenary of the Initial Encounter of St. Francis de Sales and St. Jane Frances de Chantal* [2007]), as well as numerous articles published in peer-reviewed, refereed scholarly books and journals. Among his recent publications are "The Dynamics of Divine Love: Francis de Sales's Picturing of the Biblical Mystery of the Visitation," *Intersections: Interdisciplinary Studies in Early Modern Culture* 48 (2017); "*Lectio divina* and Francis de Sales's Picturing of the Interconnection of Human and Divine Hearts," *Intersections: Interdisciplinary Studies in Early Modern Culture* 33 (2014); and the article on Francis de Sales in *The Oxford Guide to the Historical Reception of Augustine* (2013). Fr. Chorpenning's current research focuses on the founding of the Oblates of St. Francis de Sales as a retrieval (*ressourcement*) and contemporizing (*aggiornamento*) of Francis de Sales in nineteenth-century France.

Suzanne Toczyski, PhD is professor of French at Sonoma State University in northern California. Her research includes work on French seventeenth-century theater (Pierre Corneille, Jean Racine), women's writing (Madeleine de Scudéry, Jacqueline Pascal, Gilberte Pascal), moralists (Blaise Pascal), and the travel narratives of the French missionary Jean-Baptiste Labat, with a focus on food and culture. She has also published articles on contemporary Caribbean novels by Gisèle Pineau and Patrick Chamoiseau. In addition to her work in *The Salesian Pentecost*, her current project is a series of articles examining the representation of women in St. Francis de Sales's *Treatise on the Love of God*, published in 1616. Dr. Toczyski has also made brief forays into works by Lilas Desquiron, Virginia Woolf, Camara Laye, Eugene O'Neill, Charles Baudelaire, Antoine de Saint-

Exupéry, Jean-Jacques Rousseau, and Choderlos de Laclos. Dr. Toczyski was editor of *French 17: An Annual Descriptive Bibliography of French Seventeenth-Century Studies* from 2000 to 2008, having served as a contributing editor from 1997 to 2000. She received the Sonoma State Teaching Excellence Award in 2006.

Wendy M. Wright, PhD is professor emerita of theology at Creighton University, and affiliated faculty at the Institute of Contemporary Spirituality at Oblate School of Theology, San Antonio. Professor Wright's scholarly work has focused on the Salesian spiritual tradition. Among her books are *Bond of Perfection: Jeanne de Chantal and François de Sales (1985/2001)*; *Francis de Sales and Jane de Chantal: Letters of Spiritual Direction* in the Paulist Press Classics of Western Spirituality Series (1988); *Francis de Sales: Introduction to the Devout Life and Treatise on the Love of God* (2005); *A Retreat With Francis de Sales, Jane de Chantal and Aelred of Rievaulx: Befriending Each Other in God* (1996); *Sacred Heart: Gateway to God* (2002); and *Heart Speaks to Heart: the Salesian Tradition* (2004). Recent articles include "The Visitation Stream of Salesian Spirituality" in *Love Is the Perfection of the Mind: Salesian Studies in Honor of Alexander T. Pocetto, OSFS* (Salesian Center, 2017); "Abandoned for Love: the Gracious Legacy of French Spiritual Traditions," and "Captured Yet Free: the Rich Symbolism of the Heart in French Spirituality" in *Surrender to Christ for Mission: French Spiritual Traditions* (Liturgical Press, 2018); "The Doctor of Love and Fear of the Lord" in *Saving Fear in Christian Spirituality* (University of Notre Dame, 2019); and "He Opened His Side: Francis de Sales and the Exchange of Divine and Human Hearts" in *Mysticism and Contemporary Life: Essays in Honor of Bernard McGinn* (Crossroad, 2019).

I

INTRODUCTION

The Nineteenth-Century Salesian Pentecost

Wendy M. Wright

Here we are, like new Apostles blazing with the sacred fire
  of love;
may we carry it everywhere, and, like them,
win all hearts in order to bring them all to you!
Give us Souls, Lord, and we will leave the rest to you.

Caroline Carré, *Journal*, Pentecost, May 16, 1875[1]

The story of Roman Catholicism's European flowering during what historians refer to as the "long nineteenth century" (1789–1914) is complex and dramatic.[2] Arising from the turbulent political and social transformations that began with the French Revolution (1789–99), which swept away the very bases upon which European monarchies and the Roman Catholic Church were grounded, this unanticipated flowering of Catholic life and practice is a story of spiritual renewal and innovation lead by persons enlivened by a vision of the beneficence of divine love that ardently seeks human response. A significant chapter of that story is associated with the name of seventeenth-century French-speaking Savoyard bishop Francis de Sales (1567–1622) and the Salesian spiritual tradition that springs from his unique insights.[3]

So many fresh expressions of the Salesian spirit came to life in the nineteenth century that the widespread movement has been

1

described by French scholar Henri l'Honoré as the "Salesian Pentecost."[4] The Pentecost l'Honoré invoked is, of course, the seminal event marking the birth of the Christian church as recorded in the Acts of the Apostles (Acts 2:1–31).[5] Scripture records that fifty days after the Jewish feast of Passover, when Jesus's apostles were gathered together in Jerusalem in the upper room they had often frequented with their now-risen Lord, a powerful wind filled the entire house and the Holy Spirit descended upon each of them in the form of tongues of fire enabling them to speak in diverse languages. This dynamic action displayed the nature of the divine itself: a self-giving, communicative, and inspiriting life that connects heaven and earth and binds diverse persons together in unity. Thus, the Pentecost theme aptly captures the essence of what happened among a diverse group of Roman Catholics in that long nineteenth century who found the spiritual vision of Francis de Sales resonating with the promptings of their own hearts.

In that era, when miracles, apparitions, and prophecies dominated the European Catholic imagination, mass-produced holy cards were exceptionally popular. Cards like those depicting the legendary virgin martyr Philomena, venerated for her healing powers by the celebrated country priest-confessor, the Curé d'Ars (1786–1859), were widely circulated.[6] But holy cards of saints associated less with miraculous powers and viewed more as exemplars of the fullness of Catholic faith were also in vogue.[7] In this way Francis de Sales was recalled and so his image was frequently reproduced. During his lifetime, de Sales had been much admired, especially as a model bishop of the Catholic reform, for his artfully written books, and as founder of the Order of the Visitation of Holy Mary, an innovative women's congregation.[8] That legacy endured and resulted in his relatively rapid beatification (1661) and canonization (1665), as well as his subsequent declaration as doctor of the church (1877).[9]

Those nineteenth-century "Sulpician" style mass-produced holy cards (so named because they could be purchased in the center of Paris at the famous church of St. Sulpice), always depicted Francis de Sales with a fiery heart either held in his hand or hovering in the air above him. Sometimes the enflamed heart depicted was the Sacred Heart, but the bishop's own heart was always explicitly referenced. This iconographic identity was not new: the flaming heart had long been seen as an appropriate image to express the essence of Salesian spirituality. In a more artistically sophisticated way, the imagery had been highlighted at the celebrations of the beatification and canonization of the Savoyard. The renowned Jesuit impresario Claude-François Menestrier designed the plans for the celebrations held in Annecy as well as in Grenoble. He made extensive use of emblems, processions, fireworks, and sermons: religious theater of all sorts. Chief among the persistent visual and auditory elements of these celebrations were fire and light, thought to capture the essence of the saint's spirituality. A fiery globe set off during the fireworks and a heart enflamed by rays of sunlight poised upon a bonfire were among the dramatic offerings. These recalled a fiery globe believed to have appeared in the bishop's room while he was composing his magisterial work, the *Treatise on the Love of God* (1616). Other emblematic treatments of the saint's life, notably Adrien Gambert's popular 1664 *La Vie symbolique de François de Sales*, circulated and fixed what was to become the distinctive iconography of de Sales—the fiery heart, symbol of the saint's heart set aflame by divine love, which, like a mirror, reflects that love to other human hearts.[10]

Likewise, the Salesian Pentecost that emerged two centuries later is a movement aptly captured by the image of the heart on fire with divine love: a powerful, communicative fire that spreads with vigor, enlightening and inspiring all who are swept up in its warmth. In the wake of the upheavals that launched the long nineteenth century and that ultimately transformed Western Europe and the Catholic Church, a network of individuals formed to promote a freshly invigorated faith. The spirit of Francis de Sales, the saint with the heart enflamed with divine love, animated them. In the centuries after his death, de Sales was especially revered in the regions surrounding his homeland of Savoy.[11] The Salesian Pentecost radiated out from there.

In the Diocese of Annecy, presiding bishop Pierre Joseph Rey (1770–1842), charismatic preacher Joseph-Marie Favre (1791–1838), and parish priest Pierre-Marie Mermier (1790–1862) were spurred by the missionary example and spirit of their earlier Savoyard countryman Francis de Sales to launch missions for the re-evangelization of Savoy. Under Bishop Rey, Mermier, along with five other diocesan priests, formed the Missionaries of St. Francis de Sales of Annecy (later the Fransalians), a congregation that conducted missions in the Salesian style.[12] In time, Mermier collaborated with Claudine Echernier (1801–69) to found the Congregation of the Sisters of the Cross of Chavanod for the purpose of educating poor country girls. Before long, what had begun as an internal project to re-evangelize Savoyard territory soon became an order that worked mainly overseas, principally in India.

From the Piedmont came seminary instructor Giuseppe Cafasso (1811–60), one of the luminous "social saints" of Turin, also known as the "Saint of the Gallows," and his remarkable pupil John (Don) Bosco (1815–88), who hailed from the rural hamlet of Becchi in the Piedmont and whose deep immersion into the spirit of de Sales under Cafasso was to indelibly shape his vision. The gentle Salesian, heart-to-heart way of proceeding was to be the hallmark of the religious family Don Bosco would eventually establish. Bosco's Festive Oratory of St. Francis de Sales became the site where he and his fledgling group ministered to the neglected and abandoned boys of Turin. The revival of the Salesian spirit in the Piedmont was typically linked to efforts to address social needs.[13] Eventually, a vast Salesian family blossomed under Bosco's supervision, comprising a men's community, the Salesians of Don Bosco; a parallel women's group, the Daughters of Mary Help of Christians dedicated to the education of poor girls; and a lay confraternity known as the Union of Salesian Cooperators. Maria Mazzarello (1837–81) from the rural Piedmontese region of Mornese was the Daughters' first superior.[14]

Although during his lifetime Francis de Sales as bishop of Geneva was never able to reside in his episcopal see, which was a Calvinist stronghold, his memory remained vitally alive there among the Catholic community. His later successor, Swiss-born Gaspard Mermillod (1824–92), had dreams of evangelization fueled by the Salesian spirit. Among Mermillod's most successful efforts was the initial sponsorship of the lay Association of St. Francis de Sales, an initiative approved by Pope Pius IX that was originally designed to convert "strayed brethren" of the Protestant persuasion. That association would flourish and eventually spread the Salesian spirit across Europe.

De Sales may have been especially alive for those who claimed him as their regional saint but, just as in his see, the Savoyard would posthumously win the hearts of Paris as well. Chief among his disciples in the capital was Louis-Gaston de Ségur (1820–81), a man of noble heritage whose immediate family was religiously indifferent but who was converted by a gift of a copy of de Sales's *Introduction to the Devout Life* from his pious Russian grandmother. Once ordained and later elevated to the episcopal office, de Ségur was filled with a desire to evangelize among the people of the capital, notable for its lack of religious adherence. To this end, he was in contact with like-minded ecclesiastics like Genevan bishop Mermillod, who appointed de Ségur president of the central governing committee for his lay Association of St. Francis de Sales. Archbishop de Ségur contacted fellow bishops all over Europe and convinced forty dioceses to sponsor the association. By the time of his death, worldwide membership of the lay group was estimated at close to two million. Its goals were the defense of the faith against the Protestant challenge and the reanimation of faith among a de-Christianized and religiously indifferent French society.

The association was not the only initiative designed to spread the Salesian message that Archbishop de Ségur nurtured. Among his protégés who played a role in the burgeoning Catholic revival was Paris-born Henri Chaumont (1838–96), who made a special study of Francis de Sales's writings and conceived of an association of laity dedicated to a program of perfection under the principles outlined in de Sales's *Introduction to the Devout Life* (1609).[15] It was in the confessional of his parish of Sainte-Clothilde that Chaumont became aware of the presence of Madame Caroline Carré de Malberg (1829–91), wife of military commandant Paul Carré and a former pupil at the Visitation monastery school in Metz. Under Chaumont's direction, this spiritually mature woman flourished: he encouraged her to follow the rule of life that he had synthesized. Eventually, amid disruptions caused by chaotic political upheavals, Chaumont and Madame de Carré went on to found the Daughters of St. Francis de Sales.[16] The aims of this group of women were personal sanctification and apostolic action on behalf of the faith. Eventually, the Daughters, impelled by the dynamism of those they attracted, branched out and gave birth to several different apostolates, including overseas evangelization. Archbishop de Ségur was deemed "grandfather" of the lay society. For his part, Chaumont went on to found two other associations inspired by Salesian spirituality, a society of priests and a men's association.

The networks of Salesian evangelization spread out from Paris into the Champagne region and the city of Troyes. It was from that commune that the remarkable superior of the Visitation monastery, Mary de Sales Chappuis (1793–1875) would exercise profound influence on the spreading Salesian Pentecost.[17] In 1826, Mary was sent as superior to the Visitation monastery in Troyes, which had lost much of its original spirit, where she instilled a profound love for the distinctive Salesian spirituality and became known as the "Good Mother." At the Visitation boarding school attached to the community, de Sales's *Introduction to the Devout Life* was the instructional centerpiece for the students, the majority of whom would embrace marriage and family life.

In 1841 the newly ordained priest Louis Brisson (1817–1908) was assigned as catechist and confessor for the school. Before long, he became chaplain of the monastery itself and formed a unique partnership with Mother Chappuis. When Louis Gaston de Ségur's appeal regarding the Catholic association reached the Diocese of Troyes, the response of both Brisson and Mother Chappuis was enthusiastic. He was appointed diocesan director, and she assumed the role of treasurer of the association. As theirs was a region with few Protestants to convert and where the needs of migrant youths were critical, it became another aim of the regional association to safeguard morals among poor and working-class young women.[18]

A former student of the Troyes Visitandine convent boarding school, Léonie Aviat (1844–1914), had approached the Good Mother about joining the Visitation community. When she presented herself as an entrant, Brisson and Chappuis were in discernment about the need for ministry to young women flooding the cities in the wake of industrialization. On retreat, Léonie became convinced that God was calling her to this fledgling venture and soon assumed the name Sister Frances de Sales and the leadership of an active religious community named the Oblate Sisters of St. Francis de Sales.[19] Léonie was invested in the habit of the new congregation by Bishop Gaspard Mermillod, who over the years had closely followed the expanding fire in Troyes.

The men's congregation charged with spreading the Salesian spirit that Mother Chappuis perceived as destined to come into being next emerged from the Pentecost at Troyes. Formation for both this men's community and the Oblate Sisters was rooted in the *Spiritual Directory* that de Sales had originally composed for the nascent Visitation community. The immediate need that prompted the creation of the men's institution was the education of young men. Despite opposition and the chaos generated by the declaration of the Franco-Prussian War (1870–71), the college of St. Bernard opened, as funding and vocations to the new congregation—the Oblates of St. Francis de Sales—presented themselves and students for the school appeared. Soon requests from nearby dioceses flooded in. As the group grew, their outreach extended beyond the classroom to care of working-class children and the ministry of preaching. The leaders of the Troyes Pentecost responded to the changing industrialized urban world, both in the outreach of their ministries and in their positive valuation of labor and laborers.[20]

The Salesian Pentecost thus flourished throughout Europe, sustained by these diverse local efforts linked through a trans-European network of similar endeavors. Archbishop de Ségur was to have repeated contact with the promoters of the Pentecost in Troyes and Paris. Brisson went on pilgrimage to Annecy and to Geneva, meeting with Mermillod.[21] The year 1859 saw Brisson in Paris gathering information about hostels for young women. And it was there that de Ségur accepted Brisson's invitation to come to the annual meeting of the association in Troyes. In 1866, Mermillod, now coadjutor bishop of Geneva, was invited to preach for the association while visiting Troyes. The year 1867 saw Brisson in Geneva consulting with Mermillod about the constitutions for the emerging Oblates of St. Francis de Sales. That same year Mermillod again visited de Ségur in Paris. The following year Mermillod was in Troyes for the investiture of the Oblate Sisters and, with de Ségur, was present at their profession. The year 1888 marked a reunion of Brisson and Mermillod in Rome. That same year the Genevan bishop sponsored a eucharistic congress in the French capital that Brisson also attended. During a period when he was experiencing difficulties with his bishop, Brisson had made a trip to Rome and on the way, he stopped in Turin and met with Don Bosco, whose work on behalf of marginalized youth was by this time well known by de Ségur and others. The Frenchman consulted his Piedmontese host about the difficulties of founding a community and encountering episcopal opposition, realities Bosco knew well.[22] For his part, Don Bosco kept abreast not only of the Troyes Pentecost but the far-flung efforts of evangelization emanating from Paris among the Daughters of St. Francis de Sales, especially commending them for their support of mission work overseas.[23]

Brisson was similarly consulted by others engaged in the Salesian Pentecost. Henri Chaumont, protégée of de Ségur, was tightly linked to the Troyes Pentecost. His dream of founding a lay society emerged at the same time that Mother Chappuis and Brisson were founding the Oblate Sisters. Chaumont was inspired to establish, if not quite a parallel, another sort of women's association nurtured by Francis de Sales's vision. In 1868, Chaumont made his first pilgrimage to Annecy, stopping en route to Troyes, where he was welcomed by Brisson and sat at the feet of the Good Mother, whom he considered an "oracle" and "one of Our Lord's most privileged souls just like St. Francis de Sales."[24] This was followed by a stop in Geneva, where Gaspar Mermillod, fueled by his own dreams of spreading the Salesian charism, approved Chaumont's plan for a lay society "in the spirit of St. Francis de Sales."[25]

All these comings and goings point to the extraordinary and widespread network of creativity known as the Salesian Pentecost. Whether fueled by the Visitation monasteries, by Francis de Sales's literary productions or the works of those who were influenced by the Savoyard, by the reputations of the Salesian saints, or by de Sales's memory as missionary and evangelist, the Salesian spirit came to full flower in the nineteenth century. It was indeed a Pentecost with women and men from diverse regions and social backgrounds enflamed with the fire of the love of God, communicating that love heart to heart in myriad ways.

As does any living spiritual tradition, the Salesian one at its seventeenth-century origins reflected the intellectual, ecclesial, social, and political era in which it came into being. Yet, as does any enduring tradition, Salesian spirituality developed and grew over the centuries, continuing to reflect the changing world in which its adherents found themselves. An essence perdures, an essential vision is maintained, yet creative adaptation takes place. Fresh rich insights are mined from the legacy. The varied communities and thinkers that make up the Salesian Pentecost of the long nineteenth century forged innovative communities with differing emphases and fresh ministries that took the Salesian spirit into new territory. What *can* be said is that what united these varied expressions of Salesian spirituality is the cultivation, in diverse ways, of a particular quality of heart. This remains true for all the manifestations of Salesian lifestyle and charisms that emerged over time.[26] That vision of a world of hearts transformed was the essence of the spirituality that Francis de Sales lived and wrote of so persuasively.[27]

"LIVE JESUS!" THE TAPROOT OF SALESIAN SPIRITUALITY

It can be said that persons known as "founders" of Christian spiritual schools or traditions each seized upon a particular scriptural passage or image that became the lens through which they interpreted the entire Christian message and the way it is most authentically lived. For Francis de Sales, Matthew 11:28–29, "Come to me... and learn from me; for I am gentle and humble in heart," is the clarifying optic through which not only the Christian life but the entire divine-human enterprise can be focused. De Sales, bishop of Geneva though resident in Annecy due to the Calvinist occupation of his see city, was propelled by the energies of the Catholic reform movement to employ his considerable talents in progressive pastoral work that included evangelization,[28] preaching,[29] writing,[30] spiritual direction,[31] and, with widowed baroness Jane de Chantal (1572–1641), the foundation in 1610 of a women's community, the Visitation of Holy Mary.[32]

Trained as a young man in the tradition of Christian humanism at the Parisian Jesuit College of Clermont and then more broadly at the University of Padua, Francis was well schooled in the depth and breadth of classical learning, literature, rhetoric, philosophy, canon and civil law, patristic and medieval thought, Scholastic theology, and Scripture studies.[33] As Francis was intimately familiar with the biblical word and hermeneutically well informed,[34] Matthew 11:28–29 was certainly not the only biblical inspiration from which his unique spiritual vision emerged. Francis's sense of the divine-human drama is saturated throughout with the language of the Song of Songs read as a love story between the human person and the divine lover.[35] But it is that passage in Matthew 11 that gives the clearest view of the underlying vision that he preached and taught so eloquently. That vision has been described as a "world of hearts."[36]

God, in the Savoyard's spiritual vision, can be said metaphorically to be possessed of a heart that is the source of all that is. God's heart is life-giving: a womb, a fountain, a vital restless energy that breathes and beats, pulses and acts. In its trinitarian essence the divine heart consists of the mutual and reciprocal love of the Father and Son, which in turn breathes forth the Spirit and in its generative dynamism overflows, creating all that exists. The divine heart imminent in creation acts relationally and dynamically as well. Human hearts are then, for the Savoyard, the site where the divine image and likeness is most clearly discovered. Human hearts are created to know and love God and they are, like their divine counterpart, dynamic and creative. For de Sales, all human hearts are oriented toward the good and toward God. Divine and human hearts are designed for union, to breath and beat together. This "optimistic" view of human capacity is linked to a corresponding view of the gracious and beneficent desire of God, who is love itself, to be united with humankind.[37]

But clearly human hearts, tarnished by sin, are not one with the heart of God. Thus, what is needed is an intermediary heart, fully divine yet fully human, that is model and mediator, allowing human hearts to become what they were created to be. That is the crucified heart of Jesus Christ, who invites all to come and learn from him for he is gentle and humble. Francis de Sales read this Matthean passage as an eschatological one, a disclosure of the very heart of God: a revelation of what the entire gospel ultimately preached. God's-kingdom-realized was thus revealed in a gentleness and humility that completely over-turns the values of the accepted order.[38] It is not power over others, self-assertion, or wealth that characterizes God's reign but love itself, the "queen" of all virtues, exercised primarily through all the intimate, "little" relational virtues, such as humility, gentleness, patience, simplicity, and cordiality.[39] In his typical charming style, de Sales wrote,

> The queen of bees never takes to the fields, without being surrounded by all her workers. And love never comes into a heart to dwell there without its entourage of other virtues.... There are virtues that have an almost universal use and that should not only act on their part, but also spread their qualities to the actions of all the other virtues. Occasions do not often present themselves to practice bravery, magnanimity, or brilliance, but gentleness, temperance, honesty, and humility are virtues that ought to tinge all the actions of our lives. There are more noble virtues than these but the use of these is more important.[40]

This was not a sentimental vision but a prophetic one, for it was born in the context of the violent tumult of the French Wars of Religion (1562–1629) that played out the continuing drama of the splintering of Western Christendom on the theater of French soil.[41] France especially was rent in two as a country with a religiously divided population and a crisis of succession.[42] The result was a prolonged bloody conflict that divided the country, Catholic versus Protestant and militant Catholics versus their moderate coreligionists, and affected the surrounding regions for decades. Francis de Sales's youth and adult ecclesial ministry was enfolded in this violent atmosphere. His irenic vision was both deeply personal, emerging from spiritual crisis, but also reflected his land of origin: during de Sales's lifetime the duchy of Savoy was notable for its political moderation and toleration.[43]

Francis lived amid not only these virulent conflicts but also a period of spiritual renewal and creative experimentation within the Roman Catholic world. Reform, renewal, and innovation characterized the church in his era. New orders, new spiritual movements, new translations of classic spiritual literature, and newly penned treatises fueled the widespread and intense desire for a deeper and more authentic interior life among all segments of society. Spiritual direction flourished as did collaboration between reform-minded men and women.[44] Even as the most overt conflicts in France were somewhat quelled during the reign of Henry IV (1553–1610), the spiritual dynamism of reform continued, and innovative charitable works flourished.[45] Francis de Sales would become one of the leading lights of this significant and powerful renewal. His vision, appropriately described as mystical theology, captured the imagination of his contemporaries.[46]

Salesian discipleship was thus about both deepening the life of faith and a prophetic witness born of the energy of religious reform in the midst of a violent civil and religious conflict and fueled by the fires of a widespread spiritual awakening. Discipleship consisted in a radical exchange of hearts, the practice of "living Jesus" through the cultivation of virtue, especially the "little virtues." Both individual and communal discipleship required the lifelong opening of hearts to be transformed and inhabited by the heart of the crucified one. To his followers Francis wrote, "I have wished above all to engrave and inscribe on your heart this holy and sacred motto, 'Live Jesus!'…With St. Paul, you can say these holy words: 'It is no longer I that live but Christ lives in me.'"[47]

This profound transformation was not to take place solely between the individual and God. Prayer, participation in the sacramental life of the church, and various forms of individual spiritual practice were absolutely essential, but human hearts were meant to beat not only in rhythm with the divine heart but also with each other as well. All forms of love, in this Salesian universe, have their source and end in divine love. Love of God, love of others, spousal love, celibate love, familial love, love of friends, love of enemies, and love of self, if rightly understood and directed, are all channels through which love itself flows. All forms of human interaction are therefore significant in the Salesian "world of hearts." Created by and for love, women and men realize their true identity as they allow all their relations to be guided by and attentive to the ultimate source of love. Hearts claimed by the gentle, humble heart of Jesus thus in this way draw other hearts to themselves with the force of love itself. For the bishop then, all forms of communications are imagined as "winning hearts" by and for the gentle Jesus, whose heart opened wide on the cross to reveal the infinite depth and breadth of divine love itself.[48]

THE LEGACY

Of his many accomplishments, it was chiefly de Sales's own writings, the Order of the Visitation of Holy Mary (which later would come to be identified with the emergent devotion to the Sacred Heart), and his enduring reputation for sanctity, fueled by a series of widely circulated biographies, that would carry this vision of a world of hearts beyond the early modern period into the modern world.[49] As a spiritual teacher, Francis de Sales had a special gift for directing laity, especially women.[50] In the overall revitalization of the early modern Catholic Church he felt that the engagement of all segments of society was crucial. Others of his notable contemporaries focused on reform of the priesthood,[51] took up care of the poor and marginalized,[52] and promoted a revitalization of religious life.[53] For de Sales, women and the laity were key, as is illustrated by the publication of his ever-popular *Introduction to the Devout Life*.[54]

The *Introduction* grew out of his correspondence with women seeking a deeper faith life. Its pages are addressed to "Philothea" (feminine for "Lover of God"), and they introduce readers to advice about spiritual growth in such a way as to adapt it to their vocational, social, and civic circumstances. Composed of structured meditations, devotional practices, advice for the practice of virtue in daily life and relationships, chiefly marriage and friendship, and remedies for the pitfalls that plague spiritual practice, the *Introduction* is a manual that directs its readers in the cultivation of an ordinary life transfigured by the Spirit of God. The *Introduction* was widely popular during its author's lifetime and beyond, being translated into Italian, English, German, and Dutch in a variety of (sometimes expurgated) editions.[55] It retained much of its popularity even during the Enlightenment, when religious literature diminished in circulation, and would receive renewed interest during the Salesian Pentecost.

His much denser *Treatise on the Love of God* addresses "Theotimus" (masculine for "Lover of God") and lays out, in the bishop's characteristic persuasive and image-rich language, his vision of the "birth, growth, decline, activities, qualities, benefits, and perfection of God's love."[56] This heftier and more theoretical work (although its author's intent was to present his topic "simply and clearly") was intended for a wide readership as well. But its presentation and themes suggest its suitability for a fairly spiritually mature audience. As a dense summary of the bishop's reflection on the nature of love, the *Treatise* might be described as a rhapsodic prose commentary on the biblical Song of Songs. The *Treatise* presents Francis's profoundly optimistic vision of the cultivation and full realization of the divine-human love relationship intended by God from the beginning.[57] At the core of the vision is de Sales's perspective on the incarnation as God's desire from all time to be in union with humankind. Indeed, he conceived of that mystery as a divine visit, a transformative "kiss" that inaugurated an ongoing relationship with humankind.[58] While singular, this event was designed to be recapitulated, as divine love's action is intrinsically dynamic and creative. God continues through time to visit women and men, through his presence in the Eucharist and through quotidian divine inspirations, which Francis deemed "arrows of love" that transfix the human heart.[59] Those visited, filled with the fire of the Spirit, in turn visit others, transforming them with the fire of love. Like the *Introduction*, the *Treatise* was an immediate success that required repeated printings throughout the century. Continued use, especially in regions near his homeland and the Italian peninsula, kept the mature vision of a world of hearts alive.

As for the Visitation, the congregation de Sales founded in 1610 with widowed baroness Jane de Chantal as first superior, it too gained popularity during his lifetime and beyond.[60] By the time of Jane's death, nineteen years after Francis's own, there were over eighty houses of the Visitation, which in 1618 had become a formally recognized contemplative religious order.[61] The original diocesan congregation had several ends, but existed especially for the cultivation of the distinctive Salesian spirit. For some time before its institution, de Sales had been dreaming of a unique community that might serve the needs both of the Catholic reform and of the faith-filled women that he encountered. When he met the baroness in 1604 in the city of Dijon, where he had been invited to preach a series of Lenten sermons, the seeds of the future Visitation community were planted. Jane de Chantal's children were young, and she was living in difficult circumstances under the control of her father-in-law, but she took the bishop as spiritual guide and over the years, as their relationship grew into a profound spiritual friendship,[62] the idea of the new congregation took shape.[63]

The Visitation of Holy Mary was to be a distinctive community for widows like Jane or others of frail health or disability with a deep capacity for God yet without a call or eligibility to enter an austere cloistered order. Neither apostolic nor traditionally contemplative, the new community was to be a sign of an eschatologically oriented way of being, an "oasis of gentleness" in a sea of militant Catholicism,[64] indeed, like the gospel mystery for which it was named, a "proto-Pentecost."[65] The name of the new congregation of course recalls the visit of the Virgin Mary to her cousin Elizabeth described in Luke 1:39–56. In the eyes of the two founders, this passage was a dense symbol of the very way divine love works in the world: The Virgin Mary, having been visited and transformed by love's invitation, in her turn was inspired to visit her older cousin, carrying divine life within. Elizabeth and the child she carried were likewise animated by Mary, who bore the divine child hidden in the womb.[66] The two women in turn would animate those around them.[67] The Visitation mystery was a sign of the church itself as it moved through time toward the realization of God's plan for the world.[68] As the Visitandines sought to "Live Jesus!" through the exchange of their hearts for the heart of Christ, they would witness to the divine desire for a world transformed. The community was to be the realization of love itself brought to fullness through the cultivation of the little relational virtues, those qualities displayed in the heart of God. Jane de Chantal is remembered as speaking of this distinctive charism to her spiritual daughters:

One cannot better define the spirit of our institute than to recall the words that best capture the teaching of our Blessed

Father [Francis de Sales]: "The religious of the Visitation who are content to faithfully observe their rule, will truly bear the name Evangelical Daughters, established particularly in this century to be imitators of the two dearest virtues of the Sacred Heart of the Incarnate Word, gentleness and humility, which are the basis and foundation of their order, and which give them the special privilege and incomparable grace of accepting their calling as Daughters of the Heart of Jesus."[69]

Among the formative exercises that the bishop proposed for the community was the practice of these virtues and fidelity to his *Spiritual Directory*, daily practices designed to nurture a constant awareness of and responsiveness to God's inspirations and presence.[70]

The Visitation would garner more prominence in the latter decades of the seventeenth century as it became identified with the emerging devotion to the Sacred Heart associated with the visions of Margaret Mary Alacoque (1647–90) at the Visitation monastery of Paray-le-Monial. Although at the cusp of the long nineteenth-century, the Visitation's presence in France and elsewhere in Europe was severely compromised as the revolutionary suppression of religious orders took place—many of the French communities did not survive. The order, along with the bishop's writings, would be the chief carriers of Salesian spirituality into the modern world. These, and the reputations of both Jane de Chantal and Francis de Sales as models of the early modern Catholic reform and the later visionary reputation of Margaret Mary Alacoque, took hold in the public imagination.[71] Laudatory biographies and *mémoires* of all three figures enhanced and promoted the continuation of the Salesian heritage over the centuries and across the European continent.[72] The canonization of Jane in 1767 and the beatification of Margaret Mary in 1864[73] placed these Salesian figures on the universal Roman calendar alongside Francis de Sales and cemented their reputations across the global Roman Catholic world.[74]

PROXIMATE BACKGROUND TO
THE SALESIAN PENTECOST

The Apogee of the *Ancien Régime*

By the mid-seventeenth century both French and the wider European society, as well as the Roman Catholic Church, had radically altered from the era in which de Sales formed his spiritual vision. The diversity and local autonomy of the earlier decades gradually diminished until by mid-century consolidation of power and centralization were characteristic of French political, social, and religious life. Absolute monarchy, supported by and aligned with the French church arose.[75] Louis XIV (1638–1715) withdrew all privileges from the Huguenot minority with the Edict of Fontainebleau (1685), resulting in their expulsion and establishing Roman Catholicism as the sole faith of his triumphant nation. Reformed Catholic religious orders were sent to evangelize in areas that were previously strongholds of this Protestant minority.[76] What emerged was a confessional state, in which civil status was identified with conformity to the established religion and its practice.[77]

Louis also demanded that the aristocracy, with their regional power and very real opposition to his monarchical aims, attend him on all his royal tours and then permanently at his royal headquarters at the palace of Versailles. Centralization was key to financing Louis's continual foreign wars and consolidating his power; the entire French nation was to revolve around the Sun King. Alongside the ascendant French monarchs, the French Catholic hierarchy, notably in the figures of Cardinal Richelieu (1585–1642), chief minister for Louis XIII and Cardinal Mazarin (1602–61), minister for Louis XIII after Richelieu's death and virtual ruler during the minority of Louis XIV, held sway. After his majority, the Sun King exercised his autocratic power in the religious realm as well. By the end of the seventeenth century, the *ancien régime*, with its conjoined royalist and ecclesial power base, was firmly established.

In that religious arena and in keeping with current trends, the tone of French Catholicism of the later seventeenth and eighteenth centuries also moved in the direction of rigidity, centralization, and uniformity. The solidified reforming energies emanating from the Council of Trent (1545–63) were by that time fully integrated into the French context.[78] Distrust of the emerging "heresies" of Quietism and Jansenism permeated French religious culture. Indeed, Louis XIV saw those supporting these movements as threatening his power.[79] Quietism, broadly identified as the spiritual teaching that perfection and spiritual peace are attained by annihilation of the will and passive absorption in the contemplation of divine things, was publicly contested in France between high profile ecclesiastics Jacques-Bénigne Bossuet, bishop of Meaux (1627–1704) and François Fénelon, archbishop of Cambrai (1651–1715). Despite the fact that Fénelon had invoked the recently canonized Francis de Sales in defense of his positions,[80] the result of the quarrel was the prohibition of Fénelon's *Maxims of the Saints* and the incarceration and subsequent exile of laywoman Jeanne-Marie Bouvier de la Motte, Madame Guyon (1648–1717), whose popular teaching (for a time she was a favorite at the French court) the archbishop had defended. The quarrel represented a growing "antimystical" climate and repression of any creative spiritual challenge to a traditional and centralized church.

This same antimystical spirit was reflected in internal conflicts among members of the powerful Jesuit order in France. The considerable cadre of followers of spiritual luminary Louis Lallement (1578–1635) called for the cultivation of a deep contemplative practice to undergird the Society's mission, but they were sharply opposed by Fathers General of the order, Claudio Aquaviva (1581–1618) and Muzio Vitelleschi (1615–45), who viewed this approach as unsuited for an apostolic community.[81] The conflict continued to rile the Society of Jesus for over a century. In a parallel mode, fear of Quietist tendencies surrounded some Visitation monasteries. In the town of Nancy, Jesuit spiritual director Jean-Pierre de Caussade (1675–1751), who was closely associated with the Visitation monastery there, was for a time suspended for promoting ideas that were considered close to Quietist heresy. The work most associated with his name, known posthumously as *Abandonment to Divine Providence*, was perhaps not his own but a compilation by the Visitandines of notes taken at his conferences or the work of a lay associate of the community. Be that as it may, both Caussade's suspension and the later suspicion surrounding the writing that bore his name is telling.[82] De Sales's reputation managed to emerge generally unscathed from the Quietist controversy but suspicion of spiritual teachings that seemed to hint of Quietist thought continued.[83]

Jansenism, as a distinct set of teachings, was identified with the posthumous writings of Dutch theologian Cornelius Jansen (1585–1638). Jansen's theological position, conceived as being in continuity with the theology of Augustine of Hippo, was taken up in France by a circle of prominent figures that eventually centered at the Cistercian convent of Port Royale, southwest of Paris, which included figures such as Abbess Angelique Arnauld (1591–1661), theologian Antoine Arnauld (1612–94), and philosopher Blaise Pascal (1623–62). Theologically, the Jansenist movement emphasized original sin, human depravity, bondage of the will, the necessity of grace, and the reality of predestination, and discouraged the practice of frequent communion, arguing that a high degree of human perfection was required to approach the sacrament. This theological imbroglio went well beyond the realm of religion, however, pitting Jansenists against Jesuits and their royal patrons. In fact, through it, much of the powerful eighteenth-century factions among the French elite developed. A Jansenist-pro-Augustinian-Gallican faction supported by the Paris *parlement* was opposed to a Jesuit-monarchical faction aligned with the papacy. Although Jansen's heretical propositions were officially suppressed, by the eighteenth century at this elite level, the quarrel went on at the highest levels of power-broking: a Jansenist-leaning book by Pasquier Quesnel (1643–1719) condemned by the papacy was supported by an episcopal group that included the archbishop of Paris. This, in turn, provoked the promulgation of the papal bull *Unigenitus* in 1713. Refusal to endorse that bull became the focus of heated church-state conflict.

In fact, to a great degree on the pastoral level, the French church had taken on a rigorous spirit that can be described as "Jansenistic." A fear-based pastoral approach through which the clergy discouraged frequent communion and refused absolution to sinners was commonplace. The confessional more and more became an instrument of interior discipline and asceticism, focused not on God's love and mercy or love of neighbor but on the sin of the individual, especially spiritual and sexual sin. Increasingly, God was imagined as distant, angry, and disgusted with human impurity and sinfulness.[84] The expansive love of God for humankind and the loving human response seems to have lost currency. This morally demanding Tridentine faith that dominated the *ancien régime* was spearheaded by an urban seminary-trained clergy that was generally hostile to popular expressions of religion. Confraternities, festivals, and the celebration of local saints, long the staples of rural religiosity, were discouraged and conformity to rigorous moral codes was imposed on the laity by threats of hell, punishment, and damnation.[85] Emphasis was placed on moral behavior and intellectual assent: on what one must do and what one must believe.

Corresponding with this changing spirit, the Visitation of the late seventeenth and eighteenth centuries would shift focus somewhat as the landscape of European culture and church changed. Although the writings of de Sales, the *Custom Book*, compiled by Jane de Chantal, and the *Constitutions* of the order were the sources of Visitandine identity, the communities often took on the spirit of the times. The aforementioned case of the Nancy Visitation in the eighteenth century is a case in point. Most significantly, the entire Visitation would become closely identified with the developing devotion to the Sacred Heart that was disseminated by published accounts of the experiences of Visitandine Margaret Mary Alacoque.[86] Her series of visions of Jesus displaying his heart and requesting the institution of an annual feast and monthly devotional exercises (First Friday observance and a Thursday night holy hour), were authenticated by her Jesuit confessor Claude La Colombière (1641–82). These devotions called for intensified adoration of the Heart of Jesus, identified with the sacrament of the Eucharist, and reparation for sins committed against the Divine Heart. Although the imagistic language of the heart had permeated the thought of Francis de Sales, emerging in contrast to the violence of the French Wars of Religion, this new approach bore the imprint of the sociopolitical and intellectual shifts of a later European era. The practices, as given expression by Alacoque, contained an implicit critique both of the gathering secular rejection of religion and of Protestant and Jansenist theologies of the Eucharist. This new iteration of the imagery was characterized especially by the emphasis on sin and necessity for reparation.[87]

Dissolution of the *Ancien Régime*

At the same time that the regime of absolute monarchy aligned with the Roman Catholic Church reached its height, an even more foundational yet gradual epistemological shift was taking place in Europe, as new modes of knowing, especially scientific method and reasoned philosophical discourse, challenged hegemonic assumptions that undergirded not only mystical and intuitive modes of knowing but also political and cultural assumptions upon which the traditional ordering of society rested.[88] The French Enlightenment dawned. Denis Diderot (1713–84) emphasized the importance of reason, thought, and the power of individuals to solve problems. Voltaire (1694–1778) launched a crusade against superstition and prejudice and wittily championed freedom of political and religious thought, and Jean-Jacques Rousseau (1712–78) proclaimed the natural and civil rights of all persons and offered a nascent vision of a democratic government in which liberty, equality, and fraternity, rather than the oppression of the ruling classes, were operative. Reason replaced revelation, ideas of progress ruled out original sin, morality was to be based on happiness, and positivism asserted that every rationally justifiable assertion is capable of logical or mathematical proof, thus outmoding metaphysics and theism.[89] These new philosophical ideas would have profound consequences.[90]

While Enlightenment thought uncoupled from religious belief would eventually be instrumental in undermining not only the credibility of the political and social order but also the religious dogmas and establishment that supported that order, this was not inevitable. During the first half of the eighteenth century, a generation of Catholic thinkers took the new ways of thinking seriously. In fact, it cannot be claimed that there was a single French Enlightenment that universally challenged religion, but that there were a series of Enlightenments, including examples of Catholics in France and across the globe motivated by lingering Tridentine aspirations of reform who were open to enlightened ideas.[91] In France, the intellectual landscape was richly diverse: thinkers from across the ideological and theological spectrum engaged with the challenges posed by Locke, Descartes, Newton, Spinoza, and others. There were not only Catholics who wished to explain and maintain the world as it was, there were also "prophetic" Catholics who wished to change it.[92] Be this as it may, by the 1750s this creative engagement in the French milieu would collapse under the political-theological quarrels surrounding the Jansenist-Jesuit standoffs. This, in turn, brought antireligious focus to the secularized radical Enlightenment. In the end, the profound disruption of religious practice that would eventually take place in the midst of political and social upheaval would forever alter European Catholicism and, for a long time, pit many of its adherents and the leadership of the church against emerging secular powers.[93]

But these conflicts were not the only harbinger of change. Even within the Catholic tradition of pastoral and theological reflection itself, a distinct shift was taking place in the direction of modifying the rigorist spirit that predominated and anticipating the fire that in the next century would animate the Salesian Pentecost. This gradual turn to a more affective and pastorally sensitive faith was notably encouraged by Neapolitan bishop and moral theologian Alphonsus Liguori (1696–1787). Liguori had trained as a lawyer at the University of Naples but, disillusioned with this secular path, underwent formation for the priesthood with a sodality attached to the Neapolitan cathedral. It was through this community that he became familiar with the writings of Francis de Sales, especially the *Treatise on the Love of God*. He had been trained in the rigorist moral theology that held sway on the Italian peninsula, but as soon as he began his pastoral ministry among the unlettered poor of Naples, Alphonsus changed his mind about rigorism, a stance that seemed to him to cause damage to hearts and minds and lead people to despair.

Liguori dreamed about founding a missionary society dedicated to preaching God's word among the most abandoned. Eventually that group was formed and given the name the Congregation of the Most

Holy Redeemer (the Redemptorists). Throughout his life, its founder was an avid writer, his pen turned to both pastoral concerns and to moral theology. It seemed to him that the ideas of the Enlightenment, which had spread among intellectuals of his day, were to be avoided, but even more pernicious was the cold, forbidding Jansenistic spirit that leeched warmth and tenderness from Christian piety.[94]

Liguori's early devotion to Francis de Sales never left him, and all of his writings are liberally seeded with quotes, both direct and paraphrased, from the Savoyard's works. In fact, he clearly used de Sales as a spiritual master whose theological orientation and pastoral perspectives on the Christian life announce good news to counteract the entrenched perspectives of the day.[95] This battle, Alphonsus believed, was not merely to be fought among the theological elite but among ordinary people, fostered by the publication of manuals of popular devotion. He encouraged frequent reception of the Eucharist, Marian and Sacred Heart devotion, and other expressions of popular piety. Thus, both his pastoral writings (which gained an immediate following) and his moral theology (which was only gradually accepted) were direct critiques of current sacramental practice and the severe spirit that animated it. Despite entrenched resistance, his ideas gradually gained favor as the idea of a God of love and mercy gained traction. The dissemination of Liguori's work in the nineteenth century often went hand in hand with the revival of enthusiasm for all things Salesian.[96]

The Collapse

Despite the astonishing French cultural and political dominance in Europe and the concentration of power amassed during Louis XIV's reign, the autocratic opulence of the *ancien régime* was to prove its downfall. By the late seventeenth century, the Sun King's lavish lifestyle, the economic losses that accompanied the Huguenot suppression, and thirty years of expensive foreign wars had eroded state finances. The French Catholic Church, which controlled a vast percentage of the nation's land and most of whose leaders were of the nobility, was inextricably aligned with the doomed monarchy. When the long reign of the Sun King ended, his great-grandson, Louis XV (1710–74), inherited a failing state. This king's political missteps and lavish spending did little to reverse the fading influence of the monarchy. His ill-fated grandson took the title of Louis XVI (1754–93) and, with the help of his ministers, unsuccessfully attempted to rectify France's financial crisis. But the tide of the nation's fortunes had irreversibly turned. Poverty was widespread, and high taxation inflamed long simmering resentment of class and clerical privilege. The new philosophical ideas championing democracy and scientific reason increased civil unrest. Rumors of the luxurious and reportedly scandalous lifestyle of the royal household stirred up the populace. In this context, Louis XVI's desperate attempt to levy a new tax on an already overtaxed citizenry was fiercely resisted.

To avert the deepening crisis, in May 1789 the young king agreed to summon the "Estates General," a body consisting of the three estates—clergy, nobles, and commoners—that had not met since 1614 and had little real influence. Angered by the king's refusal to allow them to meet simultaneously with the other estates, on June 17 the commoners' Third Estate proclaimed itself a National Assembly, declaring that it alone had the right to represent the nation. Rumors that the king intended to suppress the assembly sparked a popular uprising and on July 14th the Bastille prison, symbol of royal repression, was stormed. After a series of compromises brokered with the escalating revolutionary factions, Louis and his family attempted to flee the country aided by monarchies outside France. The escape failed and the family were forced to return to Paris, where they were confined in the Tuileries palace. Louis reluctantly accepted a new constitution, thus establishing a constitutional monarchy. Soon, the "Declaration of the Rights of Man and the Citizen" established the precedent of equality of rights for all designated as citizens.[97] This solution lasted a short time but, as revolutionary leadership was increasingly radicalized and faith in the good intentions of the king dissipated, in 1792 the monarchy was abolished, and France declared a republic. Louis was tried for treason and guillotined the following year.

THE LONG NINETEENTH CENTURY

Revolution and Disruption

This was the first moment in what was to be a long, bloody, and convoluted ascendancy of the French people and the overthrow of the *ancien régime* with its attendant powerbroker, the Catholic Church. It was to have profound consequences for the religious life of the nation and for the rest of Europe.[98] One attempt at governance swiftly followed another. Constitutional monarchy was followed by the First Republic proclaimed by a new convention, which in turn devolved into the dark and bloody period known as the Reign of Terror (1793–94), during which thousands suspected of antirevolutionary sentiments were executed. The Terror ended with the execution of Maximillien Robespierre (1758–94), one of the revolution's leading lights, as a directory took over from the convention. It was during this extended turbulent period that the various governing forces dismantled the power and apparatus of the Catholic Church that had been so aligned with the monarchy. It is true that at first, the revolution did not intend to destroy Christianity. A continuity between the old and new regimes was envisioned with religious feeling being harnessed for the new government. Instead, what is sometimes described as the "de-Christianization" of France took place. This was fueled by strong sentiments of anticlericalism among the middle and lower classes.[99]

At first, clerical corruption and wealth were targeted: the privileges of the first and second estates were abolished, tithes traditionally owed to the clergy were done away with, all church property (a vast percent of all French land before the revolution) was confiscated and given to the state. Then religious communities were disbanded, and a Civil Constitution of the Clergy in 1790 declared all clergy subordinate to the civil authorities as employees and required that they take an oath of allegiance to the revolutionary government. All who refused ("nonjuring" or "refractory" priests) were subject to loss of income, conscription, banishment, or death.

From the perspective of the varied revolutionary forces, and as a logical extension of much radical Enlightenment philosophy, which championed reason and often viewed traditional faith as superstition, the church was perceived as antirevolutionary. Thus, attempts were made to prohibit or destroy traditional symbols of worship (bell ringing, statuary, crosses, etc.) as well as to impose alternative civic cults and events—the Festival of Reason, anticlerical parades, the Cult of the Supreme Being, and the Cult of Reason—to replace traditional observances.

By the end of the decade, perhaps twenty thousand priests had been forced to leave France, and hundreds who did not leave were executed. Monasteries and religious houses were abandoned. By Easter 1794, few of France's forty thousand churches remained open; many had been closed, sold, destroyed, or converted to other uses. Most French parishes were left without the services of a priest and deprived of the sacraments. Two generations of Frenchmen would be uncatechized and many, whether sympathetic to the various permutations of the revolution or not, would adopt the skeptical, deist, or atheist positions of the *philosophes* or simply come to consider religious practice unnecessary. Families and individuals remaining loyal to the Catholic faith during this period either fled France or went underground.[100]

The revolutionary impulse bled out beyond the borders of France itself. Ideas of liberty and equality gained ground and, although frequently opposed by local governments, many Italians came to view the Revolutionary French legal and administrative system as the only answer to their own grievances against traditional elites. In Piedmont and Naples, where discontent was especially widespread, proponents of democratic ideas organized and became influential and active.

To compound matters even more, the gathering momentum of the industrial revolution further altered the European landscape, transforming a largely rural, agrarian society into an industrialized, urban one. First, the introduction of new machines and techniques in textiles, iron making, and other industries began the transformation. Eventually the development of steam power would change industries, transportation, banking, and commercial activity. Factories grew up, turning smaller towns into urban centers. A general shift of the largely uncatechized younger population, from the rural countryside to the cities in search of work, was taking place, creating new social issues and needs for pastoral care.

Resurgence of the Catholic Faith

Gradually a return to some form of religious faith began to reassert itself. The revolutionary efforts to create alternative cult symbols to replace traditional religion failed to win popular allegiance. Moreover, varied mismanaged and corrupt attempts at governance following the revolution in turn quickly became unpopular. Soon, a young general, Napoleon Bonaparte (1769–1821), taking advantage of the chaos, staged a coup by creating the position of First Consul, which he filled, thus securing for himself control of all France. Ambitious to bring political and financial stability to the country, in 1804 Napoleon crowned himself emperor and inaugurated the First Empire, a political solution that survived for a decade. Under Napoleon, who perceived the church's social usefulness, a law legalizing limited public worship was passed and negotiations with Pope Pius VII were entered into which led to the Concordat of 1801. Ultimately, this ended the overt de-Christianization process and established a framework for a relationship between the Catholic Church and the French nation. However, this was often a fraught affiliation. Although the confessional state of the *ancien régime* was not restored, the Imperial Catechism made loyalty to Napoleon the essence of religious obligation. Church personnel were considered state employees and bishops were unable to communicate with the papacy except through government channels.[101] In this climate, new attempts at establishing faith-based communities and apostolates were frequently subverted, both by the severely limited authority of ecclesial figures and by the oversight of secular authorities.

The response of French Catholics to this upheaval was varied and complex and cannot be summed up as simply rejection of the revolutionary legacy or as a straightforward contest between liberals, modernists, Ultramontanists, or Gallicans. There were those who believed that the appropriate role of faith was to support the political and social status quo and willingly or gladly accepted the role of the church as subsidiary to the new republic. There were those whose focus was on the restoration of church and society as they had been before the revolution. Some of that response took the form of nostalgia for the past linked with a desire for restoration of the monarchy. Over time, devotion to the Sacred Heart became associated with this stance, and in the aftermath of the revolution, accounts of visions and prophecies emanating from Visitation monasteries circulated widely.[102] The new republic was characterized as a conspiracy against throne and altar and the Sacred Heart as the symbol of resistance. At the end of the nineteenth century, the monumental Basilique du Sacré-Cœur was constructed on Montmartre in the capital. Originally conceived as a citadel of the "National Vow," a place of penance for France's defeat in the Franco-Prussian war and the upheaval of the Paris Commune, the basilica became a concretization of the marriage of monarchy and a church that had resisted the aims of revolutionary France.[103]

But the desire to explain and maintain the world as it had been or had become was far from a universal response. There were Catholic approaches that were not backward gazing but forward looking. A few, like utopian thinker Hugues-Félicité Robert de Lamennais (1782–1854), looked to the dogma and treasury of faith to utterly transform and replace the social order itself.[104] Others such as Frédéric Ozanam (1813–53), founder of the lay Society of St. Vincent de Paul, accepted many of the egalitarian principles of the changed world but critiqued its liberal individualism and secularism and longed instead for an expansive and forward-looking re-Christianized society.[105] Scores of faithful, often from families profoundly affected by revolutionary upheaval, simply set out to reconstitute a vital society from the shards of a shattered Catholic Church. Freshly created apostolic religious communities sprang up to fill the vacuum left by the earlier de-Christianization: education, health care, care for the poor and marginalized, and basic catechesis were needed. Rural areas especially lacked pastoral attention. The number of local religious congregations that sprang up to address these needs across Europe is astonishing.[106] Women's congregations especially proliferated.[107] Social concerns certainly motivated most of these "useful" religious communities, but a desire to teach the faith to a generation that had been left without sacramental and liturgical life and catechesis was an even more pressing motivation. The congregations of the Salesian Pentecost were among the most vital of these.

Much more began to shift on the pastoral landscape. A new sort of diocesan clergy reconstituted itself, drawn mainly from the peasant and artisan classes rather than from the elite who had dominated clerical leadership in the past. These new priests valued piety over intellectual inquiry and were comfortable with expressions of popular religion. New eucharistic devotions of nocturnal and perpetual adoration came into vogue, and interest in pilgrimages, apparitions, and miracles flourished amid a populace seeking a different surety than the dominant secular scientific one that held sway.[108] Unlike the rigorist and fear-based spirit of the church that was passing away, a more affective and love-based spirituality appeared.

A parallel certainly can be seen in the cultural upswing of Romanticism, the artistic, literary, musical, and intellectual movement that was at its peak mid-century. Romanticism's emphasis on emotion and its glorification of the past and nature was partly a reaction to the Industrial Revolution, the aristocratic social and political norms of the Age of Enlightenment, and the scientific rationalization of nature—all components of modernity. In like fashion, Catholicism responded to the advent of the modern world. Increasingly, as the long nineteenth century progressed, pastoral emphasis throughout Europe was put on affectivity and on the love and forgiveness of God. The reciprocity of divine-human love was perceived more and more as expressed in Christ's presence in the Eucharist. Frequent communion was encouraged, and a multitude of devotional practices and pilgrimages flourished.

Typical of this new mood was the startling upsurge in Marian devotion.[109] The figure of the Virgin had long been central to Catholic piety, but in this era special significance was assigned to her. In 1814 Pope Pius VII, who had been held captive in France by the Emperor Napoleon, made a triumphal reentry into Rome as the latter suffered defeat in Russia and abdicated. During his incarceration, the pope had invoked the Virgin Mary under the title "Help of Christians," a name associated with Christian victories over non-Christian forces since the sixteenth century.[110] The pontiff's first act upon return was to proclaim May 24 a feast day honoring Mary Help of Christians.

This became a popular nineteenth-century invocation for Catholics facing a hostile, secularizing world. Less than a quarter century later, in 1830, during the uprising in the French capital, the young postulant Catherine Labouré (1806–76) received a series of visions of Mary at the Daughters of Charity motherhouse on the rue du Bac in Paris. During one of these appearances the Virgin, draped in white, revealed the design of a medal that promised to bestow grace on all who wore it. The front was to bear the Virgin's image surmounting the globe. The initial *M* and the twin hearts of Mary and Jesus were to be displayed on the reverse side.[111] At the request of Catherine's confessor, this "Miraculous Medal" was struck. Its popularity was swift and widespread. Another Marian appearance destined to catalyze popular enthusiasm was the Virgin's appearance to the peasant girl Maria Bernada Sobirós (Bernadette Soubirous) in 1858 at a grotto near Lourdes. The presence of a miraculous spring at the site was revealed, and supplicants soon began to make their way on pilgrimage in search of healing there. The Lourdes Virgin identified herself as the Immaculate Conception, a title echoing the recent papal proclamation of 1854 that established the Marian title as a dogma of the faith. Although the Immaculate Conception of Mary had been debated and discussed for centuries, its official confirmation as an article of faith in the nineteenth century fused theological, devotional, and ideological concerns of Ultramontanists and legitimists and served as an attack on liberal views of human nature, politics, and disdain for the papacy.[112] The resurgence of the type of Marian devotion seen at Lourdes and similar pilgrimage shrines idealized children and maternity, symbols of peasant religiosity, and family, and countered the urban culture of industrialized modern France.[113]

Miracles and apparitions not only enthused a generation of Catholics recovering their lost faith, they also provided evidence for a defensive church attempting to counter the challenges of a changing world. Theological and metaphysical explanations for human problems were being replaced by scientific and intellectual solutions. The visibility and size of prophetic and miracle cults in France at this period witness to the fact that such phenomena were not peripheral or simply a vestige of traditional society but part of the process by which the Catholic Church confronted modernization.[114] Religious cults met vital social and psychological needs and offered meaning and order in a turbulent world. Belief in miracles even became a test of orthodoxy and challenged the secular idea that God is unnecessary. Such cults also assisted in the development of a mass movement of conservative Catholic religious nationalism and internationalism.

The political and cultural landscape within which this renewal of faith occurred would continue to be contentious and convoluted throughout the long nineteenth century. Despite a wide range of views among Catholics themselves, the hierarchical Catholic Church in general tended to be on the defensive against much of modernity and to envision itself in stark opposition to the secular world, a position that had hardened during the social and intellectual upheavals of the previous era. Turbulent multinational wars and internal political conflicts continued in most countries. In France, the First Empire (1805–14) was replaced by a restoration of the monarchy with Louis XVIII (1755–1824) at the helm, a conciliatory ruler who managed to balance the liberal, constitutionalist, and ultraroyalist factions. His successor, Charles X (1757–1836), was forced to abdicate in 1830 during the "July Revolution" for aligning too closely with the ultraroyalists. In turn, he was succeeded by the long and fairly stable reign of Louis-Phillipe (1773–1850) and a return to constitutional monarchy. Then, after Louis-Phillipe's abdication, a brief Second Revolution and Republic of 1848 was followed by the Second Empire (1852–70), during which Louis Napoleon III (1808–73), his namesake's nephew, imposed a firm hand on any dissent. Continual upheavals persisted, such as the Paris Commune, a radical socialist and revolutionary government that ruled Paris for several months during 1871. The Third Republic followed in 1870, a bicameral parliamentarian democracy that lasted until France's crushing defeat by Nazi Germany during World War II. Under this government, Catholic interests were in large part defeated: the French educational system was laicized, religious congregations were restricted, and in 1905 the last vestiges of Napoleon's concordat with the papacy were abrogated, ending public support of religion and instituting the separation of church and state.

The French Revolution had set in motion a chain of political events that would affect not only France but much of Europe's Catholic population, especially in the regions surrounding de Sales's birthplace, Savoy, and throughout the Italian peninsula, which included the Piedmont. An independent duchy in the sainted bishop's lifetime, with its capital in Turin in the Piedmont, the western region of Savoy was annexed to France under the First Republic before being returned to the Kingdom of Sardinia in 1815. It was then annexed again under the Second French Empire in 1860. Eventually, the house of Savoy would rule over the Kingdom of Italy, which eventually led to the turbulent process of the unification of Italy as a nation. Similarly, the Papal States, that large swath of territory under the temporal rule of the pope, also had a tumultuous history in this era. When the Papal States were invaded by the French revolutionary government in 1789, Pope Pius VI (1717–99) was imprisoned and died in captivity in France. His successor, Pius VII (1742–1823), underwent a similar imprisonment when Napoleon's forces invaded the papal states in 1809, although he was returned to Rome. Under the Napoleonic Empire, the papal territory was annexed to France but was reconstituted with the collapse of the Napoleonic reign.

For much of the century, continuing revolutionary impulses directed toward unification on the Italian peninsula caused turmoil. From 1815 on, efforts to restore monarchical rule in varying political entities on the peninsula—the period of the Restoration— eventually gave way to the era of Italian unification—the *Risorgimento* (Resurgence), that consolidated different states of the Italian peninsula into the single state of the Kingdom of Italy in 1861. The process began with the revolutions of 1848, inspired by previous rebellions in the 1820s and 1830s and was completed when Rome became the capital of the Kingdom of Italy.

In the midst of constant political and social unrest, Roman Catholic practice was profoundly disrupted in these lands and in other bordering regions, just as it had been in France: restrictions on worship, clerical autonomy, and closures of contemplative communities were frequently implemented. Finally, in 1870, with the unification of Italy, the Papal States ceased to exist. The pontiff that presided over this dissolution, Pius IX (1792–1878), had been at first warily sympathetic to the liberalizing political movements of the era, but eventually hardened his positions, in 1864 publishing the *Syllabus of Errors*, which stands as a strong condemnation of liberalism, modernism, moral relativism, secularization, and separation of church and state. In 1869 he convened the First Vatican Council, which defined the dogma of papal infallibility.

Over all this tumult during the long nineteenth century hovered the existential question: How can a deep Catholic faith be practiced and cultivated in the context of an ever more secular, even antireligious world? A generation of ardent Catholics, many from families that had remained loyal to Rome and had either suffered during the revolutionary upheavals or who had engaged in clandestine efforts to preserve the faith, emerged in response. Many of them looked to Alphonsus Liguori and Francis de Sales for inspiration. The Salesian Pentecost was, of course, part of a much wider effort to reestablish a vital and viable Catholicism in the post-revolutionary world. Scores of apostolic religious communities emerged in local European contexts in response to the needs created by the postrevolutionary vacuum of pastoral presence and the changing social landscape created by industrialization. Many of these communities would become international in scale: European colonization with its attendant evangelical outreach led to new missionary fields with newly Christianized populations. It was in this context that the Salesian Pentecost, that network of communities united by their grounding in the vision of a world of transformed hearts as envisioned by Francis de Sales, caught fire.[115]

II

PIERRE-MARIE MERMIER, JOSEPH-MARIE FAVRE, PIERRE-JOSEPH REY, AND THE MISSIONARIES OF ST. FRANCIS DE SALES OF ANNECY

Joseph F. Chorpenning, OSFS[1]

The Missionaries of St. Francis de Sales of Annecy (also known as the Fransalians) were founded in 1838 by Pierre-Marie Mermier (1790–1862), a priest of the Diocese of Annecy. They were the first religious congregation ever to bear the name and be under the patronage of St. Francis de Sales.[2] In addition to Mermier, two others played key roles in the Fransalians' founding: Joseph-Marie Favre (1791–1838), a priest of the Archdiocese of Chambéry-Geneva, and Pierre-Joseph Rey (1770–1842), the second bishop of Annecy.

Historically, the foundation of the Missionaries of St. Francis de Sales came about as a response to the pastoral crisis precipitated by the French Revolution in Savoy, the birthplace of St. Francis de Sales (1567–1622), Salesian spirituality, and the Order of the Visitation of Holy Mary (founded in Annecy in 1610). The Revolution broke out in 1789, and three years later it arrived in Savoy, which was then part of the kingdom of Sardinia. France had long coveted Savoy because of its strategic position as the gateway to Italy. Invaded by the French army on September 22, 1792, Savoy was subsequently annexed to France.[3]

The Revolution's policy of systematic de-Christianization was vigorously prosecuted in Savoy. Priests who refused to take the oath of loyalty to the Civil Constitution of the Clergy (1790) were compelled to leave the country or face deportation to Guyana in South America: 690 out of 750 priests serving in the area that later became the Diocese of Annecy went into exile. Monasteries were closed. Roadside crosses and church bells were pulled down. Churches were plundered and converted into prisons, grain stores, stables, or military hospitals.[4]

With the ascent of Napoleon Bonaparte (1769–1821) to first consul, effectively making him dictator of France, in November 1799, the Revolution finally ended. The Concordat of 1801 between Napoleon and Pope Pius VII (1742–1823; reigned 1800–1823) stipulated that Catholicism could operate freely but was not the state religion. However, the restoration of religious practice faced significant challenges. There was an acute shortage of priests, and, consequently, standards were lowered for admission to holy orders. Jansenism and Gallicanism, well established in seminaries before the Revolution, continued to influence priestly formation and thus negatively impacted pastoral practice through moral rigorism in the confessional and aversion to frequent reception of communion.[5]

Most priests were unprepared and thus ill equipped to respond meaningfully to the post-Revolution state of parish life. An entire generation was unevangelized, and religious indifference was widespread. There were, however, exceptions, such as Mermier and Favre. The childhoods of both men had unfolded in the shadow of the Revolution, with their family homes serving as safe havens for priests on the run from the civil authorities. In the seminary, Mermier was a good and hardworking student, while Favre excelled, even refuting Jansenism by employing the new theological ideas of St. Alphonsus Liguori (1696–1787), whose works were forbidden in the seminary at the time.[6] (Mermier was also a devotee of Liguori.) Ordained a priest in 1817, Favre became renowned as a preacher, catechist, and confessor. In 1819, he was assigned to organize missions in the diocese, and it was in this context that he and

Mermier first collaborated, setting in motion the process leading to the Fransalians' founding.

Ordained to the priesthood in 1813, Mermier's first assignments included both parochial and educational ministries. In 1819, he was appointed pastor of the parish in the prosperous market town of Le Chatelard-en-Bauges. Mermier enthusiastically threw himself into this ministry: he visited his parishioners, preached, taught catechism, started a parish school, and built a chapel in a distant village. While appreciative of his efforts, his parishioners remained apathetic. This led Mermier to ask Favre for help in overcoming the religious indifference of his parishioners by conducting a parish mission. While success was not guaranteed, the mission's ultimate positive outcome was seen by both Mermier and Favre as confirmation of their vocation as mission preachers.[7]

Mermier and Favre, assisted by several other priests, now dedicated themselves exclusively to parish missions. After each mission, the group would assess its effectiveness and their conduct, in order to refine and improve their methods. The group also greatly benefited from Favre's experience in the apostolate. For example, he urged his confreres to cultivate a welcoming demeanor and to be generous and magnanimous in dealing with parish priests, so they became collaborators rather than adversaries.[8] Of paramount importance was that Favre and Mermier's diagnosis of the state of religion in Savoy led them to discover in St. Francis de Sales as the Apostle of the Chablais the inspiration and model for their missionary apostolate.

Favre and Mermier did not invent the parish mission. For example, it was an important element of the renewal of Catholicism after the Council of Trent (1545–63) that aimed to win over Protestants and lukewarm Catholics. The Capuchins, Jesuits, and Vincentians (also known as Lazarists) excelled in the ministry of rural missions. By the end of the eighteenth century, however, the parish mission was in decline. Favre and Mermier revived the parish mission because they believed that it was the only effective means for remedying the dire state of parish life. In short, the missioner's vocation was to proclaim the word of God to people who had never heard it before, as well as to those who having heard it had practically forgotten it.[9]

Favre and Mermier shared the conviction that the pastoral crisis that they faced was not unprecedented in their native Savoy: it was comparable to what Francis de Sales faced when he sought to win the Chablais region back to Catholicism, which had lapsed into Protestantism. Thus, they looked to recover the distinctive pastoral method that Francis developed during his four-year mission in the Chablais (1594–98). This mission's initial phase (1594–97) had been disappointing. Preaching to anyone who would listen, hours of individual religious instruction, and debates on theological issues had yielded only a handful of converts.[10] A fresh approach was needed, and this took the form of staging three sumptuous, lavish, and visually stunning Forty Hours celebrations in 1598 in Annemasse (September 7–9) and Thonon (September 20–22 and October 1–3): words, images, actions, and sounds in the form of rituals, processions, and theatrical performances appealed to people's senses instead of their intellects, thus stirring emotions that had been buried by Calvinism's emphasis on introspection. The result was dramatic: much of the populace returned to the Catholic fold, and Francis was henceforth acclaimed as the "Apostle of the Chablais."[11]

Favre especially had a masterful grasp of this facet of the Salesian approach. In a letter to Mermier of October 7, 1824, Favre detailed the various ceremonies that their parish missions were to include, assuring Mermier that he had personally tried and found these ceremonies effective. Of particular interest is Favre's evaluation of some ceremonies. This letter is of unique importance in the Fransalian tradition because it is the most complete extant description of the parish mission apostolate, which was the first and foundational ministry of the Missionaries of St. Francis de Sales. It opens a window on the Fransalian parish missions as no other source material does, and thus its historical importance is singular. While many of these ceremonies had long been staples of the parish mission repertoire, Favre and Mermier incorporated these into their ministry in their own particular and distinctive manner.

PARISH MISSION CEREMONIES: LETTER OF JOSEPH-MARIE FAVRE TO PIERRE-MARIE MERMIER OF OCTOBER 7, 1824[12]

1. OPENING CEREMONY.
2. PENITENTIAL CEREMONY, made on the first day at the evening conference.

Conference: mortal sin, the state of the sinner, how to get out of it? The ceremony takes place in the presence of the Blessed Sacrament exposed, with a paraphrase of the *Miserere*[13] and invocations.

3. CEREMONY of CURSES, made at the end of the discourse on the punishments for sin. It consists in cursing sin in this world, so as not to have to curse it in hell. The celebrant enumerates the sins and at each sin invites its curse: "Say with me: Cursed be my lack of faith which has caused me to lose heaven." All reply: "Be it accursed!," and so on for all the principal sins. This ceremony makes a great impression.

4. CEREMONY for IMPENITENT SINNERS, made on the day when the sermon is on the number of sins or when prayers are asked for impenitent sinners. All the priests in surplices are beside the altar where the Blessed Sacrament is exposed. The Director of the Mission asks for mercy for the impenitent and invites his confreres to ask for mercy: they sing the *Parce, Domine*.[14] The Director then enumerates the sins for which they are impenitent and at each sin invites the assembly to say: "Mercy on them!" This ceremony makes an extraordinary impression.

5. CEREMONY OF MARY'S GRACES. [In the Fransalians, this feast became that of the Seven Sorrows of the Blessed Virgin Mary.]

The celebration is announced the previous day at midday. During the night, a throne is erected on which is placed a statue or picture of our Lady. At the end of the morning religious instruction, the throne is illuminated, and the parish is consecrated to our Lady.

In the evening, there is a conference on devotion to Mary; exposition of the Most Blessed Sacrament; the clergy in surplices gather round the Virgin's throne. Verse of a hymn; the Director acclaims Mary as the Daughter of the Eternal Father and concludes this salutation with: "All honor and glory to Mary, Daughter of God the Father!" The people reply: "So be it." He goes on to acclaim her as Friend of God, Spouse of the Holy Spirit, full of grace, Mother of our redemption. Each time the assembly replies: "So be it." Before Benediction of the Blessed Sacrament, Jesus Christ is heard to speak. He is made to say that He gives His Mother to be the Mother of us all.

     6.   CELEBRATION OF THE SACRED HEART OF JESUS.[15] On the altar, a throne, which is wonderfully illuminated, is placed and on which is set a luminous Heart.

In the evening, a conference on the Kingship of Christ. This is followed by a procession from the presbytery to the church that should be very solemn. A priest leads the procession and enters by the main door. Eight acolytes dressed as angels follow; eight priest-thurifers dressed in albs and wearing sashes, thuribles in hand; six priest-cantors; a subdeacon, a deacon; priests in copes; the celebrant. A group of musicians plays in the gallery while the clergy process solemnly up the middle aisle of the church. Eight soldiers walk in front of the clergy and stand around the altar. Outside the church twelve soldiers discharge a volley of shots. After incensing the Blessed Sacrament exposed since the morning, the Director goes up into the pulpit while the *Vivat*[16] is sung in three voices. The Director acclaims Jesus Christ as King of Heaven and concludes with the words: "Glory, honor, blessing and thanksgiving be to Jesus, King of Heaven." The clergy reply: "For ever and ever." The people add en masse: "So be it." There is a minute's pause while the thurifers incense the Blessed Sacrament and then follows the threefold chant of *Vivat,* music, volley of shots. Then they start all over again and acclaim Jesus as King of the Earth, King of Hell, as Redeemer, etc.

Nothing more touching can be seen, nor which gives such a lofty idea of religion.

At Benediction is said: "Behold your King, you who are righteous. Behold your King, you who are sinners."

7. CEREMONY OF THE BLESSED SACRAMENT. Celebrated on the day before leaving and announced solemnly. In the morning, there is an instruction on the love of Christ Jesus for humanity in the Eucharist. General Communion for the men. The altar is illuminated. In the evening, there is a conference on the grandeur and goodness of Christ Jesus and on the ingratitude and insults of humankind in regard to Jesus Christ. Ceremony of reparation for insults.

8. CEREMONY OF THE RENEWAL OF BAPTISMAL PROMISES. Discourse on the two standards;[17] procession to the baptismal font; reminder of a person's state before and after baptism; the promises and the breaking of those promises. The renewal of promises.[18]

9. CEREMONY OF THE CELEBRATION OF THE CROSS.[19] A Calvary is constructed near the Communion table with a shroud and an image of Christ placed upon it. At its foot, there is a table in the shape of a coffin covered with a white sheet. The celebration is announced the day before as a funeral service. The Mission Cross is placed on the Communion table beside the Calvary. The Passion is narrated, accompanied by moving reflections. All go to the cemetery. The clergy ask for gratitude to Jesus. "Drunkards, will you not express gratitude to Jesus?"..."Yes...etc." All return to the singing of the *Miserere.*

10. CELEBRATION OF THE PROMULGATION OF THE
    LAW. On the final day, instead of the Examination
    of Conscience. After exposing the Blessed Sacrament,
    each of the priests goes to the confessionals. The one
    making the Examination relates the promulgation
    of the Law and makes the promise to keep it. "Do
    you believe?"…"We do believe."…"This is what God
    expects of you," adds one of the missioners.
11. CEREMONY OF THANKSGIVING. At the closure.
    Exposition of the Most Blessed Sacrament. The
    Director of the Mission invites converted sinners
    to thank God for the great blessing of the mission.
    Two verses of the *Te Deum*[20] are sung; they are
    paraphrased in these words: "Glory be to the
    Father, and to the Son…." And the people reply en
    masse: "So be it."
12. CEREMONY OF DEPARTURE. Before leaving, Mary
    is given to the parish as Mother and Jesus as Father
    by rousing the greatest trust in Jesus and Mary.
    Finally, the parish is given back to the pastor by
    handing him back the stole, in order to foster the
    parish's confidence in his ministry.
13. CEREMONY OF CALLING DOWN CURSES. Takes
    place around the Mission Cross at the moment
    of leaving. The men on one side, the women on
    the other, the clergy all around. The Director in
    surplice says: "I am going to pronounce blessings
    over you.…Blessed is he who did not believe but
    repented of this and will now believe forever…."
    "Blessed is he," repeat all the clergy. They go
    through all the commandments.…"Cursed be
    he who does not believe." "Cursed be he!" reply
    the clergy.…The people are blessed and then the
    missioners take their leave.
14. CEREMONY OF BLESSING. Before Benediction of the
    Blessed Sacrament, the Director speaks about the
    topic for the day, while offering remonstrations from

> Jesus Christ. The preacher, representing the people,
> replies to these reproofs by humbling himself.

> These are our ceremonies. There is still one more which
> I will not describe to you, as it has not yet been sufficiently
> tried out.

Inspired by Francis de Sales, Apostle of the Chablais, Favre and Mermier developed the parish mission as a carefully choreographed immersive communal experience, whose goal was to build up a unified faith community. The faithful tended not to attend Sunday Mass, and for those who did, the impact of the sermon was negligible. By contrast, they flocked to parish missions, which lasted from three to five weeks.[21] During the mission, all the principal truths of Catholicism were presented through liturgical and paraliturgical services, sermons, and religious instruction. Unlike the Sunday sermon, which was a "top-down" speech, missionary sermons were often dialogic in form, inviting active involvement by the listeners. Parishioners also participated in the mission's ceremonies through chants, hymns, recited prayers, responses, and acclamations.[22] Between 1832 and 1862, more than 620 missions were given in 240 parishes in Savoy. For their part, the Missionaries of Annecy, assisted by diocesan priests, gave 573 missions in 226 parishes.[23]

A great amount of time during the mission was devoted to hearing confessions. The presence of missioners made it possible for parishioners to unburden their consciences to a confessor other than their parish priest. Favre and Mermier emphasized the importance of missioners being specially trained in hearing confessions and the direction of souls, as well as in handling delicate matters of conscience. Nonetheless, this part of the mission ministry proved a constant challenge for missioners, as Mermier's letter of February 24, 1849, written to a confrere many years after the mission ministry was in its infancy and when the Fransalians were already in existence, attests.

A REPORT FROM THE MISSION FIELD: LETTER OF FEBRUARY 24, 1849, FROM FR. MERMIER IN LES ALLINGES TO FR. PHILIPPE GAIDDON, MISSIONARY AT ANNECY[24]

My dear confrere,

Here I am on the holy mountain, where I would like to stay a little longer to have more time at my disposal and to put my projects in better order. Since it is not easy and they want me to return to Annecy, I will set out for the journey a week from tomorrow, not arriving there until the end of the week, because of the visits that I am obliged to make on my way to fulfill different obligations.

On the first days of this week, we have been at Villard, where we did not find anything marvelous, though I had been quite satisfied with the retreat last year. No doubt, the times are bad; it is precisely for this reason that men should be better. It was worse still at Morzine. All the same, people have been eager to attend religious instruction and to frequent the sacraments; these were almost the only signs of contrition that we find among a great number of habitual and relapsed sinners.

Did I do well in loosening the strap so much in favor of these poor sinners for fear of making them disgusted with confession and of alienating them from the sacraments, thus making them almost hostile to religion?

I confess that all this is painful and that we should really open our eyes, especially as regards girls who have so many means of sanctification, who receive the sacraments regularly, even monthly, and some of them more frequently still, and yet are not better than the others, nor stronger for all that on occasions [of sin]. I have, however, recommended to our collaborators to go through the authors again attentively to study the extraordinary signs of conversion, taking care to insist strongly on the essential duties in the examens and in religious instruction.

In concluding, it occurs to me to ask myself why divine Providence has reserved for us and sends us very difficult times. Is it in His mercy or in His justice? When they are away from the forts of Israel, what will the weak do? When they burn the foundations of the edifice, who will be strong enough to sustain the house?

While awaiting further reflections, which I cannot give now, here are some at least: Perhaps it is the time, more than ever, to be holy, unstained, separated from sinners, made higher than the heavens. Our ministry demands that we offer ourselves to the people, to society, like other St. Francis de Sales': totally disinterested, burning with zeal for the salvation of souls, full of compassion at the sight of the evils that make people desolate, not amusing ourselves by losing our time in useless oratory, with a legitimate mission, irreproachable doctrine, and, above all, a good life. This, my dear confrere, I am happy to tell you for the moment....

I pray that you and all spend the holy days of Lent in a holy manner.

Very devotedly yours,
P.-M. Mermier
Superior

Mission work was spiritually, emotionally, and physically demanding. When not out on mission, living in community provided much-needed support for the missioners, as well as the opportunity to recharge their spiritual and physical batteries. This was another hallmark of Francis de Sales's Chablais mission that Mermier retrieved: the communal and collaborative nature of the missionary vocation. Francis did not embark on the Chablais mission alone but was accompanied by his cousin Louis de Sales. In 1597, this team of two was augmented by the long-awaited arrival of reinforcements: two Capuchins (Chérubin de Maurienne and Esprit de Beaulme), a Jesuit (Jean Saunier), and the new curé of Annemasse

(Jean Maniglier). Reinvigorated, the group immediately set to work to discuss its course of action and to address various concerns and strategies for the mission.[25]

In 1832, the Annecy diocesan mission band comprised six priests. Feeling the need of a community to sustain their spiritual life and missionary apostolate, they resided in the seminary and later in a house in the town of La Roche. However, Mermier wanted more: to form a religious congregation with vows. (Favre and Mermier had earlier considered combining forces and uniting under the name Oblates of St. Francis de Sales, but this never materialized.[26]) Mermier's wish became a reality on October 24, 1838, when the bishop of Annecy, Pierre-Joseph Rey, approved the group as a religious congregation, under the name of the Missionaries of St. Francis de Sales.[27] On this occasion, Bishop Rey exhorted the new congregation, "Yours is a triple task: to study St. Francis de Sales, to imitate his virtues, and to form your method of guiding people on this—full of gentleness to sinners."[28]

Mermier recounted the history of the founding of the Fransalians from his own perspective in his own words in a letter of October 29, 1842, which he drafted to the Holy See, petitioning for papal approbation of the new congregation, which was granted in 1843.

THE ORIGIN AND EVOLUTION OF THE FRANSALIANS AS A RELIGIOUS CONGREGATION: DRAFT OF PETITIONARY LETTER OF OCTOBER 29, 1842, TO POPE GREGORY XVI[29]

The petitioner is a priest of Savoy, born on August 28, 1790, at Chaumont in Savoy, in the diocese of Annecy. He was ordained to the priesthood on March 21, 1813. Soon thereafter, he was sent as an assistant to one of the large parishes of the diocese where he ministered for a period of three years.

From there, he was sent as [spiritual] director and professor to one of the principal seminaries of the diocese. About three years later, he was appointed archpriest [dean] of a district at the head of a parish.

With the restoration of the dioceses of Savoy, when the diocese of Annecy was re-established, he was called to its major seminary as spiritual director. A little later, he resumed the work of [parish] missions, which he had begun between 1821 and 1822, with the permission of his ordinary, who, at the time, was the archbishop of Chambéry. He has thus continued this important work up to the present. From the start, he was assisted by other diocesan priests who wished to join him and to help him in this kind of ministry, always with the permission of the ordinary, only for the time each mission lasted. Afterward, he continued this ministry with the help of some confreres, also diocesan priests, who joined him and toiled in harmony for this good work, without any other bond than that of charity and zeal. They hoped one day to form a Congregation of Missionaries, almost as it exists today. Since then, they have tried to live under a common rule, insofar as their situation and the circumstances in which they find themselves, permit. This Rule, with regard to the Constitutions and principal rules, was the same as that which was later approved by the ordinary. There have been added to it general rules, explanations of the vows, and the government of the Congregation, as well as some other particulars.

Three of the confreres who had joined have already gone to receive their reward from the sovereign Master of the Harvest [cf. Matt 9:38; Luke 10:2], all three full of merit. Two others were compelled to leave this difficult ministry, due to ill health.

At this moment, the number of missionaries has come up to twelve. They have with them seven coadjutor brothers, who serve them in household affairs and who are preparing to make the same vows as the missionaries. The majority of the confreres who have joined have already lived in community for six, eight, or ten years. They know sufficiently how to give spiritual exercises and to direct souls. They busy themselves by giving missions in the parishes of the diocese during nine months of the year, almost without a break, not to mention other public and private spiritual exercises.

Thus, he [= the petitioner, that is, Mermier] has lived with his confreres without any resource, at least for a sufficiently long time, with no financial help from the diocese where he has worked since 1822. He has not gone outside of the diocese for ministry, accepting only his food as salary and stipend, not including clothing. For most of his confreres, it is the same.

Now the good work is authorized. The funds for offering a grant to the missions established in the diocese have increased. This grant, overseen by an ecclesiastical administration, is approved by the king. It had been reduced to a capital of 2,000 francs during the French Revolution and has at this moment a capital of 50,000 to 60,000 francs.

Now, most of the parishes, where he has preached missions, have established funds for the maintenance of the missionaries who give spiritual exercises in their churches. For the present, it is in most places only for these exercises, which are repeated at specific intervals, such as every seven years.

Now, the parish priests, even those who have no funds available for the expenses of a mission, request in large numbers this favor for their parish. Often, they prefer to burden themselves with the expenses, which the maintenance of the missionaries requires, rather than to be deprived of this powerful help.

Now, Monseigneur Rey, bishop of Annecy of blessed memory —unshakeable in his confidence in divine Providence and in his great zeal, well-supported by the sacrifices of his generous clergy, and encouraged by the success of this undertaking and by the abundant blessings which heaven bestows on it today— has succeeded in having a large and beautiful house built for this precious establishment. For about six years, the missionaries have resided together in it. They have lived in community in an edifying manner, according to the Constitutions and following the Rules approved by Bishop Rey on September 29, 1836.

Now, he has canonically erected them into a religious Congregation by his decrees of October 24, 1838.

Now, finally, His Majesty, the King of Sardinia,[30] their lawful and religious-minded sovereign, at the first request made to him by His Excellency, Bishop Rey, has been pleased to authorize and permit by letters patent of September 29, 1838, the establishment of the Congregation of the Missionaries of St. Francis de Sales in the diocese of Annecy in Savoy, so that it may enjoy all the rights granted to religious congregations.

The petitioner, desiring that this work acquire permanence and that it be established on the most solid foundations, so that it becomes useful not only to his diocese, but also that it may become a stronghold against heresy, and extend itself into neighboring dioceses and even to foreign missions, comes, with the agreement of his bishop and in harmony with his confreres, to prostrate himself at the feet of His Holiness. He requests that His Holiness receive them, bless their undertaking, and approve their proposed Constitutions and Rules by making the corrections, changes, and additions that are necessary and useful.

Signature follows.

Realizing that the house at La Roche was too small for the congregation's future development, Bishop Rey made provision for the construction of a new residence on a plot of land in Annecy, near the diocesan seminary, known as La Feuillette. Moreover, so that the missionaries would be ever mindful that they were the latter-day successors of the Apostle of the Chablais, Rey made this provision in his last will and testament:

I bequeath to the dear Missionaries of St. Francis de Sales the whole of the property that I acquired at Les Allinges, including the precious chapel where St. Francis de Sales for so long celebrated the sacred mysteries for the conversion of my fatherland. Although the motherhouse of this congregation is La Feuillette, the Missionaries are to look upon Les Allinges as a center where the memory and traces of their Model and Patron are to be seen at every step. This will inspire them with fervor in the noble and holy work of preaching missions.[31]

Each night during the first five months of the Chablais mission, Francis de Sales took refuge in the fortress of Les Allinges until he was able to stay in Thonon. There he daily celebrated Mass and spent long hours in prayer in its chapel before the Romanesque fresco of *Christ in Glory* (10th–12th centuries); it was also there that he wrote *Meditations on the Church*, also known as *The Catholic Controversy*.[32] The residents of the Chablais considered Les Allinges a relic of the Apostle of the Chablais; however, over the centuries, the state of the fortress had deteriorated. Bishop Rey not only acquired Les Allinges, but also sponsored its restoration and promoted it as a pilgrimage site. To achieve the latter goal, Rey entrusted Les Allinges in 1837 to the care of the Fransalians.[33] Mermier's most well-known statement of St. Francis de Sales's patronage of the missionaries is the following text.

ST. FRANCIS DE SALES: PATRON AND MODEL FOR THE FRANSALIANS (MEMOIR OF 1839, VIII)[34]

The name of St. Francis de Sales is greatly renowned wherever he is known; his writings—luminous and full of the fire [of divine love] which was consuming him—are so widespread and held in the highest regard. His memory and cult are so universally esteemed that all the faithful of the Catholic Church who honor the cult of the saints and in particular that of St. Francis de Sales, bishop of Geneva, the glorious Apostle of the Chablais, will be happy to learn that a new religious community, under the title, "The Congregation of the Missionaries of St. Francis de Sales," is coming into existence in Savoy. The philanthropists themselves, the so-called "friends of humanity," and perhaps also many among the Protestants, would praise this undertaking. If not because it is a work of religion, it will be because of the homage and the tribute of gratitude which we pay through this institution to the virtue of a man who was the greatest friend of his fellow human beings and the most compassionate in all their afflictions.

The house of the Congregation is at Annecy, close to the tomb and relics of its illustrious and glorious protector and patron. It is from there, from its center, that the Congregation hopes to spread itself throughout the diocese and even further if it pleases the sovereign Master of the Harvest to bless it and give it growth [cf. Matt 9:38; Luke 10:2].

Mermier's conviction that the Fransalians' primary apostolate was the parish mission did not fossilize into a narrow commitment that precluded growth and development. On the contrary, from the outset, he considered the foreign missions of capital importance in the work of renewal in the church. When the Holy See requested the Diocese of Annecy to send missionaries to Africa, Mermier regarded this as a call from divine providence. Without delay, Mermier offered the services of the Fransalians and proposed that he himself lead them to Africa. In the end, Rome assigned to the missionaries the Mission of Vizagapatam in east India, on the Bay of Bengal.

Mermier conscientiously maintained communication with the missionaries in India through frequent and substantial correspondence that dealt with the spiritual life, difficulties, and successes. He also shared news about the congregation and France, while encouraging his confreres to reciprocate by writing often.[35] A good example of this correspondence is Mermier's letter of June 3, 1850, to Fr. François Decompoix (1825–1918), who had recently arrived in India, where he would minister for the next seventeen years.[36] Like Favre and Rey, Mermier was critical of the seminary formation of the day and believed in the continuing formation of the clergy, which aligned with Francis de Sales's insistence on ongoing theological study as indispensable in the life of the priest.[37] Mermier here instructs his young confrere in what he regarded as the essential qualities of the priest and suggests useful resources for him to draw on in his priestly ministry.

LETTER OF JUNE 3, 1850, FROM FR. MERMIER TO FR. FRANÇOIS DECOMPOIX, MSFS, IN INDIA[38]

+

J. M. J.

My dear confrere,

As I am writing you for the first time, my dear Decompoix, I would remind you that the work of a priest is summed up by these three words: devotion, study, and ministry.

1. To form oneself in devotion through spiritual exercises well done, first of all, in annual retreats, then followed by the daily practice of meditation, examens, spiritual reading, habitual recollection, and through a great purity of conscience. This task, in my opinion, is more difficult when we look at it as less important or we perform it only by half. In fact, we promise ourselves to do better, but this better is never attained and our lives pass in vain and useless desires. We keep giving ourselves to new projects. St. Bernard,[39] writing to a great pope, was not afraid to call such things cursed—*maledictae*—because they do harm to the first duty that well-ordered charity prescribes, namely, the obligation of each one to care for one's own soul above everything else—"what does it profit a man to gain the whole world and suffer the loss of his own soul?" [Mark 6:36; Matt 16:26]. And then, what do we offer to others? Very little or nothing because the apostle ought to give from his abundance. In vain does a famished child suck the milkless breast of a languishing mother.

I am convinced, my dear confrere, that you know to avoid this fatal danger, as you have not yet had occasion to launch yourself into the great occupations of the ministry. But today, how you are, wherever you are going to be at the head of a Christian community with the problems of housekeeping, you will need to recall some very important advice. The farsighted wisdom of Bishop Neyret[40] would have preceded me without doubt.

2. To form oneself in the knowledge that is necessary and useful for the exercise of such an important ministry, and the success or failure of which has such great consequences, that is the second motive, namely, to study. But what are the means to succeed?

We are to seek it in the Spirit of God. The Spirit of God: The Apostles received it in abundance, and they were filled with this knowledge from the first instant: "all were filled with the Holy Spirit" [Acts 2:4]. God is jealous of His glory. "I will not give My glory to another" [Isa 42:8].

Now, to obtain this Spirit of knowledge, we must ask God for it, we must ask Him to descend upon us through humble prayer and full of confidence, we should be faithful sons.

The means is in the divine Scriptures: let us examine the Scriptures…, and these are those that bear witness to me. St. Ambrose: Scripture is a sacerdotal book. We all have it in our hands, we find it daily in the Divine Office, in the Ordinary of the Mass, in all our prayers; we are as if immersed in it, and yet we do not know it at all or very little. It is indeed a wonder, not to say a monstrosity; a little schoolmaster knows his grammar! Let us pay attention to the use of [Sacred Scripture] by the Fathers of the Church, the Apostles, and Jesus Christ Himself: "It is written," He says, "let us examine the scriptures" [cf. Deut 8:3; Matt 4:4; 21:13; Acts 17:11]. I consider this study so necessary that I would like you all to have at hand a copy of Carrières's edition of the Bible, which includes the translation, together with Menochio's commentary.[41]

The means is in the theology studied, meditated upon, analyzed, compared with practice. You have with you the theology of St. Alphonsus [Liguori].[42] What a great source of help! The best means is to profit by your own experiences, even to take notes on some points so that you may reflect on them at leisure or that you may seek advice in case of doubt.

I say nothing of other means, all very useful, offered by other branches of knowledge offered to apostolic men, in view of the numerous interactions they may have with all kinds of persons, in all kinds of circumstances.

3. To form oneself for ministry, it is the third and the last word: what is its significance? To train oneself for preaching, to teach what is necessary, to whom it is necessary, when it is necessary, and how it is necessary; [this demands] such knowledge and such study, such constant diligence, such union with God.

To train oneself to administer the sacraments, to dispense them worthily, validly, usefully; to form oneself in the celebration of the Holy Sacrifice of the Mass, in the praying of the Breviary, in the performance of the ceremonies, etc., that is, to do everything in the church of God with order, charity, and in an edifying manner, worthily, attentively, entirely, and devotedly.

In 1845, the Missionaries of St. Francis de Sales consisted of a dozen priests. Four of these priests, together with two brothers, were sent to the Mission of Vizagapatam, which at the time numbered two thousand Catholics, spread over a vast area and grouped together in four stations. These seeds yielded a rich harvest: presently, this territory is divided into fifteen dioceses and has a Catholic population of more than a million. Today in India, the Fransalians have seven provinces and serve in over fifty dioceses. Worldwide, they number approximately fifteen hundred members (priests, brothers, and seminarians) and minister in thirty-two countries.[43]

Mermier died at La Feuillette on September 30, 1862, and was buried in the vaults of the motherhouse. Following the anticlerical French government's expulsion of religious congregations and the seizure of their assets (1903), the Fransalians lost La Feuillette. In 1960, during excavation of this property, Mermier's grave was discovered and opened in the presence of ecclesiastical and civil authorities: his body was incorrupt, with even his vestments intact. The diocesan canonical process for Mermier's beatification was opened on October 7, 1990, and Pope St. John Paul II (1920–2005, reigned 1978–2005) declared Mermier a "Servant of God" on May 5, 1993.[44]

Unfortunately, Mermier's cause was unable to be completed, due to lack of availability of the required canonical and theological personnel. On June 20, 2007, the remains of Mermier and Bishop Rey were reinterred in the crypt of the Basilica of St. Francis de Sales at the Monastery of the Visitation in Annecy, and on January 24, 2017, Mermier's cause was reopened by the bishop of Annecy and is currently in process.[45]

III

THE FAMILY OF DON BOSCO

Salesians, Daughters of Mary Help of Christians, Salesian Cooperators

Joseph Boenzi, SDB

Beginning in 1796, Napoleon Bonaparte had brought the French Revolution to Italian soil through the rapid conquest of the peninsula. Italy at the time was a patchwork of independent kingdoms, duchies, cities, and states. Revolutionary ideas followed the conquest including anticlerical movements. But the pendulum swung back after Napoleon was defeated at Waterloo in 1814 and revolutionary impulses were supplanted by efforts to restore elements of the older order, including the monarchy. 1815 thus ushered in the period of the pan-European Restoration (1815–48).

That year was momentous for European politics; the Congress of Vienna (November 1814–June 1815) created a new map of political power in which France, Austria, Russia, Prussia, the Netherlands, Spain, and Great Britain emerged dominant. The future of divided Italy was decided by outside forces, and each of the ten separate nation states was governed by different foreign rulers. Among these, in the Kingdom of Sardinia, composed of Piedmont, Savoy—the region of Francis de Sales's birth and ministry—Nice, and the Island of Sardinia, Victor Emmanuel I of the House of Savoy was restored to the throne. The capital was located in the city of Torino (Turin), at the heart of an area undergoing the process of industrialization that was generating a newly influential middle- and working class and supplanting the local nobility.

Eighteen fifteen was also a harbinger year for what would become the Salesian Pentecost. This was the year in which John Bosco, a Piedmontese peasant, was born in the town of Castelnuovo d'Asti. He would be one of the leading lights of the spiritual flame, first lit by Francis de Sales two centuries prior, that would catch fire across the continent in the nineteenth century.

Bosco came into the world of the Restoration, but during his lifetime latent revolutionary ideals fueled by a flowering spirit of Romanticism would create a new political-cultural climate on the peninsula. The Risorgimento (1848–70) would dawn, an era in which the ten radically diverse nation-states on the peninsula eventually endorsed the ideal of a unified Italy. The implications of this idea would bewilder and occupy the minds and hearts of the era. Monarchy or republic? What of the Catholic Church? And what of the pope and the Papal States, which formed one of those nations? Could one be both a loyal Catholic and a loyal Italian? The impact of the Risorgimento on the church and the implications of the great cultural movements of the century, including industrialization, would come to shape Bosco's world and later educative pastoral ministry.

However, the beginning of the story of Don Bosco's Salesian family, with its headquarters named the Oratory of St. Francis de Sales, are modest, rural, and seemingly far removed from the swirling political and cultural affairs that would later surround that family. In middle age, in the year 1874, Bosco himself drew up an account of the first forty years of his life and ministry with the intent that for his Salesian family, this "will be a record to help people overcome problems that may come in the future by learning from the past. It will serve to make known how God himself has always been our guide."[1]

As his quote suggests, this hindsight narrative, known as the *Memoirs of the Oratory*, is saturated with a keen sense of the guiding presence of the divine, a sense that sustained Bosco throughout his lifetime.

MEMOIRS OF THE ORATORY: CHILDHOOD

The day consecrated to Mary Assumed into Heaven was the day of my birth, in the year 1815 in Morialdo, a village belonging to the town of Castelnuovo d'Asti. My mother's name was Margaret Occhiena, and she was from Capriglio. Francis was my father's name. They were country people who earned their bread and livelihood honestly by hard work and thrift. My good father, almost entirely by the sweat of his brow, supported my grandmother, in her seventies and suffering the aches and pains of old age, three children, of whom the oldest was Anthony, son from my father's first marriage, a middle child Joseph, and the youngest John, who is me, plus two field hands to help him with the farming.

I was not yet two years old when the merciful Lord hit us with a sad bereavement. My dearly loved father died unexpectedly. He was strong and healthy, still young, and actively interested in promoting a good Christian upbringing for his offspring. One day he came home from work covered in sweat and imprudently went down into a cold cellar. That night he developed a high temperature, the first sign of a serious illness. Every effort to cure him proved vain. Within a few days he was at death's door. Strengthened by all the comforts of religion, he encouraged my mother to maintain her trust in God. He died soon afterwards on 12 May 1817; he was only 34.

I do not know how I reacted on that sad occasion. One thing only do I remember, and it is my earliest memory: we were all going out of the room where he had died, and I insisted on staying behind.

My grieving mother addressed me, "Come, John, come with me."

"If papa is not coming, I don't want to come," I answered.

"My poor child," my mother replied, "come with me; you no longer have a papa." Having said this, she broke down and started crying as she took me by the hand and led me away. I began to cry too because she was crying. At that age I could not really understand what a tragedy had fallen on us in our father's death.

This event threw the whole family into difficulty. Five people had to be supported. The crops failed that year because of a drought, and that was our only source of income. The prices of foodstuffs soared. Wheat cost as much as four francs a bushel, corn or maize two and a half francs. Some people who lived at that time have assured me that beggars hesitated to ask for even a crust of bread to soak into their broth of chickpeas or beans for nourishment. People were found dead in the fields, their mouths stuffed with grass, with which they had tried to quell their ravenous hunger.

My mother often used to tell me that she fed the family until she exhausted all her food. She then gave money to a neighbor, Bernard Cavallo, to go looking for food to buy. That friend went round to various markets but was unable to buy anything, even at exorbitant prices. After two days he came in the evening bringing back nothing but the money he had been given. We were all in a panic. We had eaten practically nothing the whole day, and the night would have been difficult to face.

My mother did not allow herself to be discouraged. She went around to the neighbors to try to borrow some food, but she did not find anyone who could help. She told us, "My dying husband told me that I must trust God. So let's kneel down and pray." After a brief prayer she got up and said, "Drastic circumstances demand drastic means." Then she went to the stable and, helped by Mr. Cavallo, she killed a calf. Part of that calf was immediately cooked and the worst of the family's hunger satisfied. In the days that followed, cereals bought at a very high price from more distant places enabled us to survive.

Anyone can imagine how much my mother worked and suffered in that disastrous year. The crisis of that year was overcome by constant hard work, by continuous thrift, by attention to the smallest details and by occasional providential help. My mother often told me of these events, and my relatives and friends confirmed them.

When that terrible scarcity was over and matters at home had improved, a convenient arrangement was proposed to my mother. However, she repeated again and again, "God gave me a husband and God has taken him away. With his death the Lord put three sons under my care. I would be a cruel mother to abandon them when they needed me most."

On being told that her sons could be entrusted to a good guardian who would look after them well, she merely replied, "A guardian could only be their friend, but I am a mother to these sons of mine. All the gold in the world could never make me abandon them."

Her greatest care was given to instructing her sons in their religion, making them value obedience, and keeping them busy with tasks suited to their age. When I was still very small, she herself taught me to pray. As soon as I was old enough to join my brothers, she made me kneel with them morning and evening. We would all recite our prayers together, including the rosary. I remember well how she herself prepared me for my first confession. She took me to church, made her own confession first, then presented me to the confessor. Afterwards, she helped me to make my thanksgiving. She continued to do this until I reached the age when she judged me capable of frequenting the sacrament on my own.

I had reached my ninth year. My mother wanted to send me to school, but this was not easy. The distance to Castelnuovo from where we lived was more than three miles; my brother Anthony was opposed to my boarding there. A compromise was eventually agreed upon. During the winter season I would attend school at the nearby village of Capriglio. In this way I was able to learn the basic elements of reading and writing. My teacher was a devout priest called Joseph Delacqua. He was very attentive to my needs, seeing to my instruction and even more to my Christian education.

During the summer months I went along with what my oldest brother wanted by working in the fields.

It was at that age that I had a dream that made a deep impression on me. In this dream I seemed to be near my home in a fairly large yard. A crowd of children was playing there. Some were laughing, some were playing games, and quite a few were swearing. When I heard these evil words, I jumped immediately amongst them and tried to stop them by using my words and my fists. At that moment, a dignified man appeared, a nobly dressed adult. He wore a white cloak, and his face shone so that I could not look directly at him. He called me by name, told me to take charge of these children, and added these words: "You will have to win these friends of yours not by blows but by gentleness and love. Start right away to teach them the ugliness of sin and the value of virtue."

Confused and frightened, I replied that I was a poor, ignorant child. I was unable to talk to those youngsters about religion. At that moment, the kids stopped their fighting, shouting, and swearing; they gathered round the man who was speaking.

Hardly knowing what I was saying, I asked, "Who are you, ordering me to do the impossible?" "Precisely because it seems impossible to you, you must make it possible through obedience and the acquisition of knowledge." "Where, by what means, can I acquire knowledge?" "I will give you a teacher. Under her guidance you can become wise. Without her, all wisdom is foolishness."

"But who are you that speak so?"

"I am the son of the woman whom your mother has taught you to greet three times a day."

"My mother tells me not to mix with people I don't know unless I have her permission. So tell me your name."

"Ask my mother what my name is." At that moment, I saw a lady of stately appearance standing beside him. She was wearing a mantle that sparkled all over as though covered with bright stars. Seeing from my questions and answers that I was more confused than ever, she beckoned me to approach her. She took me kindly by the hand and said, "Look." Glancing round, I realized that the youngsters had all apparently run away. A large number of goats, dogs, cats, bears, and other animals had taken their place. "This is the field of your work. Make yourself humble, strong, and energetic. And what you will see happening to these animals in a moment is what you must do for my children."

I looked around again, and where before I had seen wild animals, I now saw gentle lambs. They were all jumping and bleating as if to welcome that man and lady.

At that point, still dreaming, I began crying. I begged the lady to speak so that I could understand her, because I did not know what all this could mean. She then placed her hand on my head and said, "In good time you will understand everything."

With that, a noise woke me up and everything disappeared.

I was totally bewildered. My hands seemed to be sore from the blows I had given, and my face hurt from those I had received. The memory of the man and the lady, and the things said and heard, so occupied my mind that I could not get any more sleep that night. I wasted no time in the morning in telling all about my dream. I spoke first to my brothers, who laughed at the whole thing, and then to my mother and grandmother. Each one gave his own interpretation. My brother Joseph said, "You're going to become a keeper of goats, sheep, and other animals." My mother commented, "Who knows, but you may become a priest." Anthony merely grunted, "Perhaps you'll become a robber chief." But my grandmother, though she could not read or write, knew enough theology and made the final judgement, saying, "*Pay no attention to dreams.*"

I agreed with my grandmother. However, I was unable to cast that dream out of my mind. The things I shall have to say later will give some meaning to all this. I kept quiet about these things, and my relatives paid little attention to them. But when I went to Rome in 1858 to speak to the Pope about the Salesian Congregation, he asked me to tell him everything that had even the suggestion of the supernatural about it. It was only then, for the first time, that I said anything about this dream which I had when I was nine or ten years old. The Pope ordered me to write out the dream in all its detail and to leave it as an encouragement to the sons of that Congregation whose formation was the reason for that visit to Rome.

This is the first reference to the Salesian Society that Don Bosco made in these *Memoirs*. He links his dream as a nine-year-old with his life's work as an educator and evangelizer of youth people at risk and stresses the point by telling us how he first retold the dream on the occasion of his journey to Rome in 1858. That was the first of what would become twenty visits to Rome over the course of his life. In 1858 he asked for an individual audience with Pope Pius IX and the pope had him return several times during his stay in the city. At a meeting on March 21, Pius IX asked him to share everything that had influenced his vocation, even "those things that only had the appearance of the supernatural."[2] It was on that very occasion that Don Bosco presented the pope with his ideas to found the Salesian Society.[3]

John's education, religious and otherwise, continued despite the obstacles he would confront as a poor boy from a rural background.

MEMOIRS OF THE ORATORY: BOYHOOD MISSION

One thing that gave me serious concern was the lack of a church or chapel where I could sing, pray with my friends. To hear a sermon or go to catechism, you needed to go about ten kilometers, there and back, either to Castelnuovo or the nearby town of Buttigliera.[4] This was the reason why they willingly came to listen to me repeat the pastor's sermons; I invited them to come by preforming acrobatic tricks.

I was eleven years old when I made my first holy communion.[5] I knew my catechism well. The minimum age for first communion was twelve. Because we lived far from the parish church, the parish priest did not know us, and my mother had to do almost all the religious instruction. She did not want me to get any older before my admission to that great act of our religion, so she took upon herself the task of preparing me as best she could. She sent me to catechism class every day of Lent. I passed my examination, and the date was fixed. It was the day on which all the children were to make their Easter duty.

In the big crowd, it was impossible to avoid distractions. My mother coached me for days and brought me to confession three times during that Lent. "My dear John," she would say, "God is going to give you a wonderful gift. Make sure you prepare well for it. Go to confession and don't keep anything back. Tell all your sins to the priest, be sorry for them all, and promise God to do better in the future." I promised all that. God alone knows whether I have been faithful to my resolution. At home, she saw to it that I said my prayers and read good books; and she always came up with the advice which a diligent mother knows how to give her children.

On the morning of my first communion, my mother did not permit me to speak to anyone. She accompanied me to the altar and together we made our preparation and thanksgiving. These were led by Father Sismondi,[6] the vicar forane, in a loud voice, alternating responses with everyone. It was my mother's wish for that day that I should refrain from manual work. Instead, she kept me occupied reading and praying.

Among the many things that my mother repeated to me was this: "My dear son, this is a great day for you. I am convinced that God has really taken possession of your heart. Now promise him to be good as long as you live. Go to communion frequently in the future but beware of sacrilege. Always be frank in confession, be obedient always, go willingly to catechism and sermons. But for the love of God, avoid like the plague those who indulge in bad talk."

I treasured my mother's advice and tried to carry it out. I think that from that day on there was some improvement in my life, especially in matters of obedience. It was not easy for me to be submissive because I liked to do things my way and follow my own childish whims rather than listen to those who gave me advice or told me what to do.

That year [1826][7] there was a solemn mission in Buttigliera. It gave me a chance to hear several sermons. The preachers were well known and drew people from everywhere. I went with many others. We had an instruction and a meditation in the evening, after which we were free to return home.

On one of these April evenings, as I was making my way home amid the crowd, one of those who walked along with us was Fr. [Giovanni] Calosso of Chieri, a very devout priest.[8] Although he was old and bent, he made the long walk to hear the missioners. He was the chaplain of Morialdo. He noticed a capless, curly-headed lad amidst the others but walking in complete silence. He looked me over and then began to talk with me:

"Where are you from, my son? I gather you were at the mission?"

"Yes, Father, I went to hear the missioners' sermons."

"Now, what could you understand of it? I'm sure your mother could give you a better sermon, couldn't she?"

"Yes it's true, my mother often gives me some very good instructions. But I also like to go and listen to the sermons that the missionaries preach, and I think that I can understand them."

"If you can remember anything from this evening's sermons, I'll give you four *soldi*."[9]

"Just tell me whether you wish to hear the first sermon, or the second."

"Whichever you like," he said, "as long as you tell me something that was said. Do you remember what the first sermon was about?"

"The first sermon was about the necessity of giving yourself to God in good time and not putting off your conversion."

"And what did the preacher say in the sermon?" the venerable old man asked, somewhat surprised.

"Oh, I remember quite well. If you wish I will recite the whole talk for you." Without waiting to be asked again, I launched into the preamble and went on to the three points. The preacher stressed that it was risky to put off conversion because one could run out of time, or one might lack the grace or the will to make the change. There, amidst the crowd, he let me rattle on for half an hour. Then came a flurry of questions from Father Calosso: "What's your name? Who are your family? How much schooling have you had?"

"My name is John Bosco. My father died when I was very young. My mother is a widow with a family of five to support. I've learned to read, and to write a little."

"Have you studied Donato or Grammar?"[10]

"I don't know what they are, Father."

"Would you like to study?"

"Oh yes, I would!"

"What's stopping you?"

"My brother Anthony."

"And why doesn't Anthony want you to study?"

"Because he never liked school himself. He says he doesn't want anyone else to waste time on books the way he did. But if I could only get to school, I would certainly study and not waste time."

"Why do you want to study?"

"I'd like to become a priest."

"And why do you want to become a priest?"

"I'd like to attract my companions, talk to them, and teach them our religion. They're not bad, but they become bad because they have no one to guide them."

These bold words impressed the holy priest. He never took his eyes off me while I was speaking. When our ways parted, he left me with these words: "Cheer up now. I'll provide for you and your education. Come to see me on Sunday with your mother. We'll arrange something."

65

John Bosco was fourteen years old during this period, and his situation at that age was not very different from the plight of young migrant workers he would meet in Turin after his ordination when he founded the Oratory of St. Francis de Sales. In fact, all of his first Salesians who first read these memoirs would have resonated with his descriptions and would have understood his fears and worries. When Fr. Calosso told him to "cheer up," they would have sensed that phrase as being addressed to them.

The following Sunday my mother and I went along to see him. He agreed to teach me one lesson a day. To keep Anthony happy, I was to spend the rest of the day helping him in the fields. He was pleased enough with the plan because my classes would not start till the autumn, when the rush of field work would be over.

I put myself completely into Fr. Calosso's hands. He had become chaplain at Morialdo only a few months before. I opened my soul to him. Every word, thought, and act I revealed to him promptly. This pleased him because it made it possible for him to have an influence on both my spiritual and temporal welfare.

It was then that I came to realize what it was to have a regular spiritual director, a faithful friend of one's soul. I had not had one up till then. Among other things he forbade a penance I used to practice: he deemed it unsuited to my age and circumstances. He encouraged frequent confession and communion. He taught me how to make a short daily meditation, or more accurately, a spiritual reading. I spent all the time I could with him; I stayed with him on Sundays and holidays. I went to serve his Mass during the week when I could.

From then on, I began to savor the spiritual life; up to then I had acted in a purely mechanical way, not knowing the reasons.

In mid-September, I began a regular study of Italian grammar, and soon I was able to write fairly good compositions. At Christmas I went on to study Latin. By Easter I was attempting Italian-Latin and Latin-Italian translations. All this time I persevered with my usual acrobatic shows in the fields to attract my neighbors, to whom I repeated the religious instruction that I had received, or in the barn during the winter. Everything my teacher said or did—his every word, I could say—provided edifying material for my audiences.

At last, I was able to feel happy because my deepest desires were being fulfilled and everything was going so well. Then a new trial, a real catastrophe, shattered all my hopes.

MEMOIRS OF THE ORATORY: SCHOOL AND FARM WORK

During the winter, when the pressure from farm work had eased, Anthony was reasonable enough about the time I gave to my books. When spring came, however, and work was more pressing, he began to grumble that he was left to tackle all the chores while l was wasting my time and acting the gentleman. After some lively, exchanges involving Anthony, my mother, and me, it was decided in the interest of family peace that I should go to school early in the morning and spend the rest of the day working in the fields. But how could I study? How could I manage the translations?

Take note. The walk to school and back allowed me some time to study. When I got home, I would take the hoe in one hand and my grammar in the other, and along the way I would recite and repeat grammatical forms until I reached the place of work. Then glancing longingly at the grammar, I would put it in a corner and begin hoeing, weeding, or gathering greens according to the need.

When there was a rest break, I went off on my own to study, a book in one hand, a hunk of bread in the other. I did the same thing on my way home. Written work had to be done in short periods snatched at mealtimes or in time borrowed from sleep.

Despite all my work and good will, Anthony still was not happy. One day he announced very decisively, first to my mother and then to my brother, Joseph, that he could stand it no more. "I've had it up to here," he blustered. "I've had my fill of this grammar business. Look at me," he said, "I've grown big and strong without ever setting eyes on such books. It's all nonsense!" Carried away by blind rage, I retorted in a way I should not have: "Our donkey is bigger and stronger than you are, and he never went to school either. Do you want to be like him?" This so angered him that only speed saved me from a volley of slaps and punches.

My mother was heartbroken, I was in tears myself, and the chaplain was upset too. In fact, when that worthy minister of God came to know how matters stood in our family, he took me aside one day and said, "Johnny, you've put your faith in me, and I won't let you down. Leave that troublesome brother of yours and come and live in the presbytery. I'll be a loving father to you."

My mother was elated when I told her of this generous offer. In April I moved into the priest's house, though I returned home to sleep.

No one can imagine how supremely happy I was. I idolized Fr. Calosso, loved him as if he were my father, prayed for him, and tried to help him in every way I could. My greatest pleasure was to work for him. I would have died for him. I made more progress in one day with the good priest than I would have made in a week at home. That man of God lavished affection on me, and he would often say, "Don't worry about the future. As long as I'm alive I'll see that you want for nothing. And I'll make provision for you after my death."

Things were going unbelievably well for me. I could say my cup of happiness was full. There was nothing else I could wish for. Then a fresh disaster blighted all my hopes.

One morning the following autumn [1830], Fr. Calosso sent me home on an errand. I had only just made it to the house when a messenger dashed in at my heels. He said I was to get back to Fr. Calosso as fast as I could. He was very ill and wanted to see me. I did not run; I flew. I found my benefactor in bed suffering from a stroke and unable to speak. He recognized me and tried to talk but no words came. He gave me the key to his money and made signs that I was not to give it to anyone. After two days of suffering, Fr. Calosso gave up his soul to God. His death shattered my dreams. I have always prayed for him, and as long as I live, I shall remember my outstanding benefactor every day that dawns.

When Fr. Calosso's heirs turned up, I handed over to them the key and everything else.

MEMOIRS OF THE ORATORY: STUDENT YEARS IN CHIERI

Despite these setbacks, it was eventually determined that John be sent to continue grammar school studies in the city of Chieri.

After the loss of so much time, it was finally decided to send me to Chieri, where I could seriously continue my schooling. That was in [1831]. One who is raised in the backwoods and has never seen anything beyond a few small country villages is easily impressed by any little novelty [to be found in a larger city]. I lodged with a woman from my own town, Lucia Matta, a widow with one son who had decided to move to the city in order to give him the opportunity to study; she wanted me to keep an eye on him. The first person I met was Fr. Eustace Valimberti, of revered memory. He gave me a lot of good advice on how to keep out of trouble. He invited me to serve his Mass and thus he could always advise me well. He brought me to see the headmaster in Chieri and introduced me to my other teachers. Up until then, my studies had been a little of everything and amounted almost to nothing. Accordingly, I was advised to enroll in the sixth class, which today would correspond to the grade preparatory to the first year of high school [*ginnasio*].

My teacher was Dr. Pugnetti, also of dear memory. He was very kind to me. He helped me in school, invited me to his home, and was very sympathetic to me because of my age and my goodwill. He went out of his way to help me as much as he could.

My age and my size made me look like a pillar amongst my little companions. I was anxious to get out of that situation. After two months of the sixth class, I was at its head. I took an examination and moved up to the fifth class. I went gladly to my new class because my classmates were more my size, and my teacher was the beloved Fr. Valimberti. After two more months, I led the class again and, by exception, was allowed to take another examination and so was promoted to the fourth class, which is equivalent to the second year of high school.

Here my teacher was Joseph Cima, a strict disciplinarian. When he saw this student as big and stocky as himself coming into his class in midyear, he joked in front of the whole class, "He's either a simpleton or a genius. What do you make of him?" Taken aback by that harsh introduction, I answered, "Something in between. I'm just a poor boy who has the goodwill to do his work and make progress in his studies."

He was mollified by my reply and went on with unusual kindness, "If you have goodwill, you're in good hands. I'll see that you won't be idle here. Don't worry; if you have any problems, tell me promptly and I'll sort them out for you." I thanked him with all my heart.

After a couple of months in this class, something happened that gave rise to sonic comment about me. One day the teacher was explaining the life of Agesilaus in Cornelius Nepos. I did not have my book with me that day, and to cover my forgetfulness, I kept my Donato open in front of me. My companions noticed, and first one and then another began to laugh. Suddenly the whole classroom was in an uproar.

"What's going on here?" shouted the teacher. "What's going on?" he shot at me, this time. Everyone was looking at me. He told me to construe the text and repeat his explanation. I got to my feet, still holding my Donato. From memory I repeated the text, construed it, and explained it. Instinctively my companions expressed their admiration and burst into applause. The teacher was angry beyond description. It was the first time, according to him, that he had failed to maintain discipline. He swung at me, but I saw it coming and ducked. Next he placed his hand on my Donato and demanded of my neighbors the reason for all the commotion. "Bosco had his Donato in front of him all the time," my companions explained, "but he read and explained the lesson as if he had the Cornelius text."

The teacher took the Donato and insisted I go on for two sentences more. Then he said to me, "In tribute to your wonderful memory, I will overlook your forgetfulness. You have been blessed. Make sure that you put your gift to good use."

At the end of that school year [1831–32] as a result of my high marks, I was promoted to the third class, equivalent to the third year of high school.

John Bosco tells other experiences from his school days, but we move ahead to his entry into the seminary. The Archdiocese of Turin had three seminaries, and one of them was in the city of Chieri where John had come to study high school. The seminary in Chieri was conducted by the Congregation of the Mission, or the Vincentian fathers. With the advice of his confessor and help from a number of friends, he applied and was accepted in the summer of 1835. He was just turning twenty.

The seminary experience would be very different from his life on the farm and his experiences as an apprentice while studying in middle school and high school. He had overcome many difficulties and was glad that the path to the young man's leaning toward and talent for religion culminated in priestly ordination.

MEMOIRS OF THE ORATORY: DEPARTURE FOR THE SEMINARY

I had to be in the seminary on October 30 of that year, 1835. My little wardrobe was ready. My relatives were all pleased, and I even more than they. It was only my mother who was pensive. Her eyes followed me round as if she wanted to say something to me. On the evening before my departure, she called me to her and spoke to me these unforgettable words: "My dear John, you have put on the priestly habit. I feel all the happiness that any mother could feel in her son's good fortune. Do remember this, however: it's not the outfit that honors your state, but the practice of virtue. If you should ever begin to doubt your vocation, then—for heaven's sake!—do not dishonor this habit. Put it aside immediately. I would much rather have a poor farmer for a son, than a priest who neglects his duties. When you came into the world, I consecrated you to the Blessed Virgin. When you began your studies, I recommended devotion to this Mother of ours. Now I say to you, be completely hers. Love those of your companions who have devotion to Mary, and if you become a priest, always preach and promote devotion to Mary."

My mother was deeply moved as she finished these words, and I cried. "Mother," I replied, "I thank you for all you have said and done for me. These words of yours will not prove vain. I will treasure them all my life."

The following morning, I went off to Chieri, and on the evening of that same day I entered the seminary. After greeting my superiors, I made my bed, and then, with my friend [Guglielmo] Garigliano, strolled through the dormitories, the corridors, and finally into the courtyard. Glancing up, I notice a sundial with the Latin inscription: *Afflictis lentae, celeres gaudentibus horae* (For those who are sad, the hours drag by; for those who are joyful, the hours fly). "That's it," I said to my friend, "that's our program! Let's always be cheerful, and the time will pass quickly."

MEMOIRS OF THE ORATORY: ORDINATIONS AND PRIESTHOOD

When the [1839–40] school year ended, I got the idea of attempting something for which one was rarely given permission in those days—to cover the course of a year's theology during my holidays. With this in mind and without telling anyone, I presented myself to Archbishop Fransoni to ask permission to study the fourth-year texts during the holidays. In the following school year (1840–41) I would complete the *quinquennium*. I cited my advanced age—I was twenty-four—as the reason for my request.

That holy prelate made me feel very welcome and, after verifying the results of the exams I had taken till then in the seminary, granted the favor I was asking on condition that I study all the units covered in the required courses. Fr. Antonio Cinzano, my vicar forane, was enlisted to carry out the archbishop's instructions. After two months of study, I finished the prescribed units, and I was admitted to the subdiaconate in time for the autumn ordinations. When I think now of the virtues required for that most important step, I am convinced that I was not sufficiently prepared for it. But since I had no one to care directly for my vocation, I turned to Fr. Cafasso. He advised me to go forward and trust in his advice. I made a ten-day retreat at the House of the Mission in Torino. During it I made a general confession so that my confessor would have a clear picture of my conscience and would be able to give me suitable advice. Though I wanted to complete my studies, I quaked at the thought of binding myself for life. Before I took the final step, I wanted to receive the full approbation of my confessor.

From that time on, I took extra care to practice Fr. Borel's advice: a vocation is preserved and perfected by recollection and frequent communion. On my return to the seminary, I was put into the fifth year and made a prefect. This is the highest responsibility open to a seminarian.

On the day before Passion Sunday 1841, my ordination as a deacon took place; on the Ember Days[11] of summer I would be ordained a priest. The day I had to leave the seminary for the last time was very difficult for me. My superiors loved me and showed continual marks of benevolence. My companions were very affectionate towards me. You could say that I lived for them and they lived for me. If anyone wanted a shave or his tonsure renewed, he ran to Bosco; if he wanted someone to make a biretta[12] for him, to sew or patch his clothes, Bosco was the man he turned to. So you can imagine how sad I was to depart from that place where I had lived for six years, where I received education, knowledge, a spirit of Church, and all the tokens of kindness and affection one could desire.

My ordination day was the vigil of the feast of the Blessed Trinity. I said my first Mass in the church of St. Francis of Assisi, where Fr. Cafasso was dean of the conferences. Though a priest had not said his first Mass in my home place for many years, and my neighbors were anxiously waiting for me to say mine there, I preferred to say it without fuss in Torino. That day was the most wonderful day of my life. At the Memento in that unforgettable Mass, I remembered devoutly all my teachers, my benefactors spiritual and temporal, and especially the ever-lamented Fr. Calosso, whom I have always remembered as my greatest benefactor. On Monday I said Mass in the Church of Our Lady of Consolation to thank the great Virgin Mary for the innumerable graces she had obtained for me from her divine Son Jesus.

On Tuesday I went to say Mass in St. Dominic's Church in Chieri, where my old professor Fr. Giusiana was still living. With fatherly affection he was waiting for me. He was so moved that he cried all through the Mass. I spent the whole day with him, one I can call a day in paradise.

Thursday was the solemnity of Corpus Christi. I went home and sang Mass in the local church and there I officiated at the procession of the Blessed Sacrament. The parish priest invited to dinner my relatives, the clergy, and the leading citizens of the town. They were all happy to be a part of it because everyone was happy for anything that would turn out to my advantage. I went home that evening to be with my family. As I drew near the house and saw the place of the dream I had when I was about nine, I could not hold back the tears. I said: "How wonderful are the ways of Divine Providence! God has truly raised a poor child from the earth to place him amongst the princes of his people."

At this point Bosco was sent for further ecclesial education in Turin. The religious situation on the Italian peninsula mirrored that of much of the rest of Europe at this time. After the heady Enlightenment and the wild Revolution with its anticlericalism and suppression of religious institutions, the Restoration sought a return to the stability of a powerful unity of monarch and church. Under King Victor Emmanuel I a restrictive line was followed that favored the aristocracy and enforced religious observance. The great moral theological controversy of the time pitted the tendencies of Laxism (teaching that whenever possible, any opportunity for liberty should be followed) and Jansenism (stressing human moral depravity and the predestination of both damned and saved) against one another. The result was a pastoral "middle" ground with an emphasis on morality as defining Christian identity. This translated in the pastoral realm into a type of severe rigorism. Supporters insisted on frequent reception of the sacraments but linked ascetic morality with sacramental life. A rigorous religious regime that emphasized the confession of sins, penance, and the necessity to strive after "perfection" was common. God was presented as Judge, universal judgment was a common theme of sermons, and the fear of God became the predominant religious emotion.

At the same time, when Napoleon had earlier invaded Italy, he had done so by way of Savoy and many "radical" ideas such as liberty and equality and separation of church and state had circulated in Italy through the Piedmontese link. Thus in the north, in the Kingdom of Sardinia (inclusive of Piedmont and Savoy), despite the religious rigorism of the Restoration, other ideas continued to circulate. Since the beginning of the century a movement to renew the clergy had gained ground there. This movement, born on the aftermath of the Enlightenment and French Revolution, when criticism of clergy was intense, worked to foster a new apostolic interest among priests and seminarians. A key institution that furthered this renewal was the Convitto Ecclesiastico in Turin. Founded in 1818 by the moral theologian and priest of the Archdiocese of Turin, Luigi Guala (1775–1848), the Convitto offered newly ordained priests a more grounded, pastoral formation after the heady academic training they had received in the archdiocesan seminary. By the time John Bosco entered the Convitto in 1841, Guala was nearing retirement and had entrusted much of the formation to Fr. Joseph Cafasso (1811–16, canonized 1947). Fr. Cafasso, one of the so-called social saints of the era, known particularly as the "priest of the gallows" for his work with death-row prisoners, taught moral theology. He promoted the "benignist" approach of Alphonsus Liguori that presented God as a merciful father, stressing frequent communion and devotion to Mary, the helper and mother of the faithful. He had launched a renewal of piety and devotion among the laity of his day. This spirituality had a decidedly social dimension: attention for the poor. Almost all priest-educators at the Convitto were making an "option for the poor" at this time. Although the Alphonsan renewal was blocked in parts of the peninsula, like the papal states, it was supported by others, including those at the Convitto.

Cafasso was also a devotee of St. Francis de Sales, well remembered in the region not only as a renowned doctor of the church but as a local saint as well. At the Convitto students studied the Doctor of Divine Love's *Treatise on the Love of God* and celebrated his memory. In his efforts to prepare the young priests at the Convitto for new ministries in a changing society, he actively proposed Francis de Sales as a patron of a new kind of priest who rejected careerism and embraced a life among the poor who lived on the margins of society. He held up the saint as a model missionary among Protestants and an effective apostle in rural Savoy—a model that all priests should imitate. John Bosco, who had Cafasso as his confessor and spiritual director, frequently heard him champion a new style of apostolic priest in the tradition of Francis de Sales, when he instructed them:

> Which of us, brothers (for there are a certain number of us here)—which of us will save more souls? Which of us will wear a huge crown of saved souls in heaven?...Who will be? Neither I nor you can know at the moment, but we can all have the desire to save many. We can all make the commitment to

save as many as we can, since although someone works in a small village, in a hamlet, among tough and obstinate people, nevertheless with his prayers, with the purity of his intention, with groans and sighs and mortification, he can save more souls than are saved by the most famous preacher in the world. And even if our people are so stubborn that we do not save even one, that will take nothing away from our crown, and God will reward us equally, as if we had truly saved them all.

Dedicate your lives to seeking souls—souls, my brothers! Souls for Heaven. "Give me souls," Saint Francis de Sales kept repeating: "Give me souls, O Lord, if you want me to experience a little bit of happiness in this world!"[13]

Don Bosco's first assigned ministry as a priest was as a chaplain at a shelter for girls at risk, founded in Turin by the Marchioness of Barolo, Juliette Colbert Falletti (1786–1864). Other ministries included visiting prisoners, teaching catechism, and helping out at many country parishes. But what was to become the focus of his life's work increasingly presented itself to him on the streets and in the prisons of the capital city.

There were several categories of young people teaming about the streets of Turin with whom John Bosco came into contact: a few privileged elite who enjoyed educational opportunities; hardworking youth from urban and working-class families who enjoyed some education but were faced with limited work opportunities as artisans because of changes in a traditional economy that was transforming into an industrial one; unschooled migrant youth, some as young as eleven or twelve, swarming into the city from the countryside and looking for work in what was often the most dangerous and uncompensated construction sector; young offenders roaming in gangs having serving time in Turin's inhumane prisons. Encouraged by Fr. Cafasso, Don Bosco dedicated his apostolic efforts to troubled youth. The sad plight of imprisoned boys convinced him of the importance of intervening in the life of young people before they became at risk.

MEMOIRS OF THE ORATORY:
BEGINNING OF THE ORATORY

Hardly had I registered at the Convitto of St. Francis, when I met at once a crowd of boys who followed me in the streets and the squares and even into the sacristy of the church attached to the institute. But I could not take direct care of them since I had no place to host a group. A humorous incident opened the way to put into action my project for the boys who roamed the streets of the city, especially those released from prison.

On the solemnity of the Immaculate Conception of Mary (December 8, 1841), I was vesting to celebrate holy Mass at the appointed time. The sacristan, Joseph Comotti, saw a boy in a corner of the room and asked him to come and serve my Mass.

"I don't know how," he answered, completely embarrassed.

"Come on," repeated the sacristan, "I want you to serve Mass."

"I don't know how," the boy repeated. "I've never served Mass."

"You little brat," said the sacristan, quite furious, "if you don't know how to serve Mass, what are you doing in the sacristy?" With that he grabbed a feather duster and hit the poor boy about the head and shoulders.

As the boy beat a hasty retreat, I cried loudly, "What are you doing? Why are you beating him like that? What's he done?"

"Why is he hanging around the sacristy if he doesn't know how to serve Mass?"

"But you've done wrong."

"What does it matter to you?"

"It matters plenty. He's a friend of mine. Call him back at once. I need to speak with him."

"Son! Sonny!" the sacristan began to shout, as he ran after him. Promising him better treatment, the sacristan brought him back to me. The boy came trembling and tearful because of the blows he had received.

"Have you attended Mass yet?" I asked him with as much loving kindness as I could.

"No," he answered.

"Well, come to Mass now. Afterwards I'd like to talk to you about something that will please you."

He promised to do as I said. I wanted to calm down the poor fellow's spirit and not leave him with that sad impression towards the people in charge of that church. Once I had celebrated my Mass and made due thanksgiving, I took my candidate into a side chapel. Trying to allay any fear he might have of another beating, I started questioning him cheerfully:

"My good friend, what's your name?"

"My name's Bartholomew Garelli."

"Where are you from?"

"Asti."

"Is your father alive?"

"No, my father's dead."

"And your mother?"

"My mother's dead too."

"How old are you?

"I'm sixteen."

"Can you read and write?"

"I don't know anything."

"Have you made your first communion?"

"Not yet."

"Have you ever been to confession?"

"Yes, when I was small."

"Are you going to catechism classes now?"

"I don't dare."

"Why?"

"Because the other boys are smaller than I am, and they know their catechism. As big as I am, I don't know anything, so I'm ashamed to go."

"If I were to teach you catechism on your own, would you come?"

"I'd come very willingly."

"Would you come willingly to this little room?"

"I'd come willingly enough, provided they don't beat me."

"Relax. No one will harm you. Instead, you will be my friend and you'll be dealing with me and no one else. When would you like us to begin our catechism?"

"Whenever you wish."

"This afternoon?"

"Okay."

"Are you willing right now?"

"Yes, right now, with great pleasure."

Don Bosco uses dramatic language to describe this pivotal moment in his life, and then downplays it by calling it "an incident." That chance meeting with an orphan in the sacristy on the Feast of the Immaculate Conception in 1841 would set a pattern for the way he would approach abandoned youth. The scene is dramatic. In his narrative, Don Bosco tells us how he spoke to the boy after Mass. His motive, he says, was very simple. "I wanted to calm down the poor boy's spirit and not leave him with that sad impression towards the people in charge of that church." At this point, then, the newly ordained Don Bosco does not see his life's mission spreading out before him. He just hopes to ease the suffering of a migrant boy who had been the victim of prejudice and violence.

When he learned from the teenaged apprentice that he had never received communion but that he would like to do so, Don Bosco offers to give him religious instruction. He continues his narrative with a simple reference to Catholic practice and the need of a young person who felt distant from religion but not hostile to it.

I stood up and made the sign of the cross to begin but my pupil made no response because he did not know how to do it. In that first catechism lesson I taught him to make the sign of the cross. I also taught him to know God the Creator and why he created us. Though Bartholomew's memory was poor, with attentive diligence in a few feast days, he learned enough to make a good confession and soon after, his holy communion.

To this first pupil some others were added. During that winter, I concentrated my efforts in helping grown-ups who needed special catechism, above all those who were just out of prison. I was beginning to learn from experience that if young lads just released from their place of punishment could find someone to befriend them, to look after them, to assist them on feast days, to help them get work with good employers, to visit them occasionally during the week, these young men soon forgot the past and began to mend their ways. They became good Christians and honest citizens.

This was the beginning of our Oratory. It was to be blessed by the Lord with growth beyond my imagining at that time.

Before ordination he had learned that the seminary's patron, St. Francis de Sales, attracted many needy people to the love of Christ through gentleness and loving kindness. Now in Fr. Cafasso's pastoral courses, he was presented with the saint's underlying motivation: "to save souls." Those approaches described what Don Bosco now offered the criteria for his actions during the first months that he worked among poor immigrant apprentices in 1841 and 1842.

All my efforts that winter were concentrated on getting the little Oratory established. My aim was to bring together only those children who were in greatest danger, ex-prisoners by preference. Nevertheless, as a foundation on which to build discipline and morality, I invited some other boys of good character who had already been taught. These helped me maintain order, and they read and sang hymns. From the very beginning I realized that without songbooks and suitable reading matter, these festive gatherings would have been like a body without a soul. In those days, the feast of the Purification (February 2) was still a holy day of obligation. On that day in

1842, I already *had* about twenty children with whom we were able to sing for the first time "Sing Praises to Mary, O Tongues of the Faithful."[14]

What we begin to notice is that as Bosco speaks of his work among poor apprentices in Turin, his timeline is completely Marian. Everything began on December 8th, Feast of the Immaculate Conception; his group makes headway on February 2nd, Feast of the Purification of Mary—according to the liturgical calendar of his day, rather than the Presentation of the Lord, as we would reference it.

In the month of March, Don Bosco tells us, the Oratory begins to grow. Again this takes place under the guidance of the Virgin Mary.

By the feast of the Annunciation to the Holy Virgin, our group already numbered thirty members. On that day we held a little celebration. In the morning, the young people approached the holy sacraments; in the afternoon they sang a hymn of praise to Mary, and after the catechism lesson, I told them an example of Christian life during a short sermon. The small choir room where we had gathered up to then, had become decidedly too small, so we moved to the nearby chapel inside the sacristy.

This is how we organized the Oratory in those early days: every Sunday and holiday offered the youngsters the possibility to approach the holy sacraments of confession and communion; but one Saturday and one Sunday each month was designated as the time to perform this religious duty. In the afternoon, at a specific hour, a hymn of praise was sung, catechism was taught, then a story full of Christian examples. The day ended with the distribution of little prizes or treats, sometimes to everyone, sometimes by lot.

As a newly ordained priest, John Bosco found his joy in working with young immigrant apprentices. As they searched for better opportunities to earn a livelihood, he accompanied them. He looked for ways to help them learn their trades and find fair employers. At the same time, he accompanied them also as they searched for ways to love and serve God.

These experiences were key to Bosco's own discernment as he clarified his priestly vocation. So much of this took place while he was a student-priest at the Convitto Ecclesiastico. It is interesting to note that Bosco spent three years at the Convitto and was known as a diligent student of moral and pastoral theology; however, in his *Memoirs*, he does not say a word about courses. Instead, he describes the "Oratory"/Youth Center that he was developing for young people. Contact with Turin's poor youth strengthened his vocation, as did the opportunities he found to preach and give retreats to the young and the poor. And it is in connection to the young that he discovers a passion for his vocation.

> After two years at the Convitto, I passed my confessional examination. What a joy to find my confessional surrounded by forty or fifty young people seeking God.
>
> At that time, I began to preach publicly in some churches in Torino, in the Hospital of Charity, at the Hotel of Virtue, in prisons, in the College of St. Francis of Paola, directing triduums, novenas, or spiritual exercises. After two years of moral theology, I enrolled in the confessional exam. After I passed that examination, I was better able to cultivate the discipline, morality and spiritual good of my youngsters in prisons, in the Oratory and wherever they were beginning to practice their professions.
>
> It was a comforting thing for me during the week and especially on Sundays and holidays to see my confessional surrounded by forty or fifty young people waiting for hours and hours for their turn to come to be able to confess.
>
> This was the ordinary way of life at the Oratory for almost three years, that is, until October 1844.[15]

The Hotel of Virtue (Albergo dei Virtù), mentioned in this last passage, was a center for training youngsters in trades, particularly those whose families could not afford to do so. The Albergo was founded in 1580 by Charles Emmanuel I, Duke of Savoy, and continued to operate until after World War II, closing in 1954. Clearly, the young Don Bosco had already begun to ally himself with people and institutions that looked out for poor, working-class youth.

In fact, among the works of the Oratory, the guiding and training of apprenticing youths was a priority. Bosco was proficient in a number of crafts and trades, thanks to his rural background. He passed on his skills to many young people seeking employment in Turin's growing economy. He also visited his Oratory youth on their job sites, defending them when warranted. He was the first person to draw up employment contracts for young workers who were likely to be exploited had he not done so. Later we will look at how Don Bosco secured just wages for young workers, but for now, we return to Bosco's narrative.

Meanwhile, new things, mutations and even tribulations were being prepared by Divine Providence.

At the end of three years dedicated to the study of moral theology, it was time for me to apply for some specific area of the sacred ministry. The uncle of my friend Luigi Comollo, Fr. Giuseppe Comollo, rector of Cinzano was now very old and frail. With the backing of the archbishop, he had asked me to be the treasurer of the parish, which due to age and illness he could no longer sustain. Fr. Guala himself dictated a thank-you letter to Archbishop Fransoni, while I was preparing for something else.

One day Fr. Cafasso called me aside and said, "Now you have completed the course of your studies. The purpose of all you have been studying is that you become qualified to work. In these times the harvest is abundant. To which ministry do you feel especially inclined?"

"To the one that you will be pleased to point out to me," I answered.

"There are three openings," Fr. Cafasso told me. "There would be a post as vice curate in Buttigliera d'Asti; or you could take up the role of tutor in moral theology here at the Convitto; or you might accept the position of director of a small Children's Hospital now under construction next to the Girls' Refuge. Which would you choose?"

"Whatever you will judge to be the most appropriate for me."

"Don't you feel inclined to one thing more than another?"

"I feel drawn to work for young people. But after that, I bow my head and desire to do whatever God wants. I know that I will discover the will of the Lord in your guidance."

"At this moment what fills your heart? How does it come up into your mind?"

"At this moment I seem to find myself in the midst of a multitude of children, who are asking me for help."

Fr. Cafasso paused for a moment. Then he said, "Alright, then: go take a few weeks of vacation. When you return, I will tell you your destination."

That conversation seems quite intense. Bosco reproduces it to point out the importance of seeking the assistance of a spiritual guide when discerning important steps to take in one's life. To the young Bosco, it was a matter of imitating Christ, who came to "the will of the Father."

In a matter of days, Bosco left the Pastoral Institute to take up residence and ministry at the Refuge, founded and sustained by the Marchioness Barolo. Of course, on Sundays he conducted his ministry for migrant youth there. Here is how he describes the transfer:

On the second Sunday of October, dedicated to the Motherhood of Mary, I took part in the transfer of the Oratory to the Refuge with my boys. At the first announcement they felt some confusion, but when I told them that there was a large room waiting for us, reserved completely for us—a place where they could sing, run, jump, and organize games, they were overjoyed. They could not wait for the following Sunday to see the novelties they were imagining. On the third Sunday of that October, Feast of the Purity of the Virgin Mary, a little after midday, a crowd of youngsters of various ages and different conditions ran down into the Valdocco district of the city, in search of the new Oratory.

"Where is the Oratory, where is Don Bosco?" they asked everywhere.

Nobody knew how or what to say, because nobody in that neighborhood had heard of Don Bosco or the Oratory. The young people, believing that they were being mocked, raised their voices, and became more demanding. The neighbors, believing that they were being insulted, became angry and started to threaten the young people.

Things began looking grim when Fr. Borel and I, hearing the shouting, left the house. When we appeared, all noise, all altercations ceased. The young people ran up and crowded around us, asking, "Where is the Oratory?"

We told them that that the real Oratory was not yet completed, but that in the meantime it could be held in my room, which, being spacious, would have served us very well. In fact, for that Sunday, things went pretty well. But on the following Sunday, the regular pupils were joined by several from the neighborhood, and we no longer knew where to put them. The room, corridor, staircase—everywhere was crowded with teenagers. On All Saints Day, Fr. Borel and I started to hear confessions in the few minutes before Mass. Everyone wanted to confess! But what were we to do? We were only two confessors, there were over two hundred youngsters, all trying to help. One wanted to light the fire, another tried to put it out. One carried wood, another water, bucket, springs, shovels, jugs, basins, chairs, shoes, books and every imaginable object was put upside down and right side up, while they tried to sort and fix things.

"It is not possible to go on like this," dear Fr. Borel exclaimed. "We need to provide premises that are more suitable." However, we spent the next six Sundays and holidays in that narrow space, which was the room on the second floor of the vestibule of the first entrance to the Refuge.

In the meantime, we went to talk with Archbishop Fransoni, who understood the importance of our project.

"Go," he told us, "do what you judge best for these souls. I give you all the permissions and permits that you need. Talk to the Marchesa Barolo, perhaps she will be able to give you some suitable premises. But tell me: why can these boys not go to their own parishes?"

"They are mostly young migrants who spend only part of the year in Torino. They don't even know which parish to attend. And many of them are in bad shape, they speak unintelligible dialects, therefore they understand little and are barely understood by others. Some are already growing tall, and they don't dare go to school where they would need to associate with the little children."

"Therefore," the archbishop summed up, "a separate place that is suited for them seems very necessary. So move forward. I bless you and your project. If I can do anything for you, come and let me know, and I will always do whatever I can."

MEMOIRS OF THE ORATORY: UNDER THE BANNER OF ST. FRANCIS DE SALES

We actually went to talk with the Marchesa Barolo. Since the Children's Hospital would not open until the following August, the charitable lady was happy to let us set up a chapel in two spacious rooms intended for the recreation of the priests who would take up residence at the Refuge. To enter the new Oratory, one passed where the door of the hospital is now, and along a small lane that separates it from the Cottolengo Hospital. One entered the current priests' residence and took the internal staircase up to third floor.

Divine Providence chose this site for the first church of our Oratory. We named it after St. Francis de Sales for two reasons: firstly, because the Marchesa Barolo had planned to found a congregation of priests under this title, and with this intention she had the image of this saint painted and placed in entry of the residence, and it is still admired today; secondly, because our ministry with young requires great calm and meekness, we placed ourselves under the protection of this saint, so that he might obtain for us the grace from God to be able to imitate him in his extraordinary gentleness in winning of souls. Another reason to put ourselves under the protection of this saint was so that he could help us from heaven to imitate him in fighting errors against religion, especially Protestantism, which was beginning to insidiously insinuate itself in our territory and especially in the city of Torino.

Fr. Giovanni Bonetti, publishing historical notes of the founding of the Oratory of St. Francis de Sales in the 1880s, ratified Don Bosco's account. He stated that "Don Bosco desired to obtain the assistance of that great champion of the Faith who had in his own time overcome so many of the sects and accomplished great things for the good of the Church."[16]

Was this really the case? Would Don Bosco have been worried about Protestants and other evangelical sects in the 1840s? This does not seem likely. Turin, like most of the Kingdom of Sardinia, was officially and thoroughly Catholic during the era of the Restoration. And although there were pockets of Waldensians in Susa and Pinerolo at the time, just as there were Jewish neighborhoods in Chieri and other small cities, no one spoke of freedom of worship before the beginning of the Risorgimento.

In 1848, King Charles Albert granted freedom of religion and full civil rights to the non-Catholic groups. During the next decade, the Waldensian community established a center in Turin, with a church and printing press near the main train station. It was only then that they began a campaign to convert people to their beliefs.[17]

When Don Bosco began his work among the abandoned youth of the capital, he had no contact with Protestants. No Reformed or Lutheran churches existed in the city at that time, and the Waldensians would not arrive for another decade. If Don Bosco was concerned about proselytism, this was not his first thought when organizing his youth center. This means that we can discount this as a motive for invoking Francis de Sales as patron during the earliest years of Don Bosco's ministry.

What is true, however, is that he did seem to look to this saint as a model of pastoral charity. This can be discerned from Don Bosco's own wording in regulations for youth work in the archdiocese— regulations that he drew up and published between 1847 and 1852:

> This oratory is placed under the patronage of Saint Francis de Sales because those who intend to dedicate themselves to this kind of work should adopt this saint as a model of charity and affability. These are the sources of good fruit that we expect the Work of the Oratories can produce.[18]

This is the first indication we have of Don Bosco's personal reasons for choosing Francis de Sales. He did not seek out the saint in order to respond to "the sects." Nor did he settle on Francis de Sales simply to please the Marchesa Barolo, even if he credits her with the first inspiration. Don Bosco chose Francis de Sales for pastoral reasons: "because those who intend to dedicate themselves to this kind of work should adopt this saint as a model of charity and affability."

MEMOIRS OF THE ORATORY: SUSPICIONS OF MADNESS

Once the little hospital opened, Don Bosco had to find other premises in which he could gather the young people. During the week he continued to work for the Marchesa Barolo beside Fr. Borel, but on Sundays he gathered the young people in a plaza, in a chapel, in farm fields, and even in a cemetery. But those who welcomed him as a priest did not welcome the young people who seemed too many, too wild, too poor. And working six days a week as a chaplain, he had no rest on Sundays as he tried to care for the poorest migrant youth of the city. Everything was taking a toll on his health. Fr. Borel encouraged him to let go of his service among the apprentices; the Marchesa released him from his contract. His brother priests of the diocese noticed his fatigue and what they thought was a stubborn attachment to an impossible and unremunerated work among the poorest young people. He tells the story himself.

More and more rumors began to circulate that Don Bosco had gone mad. My friends were in pain; others laughed; but everyone kept away from me. The archbishop felt it was time to intervene; Fr. Cafasso advised him to procrastinate, Fr. Borel was silent. So all my friends and collaborators left me alone among about four hundred boys.

On that occasion some respectable people wanted to take care of my health. "This Don Bosco," one said, "has some obsessions that will inevitably lead him to madness. Maybe treatments will do him good. Let us lead him to the asylum and there, with due regard, we will do what prudence suggests." Two priests from the archdiocese were instructed to pick me up in a carriage and take me to the insane asylum. The two messengers greeted me politely, then asked me for news of my health, the Oratory, the future building, and church. They finally sighed and told each other: "It's true." After that they invited me to go with them on a little stroll. "A little fresh air will do you good. Come: we have the carriage, we will go together, and we will have time to talk."

I then became aware of the trick they wanted to play on me, and without showing myself to be aware of it, I accompanied them to the carriage. I insisted that they enter the carriage first, and instead of entering it myself, I quickly slammed the door and shouted to the coachman: "Go with all speed to the asylum, where these two churchmen are expected."

MEMOIRS OF THE ORATORY: THE ORATORY FINDS A PERMANENT SITE

While the above things were happening, the last Sunday had come when I was still allowed to hold the Oratory in the meadow [March 15, 1846]. I remained silent about everything, but everyone knew my embarrassments and my thorns. In the afternoon of that day, I felt terrible about what might happen to the multitude of young people as I watched them in their games. I considered the abundant harvest that was being prepared for the sacred ministry, for which there were only a handful of exhausted workers, in bad health, without knowing where in the future I could gather my boys. I felt deeply moved.

Therefore, I moved to one side of the meadow. I set out to walk alone and, perhaps for the first time, I was nearly moved to tears. Walking around and raising my eyes to heaven, I exclaimed, "My God, why don't you make things clear to me? Why don't you show me the place where you want me to gather these children? Either let me know or tell me what to do."

I finished those expressions when someone named Pancrazio Soave arrived, stammering, and saying to me: "Is it true that you are looking for a site to set up a laboratory?"

"Not a laboratory, but an Oratory," I replied.

"I don't know the difference between an oratory and a laboratory, but there is a property nearby for rent. Come and see it. It is owned by Mr. Giuseppe Pinardi, an honest person. Come and he will make a good contract."...

When I reached the place indicated, I saw a two-story shelter with a worm-eaten wooden staircase and balcony, surrounded by vegetable gardens, meadows, and fields. I wanted to climb the stairs to the second story, but Pinardi and Pancrazio exclaimed: "No!" they told me. "The site intended for you is back here." It was an extended lean-to, which on one side was built into the wall of the house, and on the other ended at a height of about one meter from the ground. It seemed suited for use as a warehouse or woodshed and no more. To get inside I had to keep my head down to avoid bumping into the ceiling.

"I can't use it, because it's too low," I said.

"I'll have it fixed to please you," Pinardi graciously resumed. "I will excavate, I will make steps, I will make another floor; but I really want your laboratory to be established here."

"Not a laboratory, but an Oratory, a small church to gather youngsters."

"A church? More willingly! I will lend my service very willingly. Let us write a contract. I am also a singer, I will come to help you with church services. I will bring two chairs, one for me and one for my wife. And then in my house I have a large lamp, I will bring it here."

That respectable man seemed to be raving with delight at the prospect of having a church in his house.

"I thank you, my good friend, for your charity and good will. I accept these appealing offers if you can lower my floor no less than a foot [50 cm]. But how much do you ask?"

"Three hundred francs; they want to give me more, but I prefer to offer it to you, who wants to use this place for public benefit and religion."

"I will give you three hundred and twenty francs, provided you also give me the strip land that surrounds the house for the recreation of the young. Promise me that next Sunday I can already come here with my boys."

"Understood, agreement concluded. Come next Sunday. Everything will be ready."

I did not look for anything else. I quickly ran to my young people. I gathered them around me, and I started shouting in a loud voice: "Courage, my sons! We will have a more stable Oratory, better than anything we have ever had. We will have church, sacristy, rooms for classes, a playground for recreation. Sunday, next Sunday we will meet in the new Oratory, which is there in the Pinardi house!" And I pointed in the direction of the new place.

My words were received with the most lively enthusiasm. Some ran or jumped for joy; some stood as motionless; some shouted loudly and cheered, and I would say with squeals and screams. But moved like those who feel great pleasure and do not know how to express it, they were carried away by profound gratitude.

That morning we had celebrated Mass in the shrine of Our Lady of the Fields. Now we knelt to thank the Holy Virgin who had accepted and answered our prayers: we knelt for the last time in that meadow, and we recited the Holy Rosary, after which everyone went home. Thus we gave a last farewell to that meadow, which each one had loved out of necessity, but which, in the hope of having another better place, we abandoned without regret.

The following Sunday, Easter Sunday, on the 12th of April, all the church and recreation equipment was transported to the Pinardi property, and we took possession of our new place.

MEMOIRS OF THE ORATORY: OPENING THE YOUTH HOSTEL

The story of the move to the Pinardi property brought the second unit to an end. The third unit covered the decade from 1846 to 1855. The first year was very eventful, and Don Bosco had to face many difficulties. He became so exhausted that he collapsed with a bad case of bronchitis that nearly killed him. After he recovered, he returned to his family for a few weeks of rest and convalescence. He convinced his mother, Margherita Occhiena Bosco, to come to Valdocco with him and help him care for needy boys. She agreed and, at the age of fifty-eight, she left the country for the first time and took up residence in the city.

"Mama Margaret," as the Oratory youth would call her, became a significant educative presence at the Oratory of St. Francis de Sales. She figures importantly in the final episode that Don Bosco recorded in the first copybook where he composed the *Memoirs of the Oratory*. That incident is a significant one.

Now it happened that one rainy evening in May [1847], after dark, that a young person of about fifteen, all soaked from the rain, showed up at our door. He asked for bread and shelter. My mother welcomed him into the kitchen, brought him close to the fire and as he warmed up and dried his clothes, she gave him soup and bread to eat.

While he was eating, I asked him if he had gone to school, if he had any relatives, and what profession he practiced. He replied: "I am a poor orphan, and I come from the Valley of Sesia to look for work. I had three francs with me, all of which I spent before being able to earn more money and now I have nothing left and it's like I'm not even a person."

"Have you already been promoted to receive Holy Communion?" I asked him.

"No, I'm not promoted yet."

"And what about Confirmation?"

"I haven't received it yet."

"And what about the sacrament of Confession?"

"Yes, I went to Confession a few times," he told us.

"Where do you want to go now?"

"I don't know. I ask for charity to be able to spend the night in some corner of this house."

When he said this, he began to cry; my mother cried with him, I was moved. "If I knew that you are not a thief, I would try to fix you, but others ran away with some of the blankets and I'm afraid that you might take the others away from me."

"No sir. Rest assured! I am poor, but I have never stolen anything."

"If you want," my mother spoke up, "I will accommodate you for tonight, and tomorrow God will provide."

"Where would I sleep?" he asked.

"Here in the kitchen."

"He'll take away from all your pots and pans," I said.

"I'll make sure that doesn't happen."

"Then, go ahead with this plan," I told my mother and the boy.

The good woman, helped by the orphan, went out, picked up some pieces of bricks, and with them made four small pillars in the kitchen, on which she laid some boards. She placed a sack on them, and in this way prepared the first bed of the Oratory. My good mother then gave them a sermon on the need for work, fidelity, and religion. Finally, she invited him to say his prayers.

"I don't know any prayers," he replied.

"Then you can recite the prayers by repeating them with us," she said. And so it was.

So that everything was then secured, the kitchen was locked and never opened again until morning.

This was the first young person to stay in our hospice. Another was soon added to his number, and then others....It was the year 1847.

The Oratory of St. Francis de Sales would soon host a large youth hostel. Shops for the training of apprentices and classrooms to prepare poor youth for high school, college, and even the seminary would also become operational. But after the account of the poor orphan from Sesia that arrived on that rainy night in 1847, the first copybook comes to an end. In fact, it ended much as it began: a bed, an orphan, a mother. The *Memoirs* began with the toddler John Bosco at the bedside of his dying father, crying and brought to safety by Mama Margaret. The same copybook ends with a boy coming in from the rain, orphaned and abandoned, crying in his loneliness, and brought to safety from the night by Mama Margaret, who makes a bed for him in the warm kitchen and teaches him to pray. John Bosco asks the hard questions to the orphan on the rainy night, just has he had asked the hard questions on the night when he lost his father...but in spite of his hard rhetoric, he is moved to tears no less than his mother. With this orphan, as with the poor apprentices that he had been serving for the first five years of his priesthood, he knows that he is called to serve young people, especially the poor and abandoned.

FOUNDING THE SALESIANS

Some of the boys helped by Don Bosco decided to do what he was doing, that is, to work in the service of abandoned boys. This was the origin of the Salesian Congregation. Among the first members were Michael Rua, John Cagliero (who later became a cardinal), and

John Baptist Francesia. In 1859, Bosco selected the experienced priest Vittorio Alasonatti, fifteen seminarians and one high school boy and formed them into the Society of St. Francis de Sales. This was the nucleus of the Salesians, the religious order that would carry on his work. When the group had their next meeting, they voted on the admission of Joseph Rossi as a lay member, the first Salesian brother. The Salesian Congregation was divided into priests, seminarians, and lay religious.

The family spirit that was prevalent at the Oratory of St. Francis de Sales became the hallmark of the Salesian Society. In the early days this was easy, since almost all of the members had been boys at the Oratory. They had grown up together; they regarded Don Bosco as their father. This fact alone was enough to create a strong, cohesive spirit—a sense of family.[19] This was an "extended family" and a "productive unit." It was this sense of family that took all rigidity out of Don Bosco's foundations. Work for poor youth became more possible as Salesian "apostles" had a sense that their contribution could make a difference; as they felt their own talents valued; as they felt their own limitations compensated by others, and vice versa.

It was also this sense of family that made it easy for priests and clerics in the Society to accept laymen as full members. Under Don Bosco's lead, Salesians were to treat one another like brothers. This familiarity brought a sense to the lay members that they were cherished. The nineteenth-century distance between clergy and laity evaporated within the walls of the Salesian institute. Furthermore, lay members felt more strongly attracted to the liturgy and the sacraments, as well as to taking on roles as catechists of the young. This is because the priests who ministered to them in church were "their own." The priests who treated them with respect and affection in community and in the educational work of the Salesian institute: these were the priests who brought Christ to them in Word and Sacrament.[20] In this way too, the family spirit of the Salesians engendered a spirituality of "daily life."

The formal foundation of the Salesian Society took place on the evening of December 18, 1859. The Salesian archives have the original copy of the minutes taken during that meeting of foundation.

MINUTES OF THE ACT OF FOUNDATION OF THE SALESIAN CONGREGATION

Torino, December 18, 1859

In the name of Our Lord Jesus Christ. Amen

In the Year of Our Lord eighteen hundred and fifty-nine, on the eighteenth of December in this Oratory of St. Francis of Sales at 9 in the evening, the following gathered in Father John Bosco's room: [Fr. John Bosco] himself, Father Vittorio Alasonatti, the Seminarians Deacon Angelo Savio, Subdeacon Michele Rua, Giovanni Cagliero, Gio. Battista Francesia, Francesco Provera, Carlo Ghivarello, Giuseppe Lazzero, Giovanni Bonetti, Giovanni Anfossi, Luigi Marcellino, Francesco Cerruti, Celestino Durando, Secondo Pettiva, Antonio Rovetto, Cesare Giuseppe Bongiovanni, and the young man Luigi Chiapale. All united in one and the same spirit with the sole purpose of preserving and promoting the spirit of true charity needed for the work of the Oratories on behalf of neglected young people at risk. For in these disastrous times of ours such young people are liable to be corrupted and plunged into godlessness and irreligion to the detriment of the whole of society.

The Gathered group then decided to form a society or congregation with the aim of promoting the glory of God and the salvation of souls, especially of those most in need of instruction and education, while providing the members with mutual help toward their own sanctification. The project met with unanimous approval. Hence, after a short prayer and to invoke the light of the Holy Spirit, the group proceeded to elect the members that would make up the central body of the Society and would lead this and future communities, if it should please God to grant increase.

The group then unanimously requested him [Don Bosco] who has been the initiator and promoter [of the work] to accept the office of Major Superior, as is becoming in every respect. He accepted the office on condition that he should have the power to choose for the office of prefect the present writer [Alasonatti], who has held that office in the house up to the present.

The group then considered the method to be followed in electing the other members of the central governing body, and it was decided to hold the election by secret ballot. This was deemed the speediest way of setting up the council, which was to consist of a spiritual director, of a financial administrator, and of three councilors, in addition to the two already mentioned officers.

The writer [of these minutes] was appointed secretary and [now] solemnly declares that he has faithfully discharged the task entrusted to him by general agreement. As the balloting progressed, he recorded the votes by the name of the individual concerned; and this was the result of the elections: the seminarian, the subdeacon Michele Rua was unanimously elected spiritual director, and he accepted the appointment. The same procedure was followed for the financial administrator, with the result that Deacon Angelo Savio was elected. He also accepted, pledging to discharge the duties of that office.

Three councilors remained to be elected. The balloting for the first of these resulted in the election of the seminarian Giovanni Cagliero. The second councilor to be elected was Giovanni Bonetti. The balloting for the third and last councilor resulted in a tie between seminarians Carlo Ghivarello and Francesco Provera. A second balloting produced a majority favoring seminarian Ghivarello. Thus the central administrative body of our Society was definitively established.

The report of these proceedings, as summarily described herein, was read before the assembly of all the members and elected officers and was approved as true to fact. It was then unanimously resolved that this original document should be kept on file, and to guarantee its authenticity the Major Superior and the Secretary affixed their signatures.

Father Gio. Bosco

Father Vittorio Alasonatti, Prefect

DOMINIC SAVIO: TEENAGE SAINT

Among his many pastoral activities, Don Bosco understood the importance of distributing good Christian literature. As a newly ordained priest he joined with others in this effort, but soon understood that there was little available for ordinary people and young people, particularly in changing times. Soon, however, he discovered that there was very little Christian literature available to the laity and the young in Northern Italy. To fill the void, he began to write and to publish. In 1850, not yet ten years ordained, he founded a periodical that he called *Catholic Readings*. Issues appeared every month, in a handy, pocket-sized, and affordable paperback format. He appealed to friends who could write on subjects that were of interest, and he also wrote quite a number of the issues himself. His style was simple and direct, understandable by young people, immigrants, and those who more readily spoke other dialects than standard Italian.

Through the *Catholic Readings*, Don Bosco published a number of textbooks for use in the local high schools—the *History of Italy for Young People, Salvation History*, and *Church History* were among best well-known works. He also published a *Guide to the Metric System* when the country changed its system for weights and measures. It was a guide written for the rural and poor urban populations where there were many who experienced confusion and who were prey to unscrupulous business sharks. He presented the new system of weights and measures through a series of comical dialogues, in order to set the readers at ease, so that they could learn the new system, and be forewarned about the common tricks of the cheats that might try to exploit them.

Many issues of the *Catholic Readings* were so well received that they were reprinted as paperbacks for wider distribution. Among the most popular of these books was the *Life of Dominic Savio, Pupil of the Oratory of St. Francis de Sales*. The *Life of Dominic* first appeared in the January 1859 issue of *Catholic Readings* and recounted the experiences of a real boy who had lived at the Oratory from 1854 to 1857, dying one month before his fifteenth birthday. This composition offered a rare look into the contemporary youth culture at a time when young people were only starting to be understood as something other than small adults. When readers understood that this was not fiction but biography, many asked for more details, both about Dominic and the Oratory where he lived. Numerous reprints were distributed, and later Don Bosco would publish two revised and expanded editions. Many secondary schools in Italy made use of the book as a reader in the Italian language for the clear and expressive style. Dominic Savio thus became well-known throughout Italy, and soon, in many other parts of the world.

In writing the *Life of Dominic Savio*, Don Bosco's purpose was educational. He wanted to offer young people examples of how they could become faithful Christians and honest citizens.

The Life of Dominic Savio

Dominic Savio was born in Riva di Chieri on April 2, 1842. We pass over the early chapters of his biography in order to pinpoint aspects that Don Bosco felt were most important.

Nothing stood in the way of Dominic's being allowed to make his First Communion. He knew the children's catechism by heart and understood very well what the Holy Eucharist was. He also had a great desire to receive Jesus into his heart. There was only one difficulty, his age. At that time boys and girls did not normally make their First Communion until they were eleven or twelve years old. Dominic was only seven. To look at him, he seemed even younger, and so the parish priest hesitated to put him forward. He sought advice from some of the other priests and they, knowing Dominic's precocious knowledge, the instruction he had received and his keen desire, said that he need not hesitate. The way was now clear, and Dominic was told that he could receive the food of the angels for the first time.

It is not easy to describe the joy which filled him at this news. He ran home trembling with excitement and joy to tell his mother. Much of his time was given to praying and reading; he made visits to the Blessed Sacrament and it seemed as though his soul was dwelling with the angels in heaven. The evening before he went to his mother and said: "Mother, tomorrow I am receiving Jesus in Holy Communion for the first time; forgive me for anything I have done to displease you in the past: I promise you I am going to be a much better boy in every way. I will be attentive at school, obedient, docile, respectful to whoever tells me what to do." Having said this, he burst into tears. His mother, who had only received consolation from him, was also emotional and found it difficult to hold back her tears, but she consoled him saying: "Do not worry, my dear Dominic, everything is forgiven. Ask God to always keep you good, and also pray for me and your father."

Dominic was up early next morning, dressed himself in his best clothes and hurried off to church. It was not yet open, so he knelt down on the steps, as he had done other times, and he prayed until other children arrived and the door was opened. Between Confessions, preparation, thanksgiving and sermon, the service lasted five hours. Dominic was the first to enter the church and last to leave. All that time he scarcely knew if he was in heaven or on earth.

It was a wonderful and memorable day for him. That day, young as he was, Dominic renewed his life for God, a life that can be taken as an example by anyone. Even years later, if someone got him to talk about his First Communion, his face would light up with joy as he said: "That was the happiest and most wonderful day of my life." He wrote some resolutions on that day which he preserved carefully in a little book, and often re-read them. I was able to have that little book in my hands, and I give you the resolutions that he wrote at that time. Here they are in their original simplicity: "Promises made by me, Dominic Savio, when I made my First Communion in 1849 at seven years of age: 1. I will go often to Confession and I will go to Holy Communion as often as I am allowed by my confessor. 2. I will try to keep Sundays and holy days holy. 3. My friends will be Jesus and Mary. 4. Death, but not sin."

These promises, which he often reviewed and repeated, became the guiding principle of his actions until the end of his life.

If among those who read this book there are any who have yet to make their First Communion, I would urge them strongly to take Dominic as their model. At the same time, I heartily recommend to parents, teachers and all those who are responsible for the young, to give the greatest importance to this religious act. Be assured that the First Communion very well made is a solid moral foundation for the rest of the child's life. It would certainly be quite surprising to find any-one who has made this great act with real devotion and care and afterwards not live a good and virtuous life. On the other hand, there are thousands of young people who have gone astray and who are the despair of their parents and those responsible for them; I would not hesitate to say that the trouble began with the little or no real preparation for the First Communion. It is better to delay making it, or not to make it at all, than to make it badly.

In developing his presentation of the life and character of Dominic Savio, Don Bosco gave a chronology of his childhood, showing how he lived those situations that young people would find familiar. He spoke of family events, life at school, getting along with peers and classmates.

Dominic Attends School in Mondonio, Where He Puts Up with a Great Injustice

It seems that Divine Providence wanted to help this young-ster understand that this world is a place of exile where we journey from place to place, as pilgrims. Or perhaps it was God's design that he should be known in as many places as possible, so that his goodness and outstanding virtue might be a source of inspiration to all who saw him.

Towards the end of 1852 his parents left Morialdo and went to live in Mondonio, a small town near Castelnuovo.

Here Dominic continued the same way of life and I need to repeat what other teachers had said about him earlier. His teacher, Father [Giuseppe] Cugliero, who had him as a student, offers a similar report. Here I transcribe only a few of the facts that Fr. Cugliero described; I have been selective in order not to repeat myself too much.

I can truthfully say that in twenty years of teaching boys I have never had one to equal Dominic. He was only a boy in age, but he had the sense and judgement of a fully mature man. He was very diligent and applied himself to his lessons, and his good-naturedness and readiness to help won him the affection both of his companions and teachers. I could not help marveling at the way he could fix his attention in church, and I often said to myself "This is certainly an innocent boy, whose heart and affections are already in heaven."

The following is an incident among others recounted by his teacher:

One day, an incident of so serious a nature took place at the school such that expulsion was the obvious punishment for those responsible. The culprits realized this and sought to save themselves by coming to me and laying all the blame on Dominic. I could not imagine that the boy had done anything so stupid, but his accusers were so insistent and emphatic about it that I believed them. I was very annoyed and went to the classroom. I left the boys in no doubt as to what I thought about the whole affair, and then I turned to Dominic and minced no words in telling him off, saying that he deserved to be expelled and that he would have been, had it not been the first time he had done such a thing, and that he should make sure it would be the last time. Dominic did not say a word, but stood there with his head bowed, accepting humbly all that was said to him.

God, however, protects the innocent, and next day it came out who the real culprits were. Somewhat ashamed of all the abuse I had heaped on his head, I took him aside and asked him: "Why did you not tell me you were not responsible?" He replied: "I knew that these boys had already been up

103

to so much mischief that this would certainly earn them expulsion, and I thought I would try to save them, as I probably would not be expelled, seeing that it was my very first time...also, I remembered that Jesus had been blamed unjustly and had not said anything, and I thought I should do the same."

No more was said, but all admired Dominic's patience, which was able to return good for evil and was even ready to accept serious punishment in order to rescue those who had told such lies about him. (from the letter by Fr. Cugliero)

In the seventh chapter of the *Life*, Don Bosco began to speak from his personal experiences with Dominic Savio. His account of his first meeting with the twelve-year-old gives us a picture of his life as an educator, as well as the personality of the boy himself.

I First Get to Know Him—Interesting Episodes on That Occasion

What I report in the pages that follow can be given with more detail, because I shall be dealing with things which happened before my own eyes and also in the presence of many young people who can bear testimony to their truth. This period begins in 1854 when Father Cugliero, whom I have already mentioned, came to see me about one of his pupils whose intellect and piety deserved special consideration. "You may have in your house," he said, "boys equally good and clever, but I do not think that you have any who can surpass him in talent and virtue. Give him a chance and you will find you have another St. Aloysius." We came to an agreement that he would arrange to have Dominic come to see me when next I visited Morialdo. It was my custom to spend a few days there each year with some of the young people from this Oratory, to allow them to enjoy some experiences in the countryside. We always went around the time of the Feast of the Most Holy Rosary, and celebrated the novena in honor of Mary most holy.

It was early on the morning of the first Monday of October that I saw a boy coming towards me with his father. His serene expression and charming but respectful manner captured my gaze.

"Who are you and where do you come from?" I asked him.

"I am Dominic Savio. My teacher Father Cugliero has spoken to you about me, and I have come with my father from Mondonio."

I took him aside and asked him about himself and his studies. We found common ground immediately and a relationship of trust and mutual confidence sprang up spontaneously.

I recognized in him a soul where the Holy Spirit reigned supreme, and I marveled at the way grace had already worked in his young heart and mind.

We talked together for quite a time and, as I was going to call his father over, Dominic said to me: "Well, what do you think? Will you take me to Torino to study?"

"Well, I think there is good material in you."

"Good material for what?"

"To make a beautiful garment for Our Blessed Lord."

"Wonderful! I am the cloth and you are the tailor. You will work on me to make something beautiful for the Lord."

"I wonder if you are strong enough for a long course of studies?"

"Don't worry, Our Blessed Lord has helped me so far and I am sure he will continue to do so."

"And what are you going to do when you finish studying Latin?"

"I should love to be a priest, if that were God's will."

"Very good. And now let's try a little intelligence test. Take this little book, go over this page (it was a copy of the *Catholic Readings*). For today, study this page; come back tomorrow and recite it for me."

I then left him free to go and play with the other boys while I had a talk with his father. No more than eight minutes had gone by when Dominic approached me again with a big smile on his face. He said: "If you wish I will repeat my lesson now." I took the book and, to my surprise, he not only recited the page by heart but explained simply and clearly the meaning, showing that he understood it very well.

"Splendid," I said. "You have been quick to study your lesson and so I shall be quick to give you my answer. I will take you to Torino, and from this moment I consider you one of my chosen sons. From now onwards, often ask God to help us both to do God's holy will in all things."

Not knowing how better to express his happiness and his gratitude, he shook my hand and then kissed it several times and finally said: "I hope always to act in such a way that you will never have reason to complain of me."

At the end of October 1854, Dominic Savio was brought to Turin by his father, and he entered the youth hostel attached to the Oratory that Don Bosco had founded in the city. Don Bosco's narrative moves from the meeting in the countryside to the beginning of the school year in the city. Those were difficult times, full of change and challenge. The steadiness of Dominic will contrast with all of that, and Don Bosco will describe his depth of character and wholesome attitudes.

Dominic Comes to the Oratory of St. Francis de Sales—His Early Attitude

It is characteristic of youth to change suddenly. Often it happens that what is wonderful today is far from being so tomorrow. At one time a boy can show great promise and soon after he can act in a way that would show the exact opposite. And if one is not careful, a career that began with the highest hopes can end with disappointment and sorrow to all concerned. It was not so with Dominic. All the virtues which had begun to grow at different stages of his life now continued their growth in a wonderful way, without any of them impeding the others.

The first time Dominic went to see Don Bosco in his office, he noticed a poster that the educator had hung on the wall over his desk. It contained a quotation from Genesis 14:21—a phrase that Don Bosco associated with St. Francis de Sales.

> As soon as he arrived at the Oratory, he came to my office in order to put himself, as he used to say, completely in the hands of his superiors. His gaze immediately fixed on the wall where there was a poster with large letters that reported the words that St. Francis de Sales often used to say: *Da mihi animas caetera tolle.* He began to read the words carefully, and I wanted him to understand their significance. So, I invited him to tell me what he thought the words meant and helped him to translate them in this sense: *O Lord, give me souls, and take away everything else.*[21] He thought for a moment and then he added: "I understand. In this place you do not deal with money, but you do business in souls. I get it. I hope that my soul will also become part of this commerce."
>
> For some time, his life was quite ordinary. I noticed nothing extraordinary, but I did admire how exact he was in observing the house rules. He carried out his schoolwork with a strong sense of commitment. He enthusiastically fulfilled all his duties. He delighted in listening to sermons, as he had already rooted God's word in his heart, convinced that it was a sure guide along the road to heaven. Therefore, every maxim that he heard in a sermon became for him an essential reminder that he would never forget.
>
> Every talk, catechism lesson, sermon, no matter how long seemed to be a delight for him. If there was anything he did not understand, he never hesitated to ask for further explanations. This was the root and source of his exemplary life and steady progress in virtue which could hardly have been surpassed.
>
> In order to make sure that he understood the rules and discipline of the school well, he went to one of the teachers and asked him to help and advise him how best to be faithful to them and to correct him if he neglected any of his duties.

His relations with his companions showed the same wisdom. He refused to have anything to do with those who were rowdy, disobedient and who showed little respect for the things of God. If there was an exemplary, studious, and diligent pupil praised by his teacher he soon became a close friend of Dominic's.

December 8, Feast of the Immaculate Conception, was drawing near. It was the director's custom to say a little word of encouragement and exhortation to the boys so as to prepare them to keep the feast in a way worthy of Mary most holy. He insisted especially that they should ask Mary for the grace they had greatest need of.

That year, 1854, the whole Catholic world was in a state of excitement because of the approaching definition of the dogma of the Immaculate Conception at Rome. At the Oratory we did our very best to keep the feast with fitting solemnity and devotion.

Savio was among those who had a great desire to keep the feast very well. He wrote out nine deeds to be done in honor of Our Lady and drew out one by lot each day. He prepared himself well and made a general confession so that his soul might be as pleasing as possible to Mary Most Holy.

On the eve of the feast, he went to Our Lady's altar and, on the advice of his Confessor, renewed the promises he had made at his First Communion, and then he repeated many times: "Mary, I give you my heart, please keep it always as your own. Jesus and Mary, always be my friends. Please, please Jesus, let me die rather than ever offend you seriously."

From this feast of the Immaculate Conception, Dominic took Mary as the guide for his spiritual life, and with such effective results that I began from that time to note down the different incidents or facts of his life, so that I should not forget them.

At this point in his *Life of Savio*, Don Bosco changed his editorial technique. Instead of offering a chronological presentation, he began to group incidents together by theme. He felt that this would allow him to present Savio to his readers with greater clarity. He therefore presented the topics that helped his readers understand Savio's stated intentions as well as his growth as a Christian. We will look at a few of the chapters where incidents in Savio's journey were especially striking to Don Bosco as a Christian educator.

A rather long chapter offers a glimpse at the seriousness with which Savio embraced his duties as a student. In fact, he came to Turin to study, with hopes of someday being admitted to the seminary. Don Bosco had not yet been able to establish a school, and perhaps he did not yet have a plan to do so in 1854 when Dominic Savio arrived at the youth hostel that was attached to the Oratory of St. Francis de Sales. Boys who were interested in studies frequented schools in the city—schools conducted by a number of Don Bosco's friends who were qualified educators. Dominic attended a private school conducted by Carlo Giuseppe Bonzanino (1810–88). As may be obvious, life in the city would be very different from life in a country town or rural village.

Dominic Savio at School in Turin

Dominic had begun his grammar year at Mondonio and, with the progress he made by his hard work and more than ordinary intelligence, he was very soon moved from fourth class or, as we say today, second year Latin grammar. Here he came under the care of the devout and kindly Professor Joseph Bonzanino because secondary classes had not yet been set up at the Oratory like we have them now. I have to speak of his behavior and example even here along the same lines as earlier teachers have done. I will just pick a few things from this year and two in particular which were noted by others who knew him and admired him for them.

Prof. Bonzanino said on a number of occasions that he could not remember having had a better pupil than Savio— one who was more attentive, better behaved, and more respectful. He was a real model in everything. His clothes were poor, but he was always neat and clean, and his manners and bearing were easily equal to those of boys who came from richer and nobler families, a good number of whom went to this school. They liked spending time with Dominic not only for his learning and piety but also for his friendly and pleasant way of treating them. Whenever there was a boy who was a bit absentminded or too chatty, the teacher would put him beside Dominic, and would skillfully lead his classmate to quiet down, to study harder, and to fulfill his duties.

There were many incidents about Dominic's experience as a student in Turin. Most of these Don Bosco came to know from what was reported to him by Dominic's teachers and, in later editions of the *Life*, from Dominic's companions and classmates. In many respects, Dominic was not only a good example to his peers, but also heroic in fulfilling his Christian duties. All of those qualities would really begin to make sense in the next chapter, which Don Bosco entitled "His Decision to Become a Saint." What the author reports in chapter 10 comes from what he himself witnessed. This is a key moment in the *Life*.

Dominic's Decision to Become a Saint

Now that we have given an indication of his studies, we will speak of his great decision to become a saint.

When he had been about six months at the Oratory, Savio heard a sermon about an easy way to become a saint. The preacher presented three main points which made a huge impact on Dominic: it is God's will that all of us should become saints; it is very easy to accomplish this; there is a great reward prepared in heaven for those who become saints. This sermon was like a spark that set Dominic's heart ablaze with the love of God. For some days he said nothing, going about very quietly without his usual joyful spirit. His companions noticed this, and I did also. My first thought was that he was not feeling well, and I asked him was there something wrong. "No," he said, "it is something good." "What do you mean?" "I mean that I must become a saint. I never saw before that it was both possible and easy. Now that I see it, I can have no peace inside until I really begin to do so. Please will you show me how I should go about it?"

I praised Dominic's good resolutions, but I urged him not to let himself get too agitated, because when one's heart is filled with commotion, it is not possible to hear the Lord's voice. I said to him that for the moment he should regain his customary cheerfulness, persevere in his regular life of study and piety, and especially not neglect being with his companions in games and recreation.

One day I told him that I would like to make him a present of something that would please him, and that I would leave the choice completely to him. "I want you to help me to become a saint," he immediately replied. "I want to give up everything to Jesus and for always. If I am not trying to be a saint, I am doing nothing at all. God wants me to be a saint, so I have to be one."

On another occasion the director wanted to show his affection for the boys and make them a little present, so he said that they could ask for whatever they wished and, if it were possible, he would give it to them. The requests were to be written down, and it can be imagined that there were some strange and bizarre requests made by some of the boys. Dominic took a piece of paper and wrote these words: "I ask one thing only, that you help me to save my soul and make me a saint."

Another day there was a group of us chatting about the meaning of names and other words, according to their etymology. "What does Dominic mean?" he asked. The reply was: "Dominic means *belonging to the Lord.*" "There you are," he said, "you see how right I am in asking you to make me a saint. Even my name says that I belong to the Lord. Therefore, I need to, and I want to belong completely to the Lord. I want to become holy, and I will be very unhappy until I do."

This craving that Dominic felt about becoming a saint did not spring from the fact that he was not living a holy life. He spoke in this way because he thought that holiness demanded severe penances and long hours in prayer, and his director would not allow these activities on any account, because they were not compatible with his age or health or duties.

His Zeal for the Salvation of Souls

In chapter 11, Don Bosco continued the theme of Dominic's efforts to grow in holiness.

The first thing he was advised to do in order to become a saint was to work to win souls for God; because there is nothing holier in the world than to cooperate for the good of souls, for whose salvation Jesus Christ shed every last drop of his precious blood. Dominic knew the importance of this practice and was repeatedly heard to say: "If I could win all my companions to God, how happy I would be!" Meanwhile, he did not miss any occasion to give good advice, to warn anyone who had said or done something contrary to God's holy law.

The thing that caused him great horror and that did no small damage to his health was blasphemy or hearing the holy name of God taken in vain. If he ever heard any similar words in the streets of the city or elsewhere, he would quickly lower his head in sorrow and say with a devout heart: "Praised be Jesus Christ."

Spending a day in the middle of a town square, a companion saw him take off his hat and whisper a few words: "What are you doing?" he said, "what are you saying?" "Haven't you heard?" Dominic asked in reply. "That wagoner took God's holy name in vain. If I thought it would do any good, I would run to warn him never to do it again. But since I'm afraid that might make him say worse things, I just take off my hat and say: Praise be to Jesus Christ. And this with the desire to make amends for the injury done to the holy name of the Lord."

That classmate admired Dominic's conduct and courage, and still speaks of this episode with pleasure, to honor his friend and to edify his companions.

On returning from school, he once heard a man that was quite advanced in age who uttered a horrible blasphemy. Our Dominic trembled at hearing it; he praised God in his heart, and then he did something certainly admirable. With the most respectful air, he ran towards the careless blasphemer and asked him if he could point him in the direction of the Oratory of St. Francis de Sales. Struck by Dominic's respect and air of devotion, the old man suppressed his ferocious anger and replied, "I don't know, dear boy, I'm sorry."

"Oh! if you don't know this, could you do me another favor?"

"Tell me, gladly."

Dominic approached him as close to his ear as he could, and spoke softly so that others would not understand, "You will please me very much if in your anger you would speak without blaspheming the holy name of God."

"Bravo," said the old man, full of amazement and admiration. "Well, you're right: this is an accursed vice that I want to conquer at any cost."

Episodes that Show Dominic's Beautiful Way of Conversing with Classmates

Dominic Savio was slight in stature, but he could be (and often was) a commanding presence. Don Bosco gives us hints of this in chapter 12 of the *Life*. We report one episode here.

Once during recess, it happened that a man walked among the young people who were having fun on the playground. He turned to one of them he began to speak, but in a loud voice that everyone around him could hear. This cunning man, to bring them closer to him, first began to tell strange stories to make them laugh. Young people drawn by curiosity soon crowded around him and hung carefully from his lips when they heard him speak of strange adventures and oddities. As soon as he saw himself so surrounded, he turned the conversation to matters of religion and, as these sorts of people usually do, he noted some frightening errors, mocking the most sacred things and discrediting all the church people. Some of the bystanders, unable to accept such impiety and not daring to oppose it, simply walked away. A good number unwisely continued to listen to him. Meanwhile, Savio arrived by chance. As soon as he understood what kind of speech the man was making, he rejected all human respect and immediately turned to his companions: "Come on," he said, "forget this unfortunate man, he wants to steal our souls." The young people listened to the voice of such a lovable and virtuous companion, and all promptly turned away from that envoy of the devil. Seeing himself thus abandoned by everyone, he left and was never seen again.

His Last Moments and His Precious Death

Dominic spent just over two years at the Oratory. At the age of fourteen he suffered a bout with tuberculosis, a disease that had nearly killed him when he was ten. Since the doctors could not find a way to treat him in Turin, they recommended that he return home to his family where the doctors hoped that he would find relief and return to health. He died at home on March 9, 1857. Don Bosco learned the circumstances of the boy's death in a letter from Dominic's father, which he recounts in chapter 25 of the *Life*.

It is the truth of faith that man gathers the fruit of his works at the point of death. *As a man sews, so shall he reap (Gal 6:7).* If in his life he sowed good works, he will reap consoling fruits in those last moments; if he sowed evil works, then he will reap desolation over desolation. Nevertheless, it sometimes happens that good souls after a holy life feel terror and fright as the hour of death approaches. This happens according to the adorable decrees of God, who wants to purge those souls from the small stains they may have contracted in life and thus ensure and make them more beautiful the crown of glory in heaven. This was not the case with our Savio. I believe that God wanted to give him all that hundredfold that he gives to the souls of the just as a foretaste of the glory of paradise. In fact, the innocence preserved until the last moment of his life, his lively faith, and the continuous prayers, his long penances and life full of tribulations certainly deserved that comfort on the verge of death.

He therefore saw death approaching with the tranquility of an innocent soul; on the contrary, it seemed that not even his body felt the troubles and oppressions that are inseparable from the efforts that the soul must naturally make in breaking the bonds of the body. In short, Savio's death can be called a rest rather than death.

It was the evening of March 9, 1857, he had received all the comforts of our holy Catholic religion. Those who only heard him speak and looked at the serenity of his face, would have thought that he was lying in bed in order to rest. The cheerful air, the still lively looks, full knowledge of himself, were things that made everyone wonder and no one other than Dominic could be persuaded that he was on death's door.

An hour and a half before he drew his last breath, the parish priest went to visit him, and seeing his tranquility he was amazed to hear him ask for prayers for his soul. He made frequent and prolonged invocations, which all tended to manifest his strong desire to go to heaven soon. "What could I suggest or recommend to the soul of someone dying with such serenity?" the priest asked himself. After having recited some prayers with him, the parish priest was about to go out when Savio called him saying: "My dear pastor, before you go, leave me with something good to remember." "For me," the priest replied, "I don't know what kind of thoughts to share with you." "A few good memories that will comfort me." "I would not be able to tell you anything better than that you remember the passion of the Lord." "*Deo gratias,*" Dominic answered, "may the passion of our Lord Jesus Christ always be in my mind, in my mouth, in my heart. Jesus, Joseph and Mary, assist me in this last agony; Jesus, Joseph and Mary, may my soul breathe in peace with you." After these words he fell asleep and took half an hour of rest. Then he woke up and looked at his family: "Papa," he said, "we've arrived."

"Here I am, my son, what do you need?"

"My dear dad, it's time; take my *Young Person's Prayer Book* and read me the prayers for a happy death."

At these words, his mother broke into tears and left the room of the sick boy. His father's heart burst with pain, and tears stifled his voice; however, he took courage and began to read that prayer. Dominic repeated each phrase carefully and distinctly; but at the end of each part, he gave the response by himself: "Merciful Jesus, have mercy on me." Coming to the words, "When my soul finally appears before you, and sees for the first time the immortal splendor of your majesty, do not reject me from your presence, but deign to receive me in the loving bosom of your mercy, so that I may sing your praises eternally," he added: "Well this is exactly what I want. Oh my dear dad, to forever sing the praises of the Lord!" Then he seemed to fall sleep again like someone seriously thinking about something of great importance. A little later he woke up and in a clear, laughing voice: "Goodbye, dear papa, goodbye: the parish priest still wanted to tell me something, and I can no longer remember....Oh! what a beautiful thing I see!" Saying this and gently laughing with an air of paradise, he expired with his hands clasped on his chest in the form of a cross without making the slightest movement.

Go forward, faithful soul, to your Creator. Heaven is open to you. The angels and saints have prepared a great feast for you! That Jesus whom you loved so much invites you and calls you saying: "Come, good and faithful servant, come! You have fought the good fight, you have won! Now come to possess a joy that will never fail you again: *Enter into the joy of your master.*"[22]

SALESIAN MARIAN DEVOTION

The boys who entered Don Bosco's Oratory in Valdocco were steeped in the language of holiness. As part of this they were immersed in a Marian environment. The one who created this "atmosphere" was Don Bosco himself, whose own training and orientation had been profoundly rooted in a family-like devotion to Mary. She was the "Shepherdess" who guided him, the "Queen" who inspired him, the "Teacher" who trained him, and the "Mother" who nurtured him in his own vocation; he presented her to his young people as personally present in their house, close to them in their daily lives.[23]

Giovanni Cagliero, who was among the first young people to enter the Salesian Society in 1859, and later became a missionary in Latin America, a bishop, a nuncio for the Holy See in Central America and the first Salesian cardinal, never forgot his teenage years in Don Bosco's house. When testifying during the canonical proceedings that would eventually lead to Bosco's beatification, Cardinal Cagliero described his mentor's contagious devotion to Mary.

> His devotion to Mary Most Holy was great. He used to speak to us very often about the devotion we should have for her and he increased our fervor with his words and example. He was filled with joy and holy delight when he sang Mary's praises with us, whether in church or in the playground, and his voice was not enough. When he intoned the hymn entitled "We are children of Mary," he would raise both his hands as a sign of joy and with holy simplicity, clap on the down beat.
>
> Then I remember that his joy brimmed over when, in the early days of the Oratory, he saw us construct little shrines in the study hall and in the dormitories to celebrate the festive month of May. Every Sunday evening, he wanted that one of us should put ourselves forward and say a few words to inspire greater filial love for Mary Most Holy among our companions. He observed the novenas in her honor to prepare for her principal feasts and encouraged us to do the

same. The love Don Bosco had for the Madonna! He did everything to increase her glory, to enhance devotion to her.[24]

In 1868 on the site of Valdocco, the Basilica of Mary Help of Christians, the church of which Don Bosco had long dreamed, was consecrated. Mary had been his guide and protector from his earliest years. The title "Help of Christians" given to the basilica had gained prominence during Bosco's lifetime (although it was much older, having been associated with her dramatic intervention in a decisive sixteenth-century battle against the Turks): reports of miraculous healings in the city of Spoleto credited to her under that title were widely circulated, and Bosco celebrated them. He later insisted that Mary was foundational in the formation of Oratory. This is clear in the pages of one of his earliest writings, "The Companion of Youth." There a young Bosco assures his readers,

> If you remain her devotees, besides filling you with blessings in this world, you will receive Paradise in the next life.[25]

This is how Don Bosco explained the importance of Marian devotion to young people. Since Mary is our Mother, she wants to cover us with blessings. Since she is the Mother of Jesus, she can. She is the queen of heaven, but at the same time she is given to us as our protector.

Mary's Month—the Month of May

If the title of Mother of God is glorious for Mary, it is all the more glorious and beneficial for us who, redeemed by Jesus Christ, become her children and brothers of her divine Son. Hence, having become the Mother of Jesus, true God, and true man, she also became our mother. The Gospel confirms that Jesus Christ in His great mercy wanted to call us His brothers and made us the adopted children of Mary. When the divine Savior, nailed to the Cross, suffered the most painful agony, His most holy Mother and the Apostle John were at His feet in deepest sorrow. Jesus opening His eyes, perhaps for the last time, saw the beloved disciple and His loving Mother. Dying, He said to Mary: "Woman, behold your son." Then He spoke to John: "Behold your mother," *mulier, ecce filius tuus: ecce mater tua.* That is why the holy Fathers unanimously recognize the will of the divine Savior who, before leaving this world, wanted to give us Mary as our loving mother and make us all her children.[26]

For him, the Mother of God was foundress of all his work. In this sense, everything about Valdocco was a monument to Mary, Help of Christians. It was a temple for promoting evangelization and religious practice; an oratory/youth center for promoting social development of young people; it had shops to train the next generation of skilled labor; schools to organize instruction and promote learning and culture. As he developed the infrastructure of his work, he also founded associations and new communities: the Sons of Mary Help of Christians to promote adult vocations for the whole church; the Institute of the Daughters of Mary Help of Christians, as the "living monument to Mary Help of Christians," will "do for girls" all that he is already doing for boys.

FOUNDATION OF THE DAUGHTERS OF MARY HELP OF CHRISTIANS

John Bosco's many itineraries took him to the hill countries of Piedmont. In the town of Mornese he encountered a group of young women who had, under the tutelage of a local parish priest, Domenico Pestarino, organized themselves into a pious union dedicated to the practice of Christian charity. Among them was a local woman, Maria Dominica Mazzarello (1837–81). At the age of twenty she invited other young women of her parish to work together with her to catechize and educate young girls. Maria Mazzarello was a member of a group called the Daughters of Mary Immaculate, and while older women in this parish group were dedicated to prayer, a number of younger ones joined Maria in her efforts to educate youth.

For some time, Bosco had seen the need for ministry among girls as well as boys, especially those who came from situations of disadvantage. After a chance meeting with Fr. Pestarino while traveling in 1860, he began to view the group in Mornese as a group that he might be able to work with for the education of rural young people. Whenever asked, he would send them pointers for their catechetical ministry, and he would visit Mornese with a large group of his orphans in the autumn of 1864. Finally, in 1871–72, he worked with the assistance of Fr. Pestarino and Maria Mazzarello to transform the parish group into a religious community of women. These Sisters would do for girls what the Salesians were doing for boys. They were formally called the Institute of Daughters of Mary Help of Christians, but they quickly became known as the Salesian Sisters. Maria Mazzarello was elected the first superior and collaborated with Don Bosco in forming the Salesian spirit among them from the beginning.

Three years after the foundation of the Institute, Don Bosco sent a group young Salesians to Argentina. They were the first group of Salesian missionaries, and were led by Fr. Giovanni Cagliero, who had been the chaplain of the Sisters in Mornese during the year since Fr. Pestarino's death. Mother Mazzarello supported Cagliero and those first missionaries and began immediately making plans with Don Bosco to send Sisters on the next missionary expedition, scheduled for 1877. Mother Mazzarello hoped that she would be able to depart as a missionary with that group; instead, she was reelected as the mother general of the Institute. In her prayers, she offered her life to God for the people in the mission territories. Her health soon broke, and she died on May 14, 1881, five days after her forty-fourth birthday. Her heroic virtues were known to all: she was canonized by Pope Pius XII on June 24, 1951.

Mother Mazzarello's Letters

Maria Mazzarello learned from her father how to read as a child. She did not learn how to write until she was thirty, with the help of her good friend, Petronella Mazzarello (no relation), whose father ran the village school. It is no surprise, then, that we have more embroidery than writings. It is also no surprise that all of her writings are heartfelt.

Letter to Don Bosco, Founder

In this first recorded letter to Don Bosco, Mary Mazzarello sends greetings for the Feast of St. John the Baptist, which Salesians celebrated at Don Bosco's name day. Catholics in nineteenth-century Italy did not celebrate birthdays; instead, they celebrated the day when their saint was celebrated in the liturgy. This explains the sentiments expressed in this letter.

House of Mary Help of Christians, Mornese, June 22, 1874
Very Reverend Rector Major:

To the many good wishes that rise to Heaven from all parts for your protection and well-being, permit me to add my own. Even though not expressed in sublime words, they are no less fervent and true.

I would like to find some way to express the gratitude that I feel towards your Reverence for all the good you continually do, not only for me but for the whole community.

Since I cannot express all that I feel in my heart, I will pray with the greatest possible fervor to your great patron to make up for my inability by obtaining from God all those graces that you most desire.

I will also ask him to obtain special blessings on all your works, so that, even in this life, you may enjoy the reward of your many virtues by seeing your efforts crowned [with success] and bearing abundant fruit for which you work so hard.

Allow me, Most Reverend Rector Major, to recommend myself to your efficacious prayers so that I may fulfill all the duties of the role entrusted to me with exactness and may be able to correspond to the expectations of your Reverence. Say one of those efficacious words to Mary Most Holy, that she may help me to practice what I have to teach others, so that all may receive from me the example which my position obliges me to give them. On your name-day I will ask everyone to offer Holy Communion for your Reverence. Please remember me and all the community.

Please pardon my inability to express myself, and read in these few, poorly expressed words, all that my heart would like to say to you, and give your special blessing to me who declare myself, Most Reverend Father, with all due respect,

Your most indebted daughter in J. Christ,
Sr. Maria Mazzarello[27]

Letter to Fr. Giovanni Cagliero, Director General

Fr. Giovanni Cagliero (1838–1926) was one of the first young people at the Oratory of St. Francis de Sales to enter the Salesians at the time of the founding in 1859. He served as "director general," that is, spiritual director general of the Institute of Mary Help of Christians for a year after the death of Fr. Domenico Pestarino. In 1875, Cagliero led the first missionary expedition of Salesians. They went to Argentina, but Salesians did not distinguish between South and North America. Mother Mazzarello heard that Fr. Cagliero would be returning to Italy to collect more volunteers for the missions. She writes him on all that was happening among the Sisters and to speak about the missions.

Mornese, July 8, 1876
Live Jesus!
Very Reverend and Good Father,

If you remember rightly, before you left, we told you that when you got to America the work would surely make you forget the poor Daughters of M. H. C. It seems as though we guessed rightly, since you never answer our letters and we have written a good number of them. If you only knew how much we long to hear from you, you surely would not make us wait so long.

We heard, I don't know from where, that your Reverence has been ill. This news really made us feel sad and we hope that by now you have recovered.

Please be kind enough to write at least once. Will you give us this consolation? We hope so.

Once again, I must announce a death. I am really sorry but what can we do about it? The Lord wants to fill the house in Heaven. On April 13 (Holy Thursday), at half-past six in the evening, our dear Mother Mistress (Sr. Maria Grosso) died. She spoke almost up to the last moment and died saying: *Fiat voluntas tua*. She edified us all with the resignation she showed throughout her three-month illness.

There have been no more defections apart from those we already wrote about, thank God. Instead, extraordinary and spectacular things happened, that would take at least fifteen days of continual talking to tell you about, so it would be impossible to write about them. You would need to have seen it....

Enough. I will try to write some of them as best I can. We had ecstasies, raptures, revelations of things hidden, real matters of conscience, you know, things that were buried in the deepest recesses of some people's hearts. And all of this through a young woman from Rome whom Don Bosco had sent here to save her from the lion's mouth. I won't stop to tell you all she did from the very beginning, suffice it to say she was so bad that she was sent away. She recommended herself to Our Lady so fervently all during the month of May that she obtained the grace for returning after only one day's absence (we will tell you how this came about when you come back). Then she began to speak of a little girl, visible only to her, who was beside her almost all the time. In the beginning it was thought that she was mad, then she became gravely ill and was instantaneously cured by Our Lady (so she said).

After this miracle, she began to reveal hidden things, and it cannot be denied that she did a great good to many people in the house. After that the ecstasies began, complete fasts, which lasted several days during which the little girl fed her with heavenly food. She claimed that she saw Our Lady, and many times made everyone (even Fr. Rector) kneel down to receive her blessing. She gave such proof of all these things that everyone believed them to be true; even Don Bosco himself believed. Then the scene changed, and we realized that she was possessed by the devil, and since we could find no cure, on Don Bosco's orders we sent her to perform a few miracles in Rome. Come back soon and we will tell you all the details of this comedy; is enough for the present.

There are no other unusual happenings. There was a reception into the novitiate on May 24, but I already wrote you about that. Sr. Teresa Laurantoni is completely cured, but now we have Sr. Mina sick with a pulmonary illness. Do not be surprised; she herself admits that she has had this illness for three years and coming into the strong air [of Mornese] it became worse. I sent her to Torino and Don Bosco sent her from there to Piedmont to stay with Sr. Elisa's mother. She wears her religious habit and is fully resigned to the Will of God. Sr. Maria Belletti I infected with the same illness; the others, thank God, are well. They are happy and as far as I know, they are also good.

At the beginning of June, a house was opened in Sestri Levante. It is not really a house. Seven Sisters went there to assist boys and girls suffering from scrofulous. The children go there for a seawater dure. Among them are Sr. Enrichetta, Sr. Angiolina (from the secretary's house), and five others whom you would not know. In September they will return to the nest.

And when will you come to visit the nest? We are expecting you soon. You should see how the number of Daughters of M. H. C. has increased! There are 30 postulants and approximately 10 novices, 36 professed Sisters and 30 boarders. You can come and choose a good number to take to [the missions in] America; almost everyone wants to go. Come soon then, we are really looking forward with all our hearts to seeing you.

Now listen to what I have to say: save me a place in America, but seriously! It is true that I am good for nothing, but I know how to make polenta and then, I would see to it that not too much soap would be wasted when washing the clothes. If you wish, I will also learn a bit of cooking. In short, I am ready to do everything possible to please you all, if only you will let me come.

In order to please the Sisters, I would have to say a word for each of them. Since that is not possible, I will leave it to you to interpret everything, and I recommend each one individually to your prayers. Everyone sends greetings and assures you that we are all praying to Mary Most Holy to bless your labors and keep you safe for many years.

Please bless me in a special way. I remember you every time I go to church. Please send us your blessing and know that I am,

> Your most humble daughter in Jesus,
> *Sr. Maria M.*

The boarders would like to write to you too but for this time it is not possible. Accept their good will and bless them. They did write on other occasions, and, like us, they never got a reply.

Please give the enclosed note to Mrs. Borgna and ask her please to say something; the three girls have absolutely nothing. The youngest is not yet eight years old, and consequently cannot do anything. They really should pay for her, at least.

Here it is very hot. If only you could send us some of the cold you are feeling we would send you some heat! Instead you have to blow on your fingers while we have to fan ourselves for air. This is how the world goes; we always want what we do not have, but in Heaven it won't be like that, will it? Oh, how wonderful. Let us go there! We will really love Jesus there![28]

Letter to a Novice, Sr. Laura Rodríguez

Laura Rodríguez was the first American vocation. She met the Sisters through her brother who attended the Salesian school in Montevideo-Villa Colón (Uruguay), and entered the Institute of the Daughters of Mary Help of Christians on May 14, 1878.

This letter from St. Mary Mazzarello is written in response to the first letter she received from the Uruguayan novice, Laura Rodríguez. She gives the young Sister some pointers as she begins to follow her vocation. The tone is warm and maternal. In the language of Francis de Sales and Jane de Chantal, she invites the young Sr. Laura to meet with her in the Heart of Jesus. She also speaks of the "one thing necessary," which is to know Jesus and his salvation (Luke 10:42).

Mornese, December 1878
Live Jesus and Mary and St. Joseph!
My Good Sr. Laura:

I understood your note even though it was written in Spanish, and it gave me great pleasure. My dear Sr. Laura, although I do not know you personally, I love you very much and pray for you. I hope to meet you one day in Heaven. Oh, what a great celebration we will have then!

Meanwhile, since you are the first Daughter of Mary Help of Christians from America, you must become a great saint so that many young American women can follow your example. Although such a great distance separates us from one another we form one heart to love our beloved Jesus and Mary Most Holy, and we can always meet [there] and pray for one another.

I believe that it would be unnecessary for me to recommend that you be obedient, humble, charitable and that you love work. It has only been a few months since you became a novice, so you must still be full of fervor. I recommend that you never allow the fervor that the Lord has enkindled in your heart to die. Remember that only one thing is necessary, to save your soul. For us religious it is not enough simply to save our own soul. We must become holy and, through our good works, help many other souls who are waiting for our help to become holy too. Take courage then, and after a few days of struggle we will have Heaven forever.

Always be cheerful, have confidence in your superiors, never hide anything from them, always keep your heart open, always obey them in all simplicity and you will never go wrong.

Pray for me and for all the Sisters. Everyone, Sisters and postulants, thank you for the greetings you send, and they reciprocate them wholeheartedly in the Heart of Jesus.

May the Lord bless you and grant you holy perseverance and all the graces necessary for you to become a good religious and a true Daughter of Mary Help of Christians. Good-bye, my good Sister; believe me to be in the Lord,

Your most affectionate Mother,
Sr. Maria Mazzarello

Letter to a Missionary, Sr. Giovanna Borgna

Giovanna Borgna attended the Sisters' school in Mornese as a boarder, beginning in 1874. She became a Daughter of Mary Help of Christians at age seventeen and joined the second Salesian missionary expedition, departing for America on November 14, 1877. Mother Mazzarello wrote to her from Sampierdarena on New Year's Day, 1879, when she had come with Mother Petronilla to accompany new missionaries to the port for their departure to America. In this letter to the young missionary Sr. Giovanna, who was not yet twenty but already vicar of the house in Montevido-Villa Colon (Uruguay), Mother Mazzarello expresses her affection and her attention. She offers simple but deeply spiritual advice.

Genova-Sampierdarena, January 1, 1879
Live Jesus, Mary! and St. Joseph!
My dear Sr. Giovanna:

Your note gave me great pleasure. I am happy to hear that you have the good will to become holy. Remember that it is not enough simply to begin, we must continue. We need to keep struggling every day. Our self-love is so subtle that when we think we have already advanced a bit in something, it makes us bump our nose on the ground. But this life is a continual warfare. We must never tire if we want to win Heaven. Take heart then, my good Sr. Giovanna, act in such a way as to always be a model of virtue, of humility, charity, and obedience. Since the Lord sees the heart, it is necessary to practice these virtues more from your heart than with external acts.[29] Then, if obedience seems a bit difficult for you, look to Heaven and think of the reward that awaits you there.

Are you glad that you will now have your sister closer to you? Giacinta is well: pray that she may become good, and rest assured that I will take good care of her. Is it true that you are feeling run down? Get better soon because you have work to do. Tell the Lord to grant you the time to become holy and to win many souls for Him. Always be cheerful, be very good, work wholeheartedly, do everything for Jesus and pray so that one day we may all meet in Heaven.

Courage, pray for me and for all your Sisters. May God bless you and make you totally His.

> I am, in the Heart of Jesus,
> Your most affectionate Mother
> *The poor Sr. Maria Mazzarello*
> *Live Mary! Do answer!*

Her Last Letter, to the Sisters of the House in Carmen de Patagones (Argentina)

Mother Mazzarello had received a letter from the Sisters of the missionary house in Patagonia while she was visiting the community in Saint-Cyr. She became ill while in France, and her health continued to decline, so she made the journey back to the new general headquarters in Nizza Monferrato. She writes to encourage all the missionary Sisters and encourages them all in a very Salesian way to become saints and win people for Christ (as per Don Bosco and Fr. Cafasso), to practice the little virtues (in the tradition of Francis de Sales) and live close to Jesus, dwelling in his heart (Francis de Sales and Jane de Chantal).

Nizza Monferrato, April 10, 1881
Live Jesus!
Dearest Patagonian Sisters,

I was very pleased to hear from you. I delayed answering in hope of recovering from my illness to be able to write in my own hand, as you wanted me to do. But seeing that I will be weak for a long time to come, I will make use of someone else's hand. You will be satisfied with that, won't you?

So, Sr. Caterina [Fina] is sick? Poor soul! Give her much encouragement on my behalf, tell her always to be resigned to the Will of the Lord, to suffer always with patience and resignation. Oh, what great merit she will obtain! I believe that she will recover soon; you are too few to let one go to Heaven. Then, too, she has not yet done enough work, so she will have to get better. She must become a great saint and win many souls for the Lord. I will not tell you to look after her because I am sure that you will.

I would like to say a special word to each Sister, but since I don't have enough space, I will say to each of you that I always remember you and recommend you to our Good Jesus in a special way every day. I highly recommend humility and charity. If you practice these virtues, the Lord will bless you and your work, so that you will be able to do great good.

All the Sisters in Europe send heartfelt greetings and always remember you. Pray for everyone, pray especially for the sick, among whom are Mother Bursar (Sr. Giovanna Ferrettino), Sr. Catterina Massa and Sr. Tersilla Ginepro.[30]

The Sisters from Buenos Aires will have given you all the news, so I finish by recommending myself very much to your prayers. I leave you in the Most Sacred Heart of Jesus, in which I will always be,

Your most affectionate Mother,
Sr. Maria Mazzarello

This is that last letter that Mother Mazzarello wrote. Passing quickly over her own recent illness (from which she had not recovered), Mother Mazzarello speaks in a teasing way and encourages them to stay well because they have a lot of work to do in the missions. Whatever the outcome, however, she wanted them to know of her affection and prayers, inviting them, as she had at other times, to meet her in the Heart of Jesus.

COOPERATOR SALESIANS

In 1874, he founded yet another group, the Salesian Cooperators. These were mostly laypeople who would work for young people like the Daughters and the Salesians but would not join a religious order. Originally, Don Bosco described the members of the Salesian Society as "priests, clerics and laity." The latter were not designed to serve the former. Together they worked for the common goal of saving souls.[31] Don Bosco moved to structure the makeup of the Salesians in a way that was inclusive of several states of life, but the Roman curia was not prepared to accept such a structure. Finally, he reached a solution. Salesians "in the world" would make up a third grouping within the Salesian constellation. These were to be members of the Pious Union of Salesian Cooperators, formally organized and approved by Rome on May 9, 1876. The Cooperators constituted something of a "third order" with regard to canon law, but in Don Bosco's mind, they were the beginnings of a vast movement of committed laity and clergy.

In that year, while negotiating for the inclusion of laity in his family, Don Bosco returned from Rome; he spoke of a coalition of laypeople he calls Pious Christians. He included three concepts into this project: a third order of religious in the world, an organization of benefactors, and a union of collaborators. Pietro Stella described this threefold project in the following terms:

Identifying the Purpose of the Association of Salesian Cooperators

The Association is really a conglomeration of six more or less distinct projects:

1. Salesian religious in the world;
2. Collaborators of Salesians in their local houses, who assist by teaching catechism and other activities;
3. Supporters of Salesian work in the world through prayer and offerings;

4. Associates in youth work and the spread of faith, in union with bishops and parish priests;
5. Members of a league to combat anti-clericals and Protestants, especially through the press;
6. Union to promote moral and civil elevation of youth.[32]

Don Bosco promoted his ideas for the Cooperators in conversations with the many who were already collaborating with the Salesian Society. To these ends he began to publish a monthly formative magazine that he called the *Salesian Bulletin*. Here is how he described the Cooperator Salesians in the year that he founded the association.

A Cooperator can do good on his own, but the fruit remains very limited and for the most part of short duration. On the contrary, united with others, he finds support, advice, courage and often with slight effort he obtains a lot, because even weak forces become strong if they are united. Hence the great saying that unity is strength, *vis unita fortior*.

Therefore, our Cooperators, following the scope of the Salesian Congregation, will work according to their strength to gather youth at risk and abandoned children from the streets, initiate them in the teachings of the catechism, keep them occupied during holidays and place them with honest employers, direct them, advise them, help them as much as possible so that they can grow to become good Christians and honest citizens. The norms to be followed in this effort will be proposed to the Cooperators, and for this purpose, these will be treated in the *Salesian Bulletin*.

The words *practical way* are added in order to note that here one does not belong to a confraternity, nor to a religious, literary, or scientific Association, and much less is he subscribing to a newspaper. This is a simple union of benefactors of humanity, ready to dedicate not promises, but action and facts, concerns, disturbances and sacrifices to benefit our fellow human beings. We use the phrase *practical way* because we do not mean that this is the only way to do good in the midst of civil society. On the contrary, we approve and highly praise all the institutions, unions, public and private associations that are dedicated to the good of humanity, and we pray that God will provide all the moral and material means needed to preserve these groups, so that they may progress and achieve their proposed goals. We in turn intend to propose a means of operating, and we propose this means in the Association of Salesian Cooperators.

We speak of *benefiting morality* to make it clear what we want to do and what our common understanding is.

In fact, we will operate completely outside the realm of politics. We will constantly keep ourselves away from anything that could become a burden of any constituted authority in either civil or ecclesiastical society. Our program will unalterably be this: Leave to us the care of the poor and abandoned young people, and we will make every effort to do them the greatest good we can, because in this way we believe we can further the moral good of society and of civilization itself.[33]

Continuing the Legacy: Salesian Calm and Gentleness

Paolo Albera (1845–1921) entered Don Bosco's Oratory at Valdocco in 1858 at the age of thirteen. He was admitted to the Salesian Society on May 1, 1860, which Don Bosco had founded less than six months previously. Paolo Albera and his peers had been formed directly by Don Bosco and modeled their apostolic and spiritual lives on all that they had seen the founder do. They had enthusiastically embraced the spirit and teachings of Don Bosco's model Francis de Sales, and strove to imitate the saint's virtues, particularly his gentleness and approachability while working among young people at risk. However, by 1893 when Don Albera took up his role on the general council, he was keenly aware that many young Salesians had neither read the writings of the patron nor heard the voice of the founder. In his role as spiritual director general, Don Albera oversaw the formation of new members and coordinated the spiritual exercises for young and old alike. It was imperative that he articulate the

The Family of Don Bosco

Salesian spirit. He did so by preaching retreats. In Don Albera's retreat notes, Francis de Sales provided the language for religious experience; St. John Bosco provided a concrete example that translated faith into practice. Chief among that language to be translated into practice is the word used by Francis de Sales, *douceur*, meaning gentleness or sweetness.

Address at the Salesian General Chapter 1910

It is hard to define. We have the beautiful face of sweetness clearly fixed in our mind's eye. We know it is the fusion of piety, charity, and goodness. We know that it manifests itself in different and truly fascinating ways. But to define it? We don't know how.[34]

Don Albera may have had trouble defining these terms, but, as he told the delegates to the Eleventh General Chapter, "sweetness" and devotion were not theoretical in nature. They were best known through experience. The virtue of sweetness, an ensemble of piety, goodness, and charity, while born of joy and gratitude for God's goodness, is in fact a virtue of great strength, that bolsters and arms Christ's disciples against any enemies.

Salesian Gentleness—Retreat Instructions 1893

It is an outstanding favor that the Lord has done for us by placing us under the banner of that master of meekness that is Francis de Sales. It is almost as if he were telling us that the weapon most apt to fight our enemies in these times is sweetness. And it is as if to make the teaching of this great saint more authoritative, the Church has declared him Doctor of the Church. How many signs of affection did the great Pontiff of the Immaculate Conception show us! Nor does his most learned successor Leo XIII love us any less.[35]

Don Albera does not confine his discussion to vague, theoretical exhortations. He asserts that one learns "sweetness" from experience. This is why he cites Don Bosco's experience as essential in the reflection of the Salesian. The founder's extreme effort to remain calm in adversity demonstrates that John Bosco, like Francis de Sales before him, had to exert great effort to acquire this virtue. Ever the master storyteller, Don Albera used the following anecdote to press his point:

> You needed to spend some time with Don Bosco and you would have seen how much it cost him to always keep calm and gentle. The story is told how once there was a woman who regularly disturbed the Oratory very much, because she had a tavern nearby. And there she gathered so many poor young people, but when it came time for church services, she would block them from going. Plus, things used to happen there which were a lot worse than eating and drinking. Now Don Bosco found the means to buy that house, and therefore to send the woman on her way. When she knew that her tavern had to close down, she went searching for Don Bosco. He was with a group of boys, because he was always among the young in the early years. Well, she started in on him and covered him with insults. Those who were near to Don Bosco assure us that first he turned red, then he became pale, then red again, but he said nothing. Finally, when the woman had vented completely, Don Bosco told the young people: "Please accompany her as far as the door." He did not even wish to reproach her for her bad manners. My dear brothers, what does it mean that he changed color? It means that he was making a great effort to control himself.[36]

IV

MARY DE SALES CHAPPUIS, LOUIS BRISSON, LÉONIE FRANCES DE SALES AVIAT, AND THE OBLATE SISTERS AND OBLATES OF ST. FRANCIS DE SALES

Joseph F. Chorpenning, OSFS[1]

The flames of the Salesian Pentecost blazed brilliantly and intensely in nineteenth-century Troyes, the capital and largest city of the department of Aube, located southeast of Paris in the Champagne region. It was there, under the auspices of a triad of remarkable individuals, that two distinctive religious communities emerged to carry forward the spirit of St. Francis de Sales (1567–1622). The Oblate Sisters of St. Francis de Sales were cofounded in 1871 by Louis Brisson (1817–1908) and Léonie Frances de Sales Aviat (1844–1914), and the Oblates (priests and brothers), in 1875 by Brisson.[2] However, neither religious congregation would have come into existence if it were not for Mother Mary de Sales Chappuis (1793–1875), the Swiss-born superior of the Troyes monastery of the Order of the Visitation of Holy Mary, who is often referred to in the Oblate and Visitandine families as the "Good Mother." It was through her influence that Brisson, the monastery chaplain, and Aviat, a former student-boarder at the Visitation school, were imbued with Salesian spirituality and

135

inspired to respond with apostolic action to the complex religious and social issues of their era. The "inspiration" for the founding of a religious community ordinarily comes through the founder, but, in the case of the Oblates, it was transmitted through Mother Chappuis, who likewise played a primary role in the foundation of the Oblate Sisters.

Born into a devout Catholic family, Marie-Thérèse Chappuis's early years were spent in the shadow of the French Revolution, during which her native village of Soyhières in the Swiss Jura Mountains was annexed to France. Her most vivid memory of this time was her elderly priest-uncle celebrating clandestine midnight Masses in her parents' home. At twelve years of age, Marie-Thérèse was sent by her parents to the boarding school of the Visitation Monastery in Fribourg to complete her formal education. She eventually entered the monastery, receiving the name Mary Francis de Sales at her clothing with the religious habit. During her novitiate year (1815–16), she received a series of "lights," or revelations, from the Lord about "His designs for her work" as an apostle of the Salesian spirit.[3] Sister Mary de Sales totally immersed herself in the writings of Francis de Sales, fully appropriated the Salesian spirit, and came to be regarded as *the* authentic interpreter of the Salesian spirit in her day. Her profound understanding of, and ability to communicate, Salesian spirituality was quickly recognized, and scarcely a year after her profession, she was sent to reestablish the Visitation Monastery in Metz. When she returned to Fribourg, she was appointed novice mistress, her youth notwithstanding. In 1826, she became superior of the Visitation of Troyes, which was in urgent need of effective leadership.[4] Complicating the situation, "Troyes was a diocese full of problems, not easy to resolve by simple fiat."[5]

The Troyes Visitation had been disbanded during the French Revolution and restored in 1807. Moreover, it had been deeply influenced by Jansenism for nearly a century, with the nuns refusing to go to confession or to receive holy communion.[6] But it was not an outlier in the Diocese of Troyes, which was a Jansenist stronghold.[7] The liturgical books used in the diocese were permeated by Jansenist doctrine.[8] Gallicanism also thrived in nineteenth-century Troyes,[9] with Gallicans and Ultramontanes bitterly divided over the restoration of the Roman liturgy.[10] Exacerbating this state of affairs, French Catholicism generally had developed a pathological obsession with damnation, hellfire, and the small number of the saved. This was communicated in the pulpit by a *théologie féroce* (ferocious theology) and *pastorale de la peur* (religion of fear), and in the confessional by moral rigorism, with absolution often being withheld or delayed. The result was an "uncompromising and frightening picture of the Catholic faith, based on fear rather than on divine love."[11] According to Ralph Gibson, who pioneered study of this phenomenon, "In some ways this was part of the influence of Jansenist austerity, but Jansenists and bitter anti-Jansenists alike shared a vision of a judicial and even vengeful God, one to be feared, rather than of a loving God, an ever-present help in time of trouble."[12] Preaching about divine punishment and eternal damnation aimed to get Catholics into the confessional, but for many the sacrament had little appeal.[13]

Simply stated, French Catholicism had lost sight of the gospel's core message that "God so loved the world that he gave his only Son, so that everyone who believes in him may not perish but have eternal life" (John 3:17 NRSV). This was the ecclesial-pastoral context for the revelation to the young novice Sister Mary de Sales that "God has looked into Himself and He has decided to open up new sources of graces"[14] by completing "the work of sanctification that [St. Francis de Sales] began on earth."[15] As Brisson would later express it, "St. Francis de Sales was a man of his time, but he is even more truly of our time than his own."[16] While not officially declared a doctor of the church until 1877, Francis de Sales had been acclaimed as the Doctor of Divine Love from at least the time of his beatification (1661).[17] The Doctor of Divine Love's teaching that holiness is accessible and adaptable for people in all walks of life, that "God's great mercy…is infinitely greater…than all the sins of the world"[18]and that the Savior "forgets nothing to prove that 'His mercy reaches out to all that He has made' [Ps 144:9],…and He wishes 'all to be saved' [1 Tim 2:4] and none be lost,"[19] and pastoral method of attracting and winning hearts through gentle persuasion were uniquely suited to addressing the specific challenges confronting nineteenth-century French Catholicism.[20]

Mother Chappuis's first reforming efforts were directed to her own Visitation community; however, her aspirations extended much more widely. A year after his ordination as a priest of the Diocese of Troyes (1840), Louis Brisson was assigned as confessor and professor at the Visitation monastery's boarding school in Troyes. Like Chappuis, Brisson came from a deeply Catholic family. Among other things, his parents instilled in the young Louis a fervent devotion to the Holy Eucharist. His mother had taught him to read, using St. Alphonsus Liguori's book *Visits to the Blessed Sacrament*. While praying before the altar of the Virgin Mary in his parish church several weeks after his first communion, Brisson had a strong feeling that God was calling him to save a great many souls and "to make the Lord loved with an infinite love, to make the love of God so strong in souls...that this love would consume everything."[21]

From an early age, Brisson had also demonstrated a keen power of observation and an aptitude for the natural sciences, chemistry, physics, and astronomy. At the Visitation's school, his fascination with science, especially astronomical observation, was put to good use as a teacher. But Mother Chappuis saw in him greater potential. Not long thereafter, in 1843, he became the monastery's ordinary confessor and chaplain, serving in this capacity for the next forty-one years. During this time, Brisson was formed and nurtured in the Salesian spirit by the monastery's superior, and together they collaborated on a number of projects aimed at revitalizing French Catholicism.

Chappuis and Brisson worked together to free Troyes from "Gallican separatism and Jansenist rigorism"[22] and "to support the return...of the Roman liturgy."[23] They also participated in the European network of the Association of St. Francis de Sales, which had been initiated by the French priest Emmanuel d'Alzon (1810–80),[24] and then launched on an international scale by two major ecclesiastical patrons of the Salesian Pentecost: the Parisian archbishop Louis Gaston de Ségur (1820–81),[25] and the Swiss bishop (and later cardinal) Gaspard Mermillod (1824–92).[26] The association's inspiration, model, and patron was Francis de Sales, Apostle of the Chablais, a "region of Savoy, where, against great odds and much opposition, he [won] thousands of Calvinists back to the Catholic fold by an irenic and truly pastoral approach that respected and highlighted human freedom and dignity, and that presented the Church as the assembly of love and the visible resurrected body of Christ without compromising its hierarchical and institutional aspects."[27] Conceived as a response to Pope Pius IX's concern about the working class's ignorance of the Catholic faith,[28] the association's "general purpose was to renew the Catholic faith and restore religious practice"[29] within Christian countries—what today is called the "new evangelization." In 1857, the association was established in the Diocese of Troyes, with Brisson as its director and Chappuis as treasurer.[30]

Chappuis and Brisson's collaboration in responding to the critical social issues of the day grew out of their involvement with the Association of St. Francis de Sales. Under Brisson's leadership, the association's membership doubled, and its fundraising activity was prodigious. However, not content with these accomplishments, Brisson initiated an apostolate (in French, *œuvres ouvrières*) to provide spiritual and social support, as well as catechetical instruction, for young women workers in Troyes.[31] What is most striking about Troyes today is its stunning Gothic and Renaissance architectural and artistic treasures;[32] however, in the nineteenth century it was primarily considered "a *ville ouvrière* (workers' town),"[33] being one of the largest centers of the textile industry in France. Troyes had traditionally specialized in the manufacture of hosiery (*bonneterie*) as a cottage industry. Industrialization brought the building of factories and increased production, but also a host of social, environmental, and moral problems.[34]

Young women working in the factories were especially vulnerable. Long and exhausting work hours (about twelve hours a day), unhealthy and unsanitary working and living conditions, unsavory conversations and crude behavior, and religious indifference and ignorance were the norm.[35] To try to remedy this situation, Brisson initially established a series of clubs and then shelters. The primary purpose of the *œuvres ouvrières* was to preserve and strengthen the young women's faith and its practice, with the shelters providing affordable lodging, safety and security, clothing, food, and childcare, as well as an opportunity for work. The operation of the shelters required full-time competent and responsible staff, which proved very challenging to find and retain. To meet this critical need, the Oblate Sisters were founded.[36]

A gifted graduate of the Troyes Visitation boarding school, Léonie Aviat had been profoundly impacted by her formative experience in the Salesian spirit under the tutelage of Brisson and Chappuis. While her non-practicing Catholic parents' plan for her was a marriage that would provide social and financial security, Léonie hoped that one day she would be able to respond to the inner call she felt to give herself to God. When she turned twenty-one and was legally free to make her own decisions, she thought of entering the Visitation. However, during a retreat with Brisson, Léonie discerned that she was possibly called instead to engage in an apostolate that he regarded as critical for the renewal of the faith.[37] In his *Life of the Venerable Mother Mary de Sales Chappuis*, chapter 47, Brisson recounts the events leading to the Oblate Sisters coming into existence and their spirit.

LIFE OF THE VENERABLE MOTHER MARY DE SALES CHAPPUIS, CHAPTER 47[38]

The homes for young working girls were established, and their direction had been entrusted to some devout unmarried women who dedicated themselves generously to this apostolate. However, as invariably happens, enthusiasm cools and courage flags in the face of difficulties. It was thus necessary to entrust the care of these homes to a religious community. But what community would be able to enter fully into the outlook of the Founders [= St. Francis de Sales and St. Jane Frances de Chantal] and into the spirit that they desired to give to this apostolate? Only the Visitation measured up to these requirements, but the Sisters of the Visitation were cloistered, and an external apostolate was impossible for them. Thus, the idea emerged of establishing a congregation that, although different from the Visitation by its exterior apostolate, would, nevertheless, practice the *Spiritual Directory*, and approximate as much as possible the Visitandine spirit and interior life. This idea seemed all the more reasonable insofar as St. Francis de Sales himself had initiated the Institute as a non-cloistered congregation, which he had given statutes and named the Congregation of the Oblates of the Visitation of Holy Mary. This form particularly appealed to him because, in a letter to Cardinal Bellarmine,[39] after having provided the details of the Sisters' external occupations and manner of life, he added that they would practice these works in all simplicity and gentleness, and consequently they should not be considered as religious or monastics, but as Oblates....This name, Oblates, he had engraved on the first stone of the church which he had built for them along the shores of Lake Annecy.

This was St. Francis de Sales's first idea. It was only through acquiescence to the will of Archbishop de Marquemont of Lyon[40] that he consented to establish cloister in the monasteries of the Visitation. This compromise cost the saintly Founder very dearly. On his first visit to Lyon after the sisters had been cloistered, Archbishop de Marquemont invited him to come to see the nuns. St. Francis de Sales replied: "What nuns?" Archbishop de Marquemont: "Why, the Sisters of Our Lady of the Visitation!" St. Francis de Sales: "Then call them yours, and not mine." Everyone knows how greatly rewarded St. Francis de Sales has been for his sacrifice: by the cloister, the Visitation has easily been able to preserve its spirit and its traditions, becoming—as Father de la Rivière,[41] the first biographer of the holy Founder, said—"the priceless pearl in the diadem of Holy Mother Church."

The Good Mother desired that the spirit of St. Francis de Sales should be communicated to the greatest number of souls possible, and the way to spread it was evidently to place among the faithful a congregation which could reach all levels of society, bringing to it the teachings of the saintly Founder. They, therefore, resolved to begin. Two boarding students at the Visitation, Léonie Aviat and Lucie Canuet, in obedience to the interior attraction that was inviting them to give themselves to God for the salvation of their neighbor, came to make a retreat in the Monastery of the Visitation in Troyes, with the Good Mother. They desired to study the will of God in prayer and to receive the advice and guidance of her whom they considered a saint and to whom they wished to entrust their future. The result of this retreat was that they felt called to set to work immediately on the project by replacing the good laywomen who had undertaken the guidance of the workers' homes, but who were no longer able to continue. Léonie Aviat and Lucie Canuet went at once to establish themselves at the home where the young girls gathered. The Good Mother took charge of enabling them to make their novitiate. So that they would learn the observance and the exercises of the Rule, she entrusted them to the Assistant Mistress of Novices, who demonstrated the greatest zeal in forming them in the religious life.

Scarcely a few months had elapsed since the retreat made by the two young aspirants, when Bishop Mermillod[42] (at the time the administrator of Geneva) arrived to find that Bishop Ravinet—for whom he had great esteem and profound affection—was now bishop of Troyes.[43] Bishop Mermillod had come to ask the new bishop to begin, in his diocese, a congregation of women living the spirit of St. Francis de Sales and whose apostolate would be the religious instruction and Christian direction of youth. He wished that after a sufficient number of these women religious had been formed, they would be sent to the diocese of Geneva. He explained: "Being the successor of St. Francis de Sales, I ought to establish in my diocese the spirit of that great saint, and for this purpose I need a congregation which professes that spirit. On the other hand, the law of the land prevents me from introducing any religious orders already in existence; however, I am allowed to introduce these new religious as being a society of which I am myself the founder and for which I am personally responsible." Bishop Ravinet told Bishop Mermillod that he should ask Mother Mary de Sales

Chappuis, in whom he had great confidence, for her insights on the subject. They then went to the Visitation and explained their project to the Good Mother, who replied that she believed that it was divinely inspired. They implored her to accept responsibility for instructing and preparing the prospective vocations who would present themselves. She promised to help them and then added: "It is already done; there are here in Troyes, at the Home for Working Girls, two young women who are suitable for what you desire. I have already prepared them. They can begin."

Delighted to see his idea coming to fruition, Bishop Mermillod examined the two aspirants, and, with the concurring favorable opinion of Bishop Ravinet, he clothed them with the religious habit. He wanted them to be called the Oblate Sisters of St. Francis de Sales. He assured them that they were truly the saint's daughters, since on his deathbed St. Francis de Sales had predicted that eventually there would be in his spiritual family an intermediary order between the cloister and the world, responsible for bringing to souls the benefits of the spiritual life; that they were destined to be the auxiliaries of the priesthood in an apostolate of doctrine and of influence. This was the same idea that the Good Mother had: "The Savior wishes me to be an apostle, and what He gives me is for making apostles." Bishop Mermillod gave to Léonie Aviat the name of Frances de Sales, and to Lucie Canuet that of Jeanne-Marie. At the ceremony's conclusion, he went to take his leave of Mother Mary de Sales. He recommended to her the young throng that was going to be formed under her guidance, and he begged her to pray for himself and for Geneva, where he soon hoped to welcome the helpers whom he had just chosen....

The clothing with the habit bestowed a first consecration on the founding of the Oblate Sisters of St. Francis de Sales. The Good Mother believed that it was appropriate to procure for them the means to enter more deeply into the doctrine of St. Francis de Sales and the practice of the interior life, and so she gave them for their directress the Sister Assistant of the

Visitation, Sister Louise David Chérot. The choice could not have been better; Sister Louise David joined to a special gift of supernatural ways those religious virtues that are most emphasized: mortification and obedience. Bishop Séguin des Hons,[44] who once had the opportunity to witness an admirable act of obedience by Sister Louise David, told the Good Mother: "You have the mold for making saints." The Oblate Sisters had been founded exteriorly, but the spiritual foundation was still to be established.

One day in December 1868, the Good Mother came to the parlor after Holy Mass and told Father Brisson that she had much to tell him: "This is the life on earth of the Sacred Humanity with God His Father. 'My Father does nothing that I do not do. He works, I work with Him. I am only one with Him, and My Father is only one with Me' [cf. John 5:17 and 10:30]. I feel that the Savior's charity urges me to achieve these goals. I see Him perfectly in this work. ...I see that He is putting into operation the resources and the industries of His love in order to obtain what He wishes. I see Him wandering through places not yet visited by the divine charity in order to find there the help necessary for the souls who will enter this way, in order to make them strong and invincible. Then those who will be found faithful will completely effect the coming of the Savior on earth." The Good Mother told Father Brisson that these things were meant for the Oblate Sisters.

Brisson left behind a sizeable number of retreat conferences, chapter instructions, and sermons, in addition to his biography of Mother Chappuis and other writings. By contrast, Léonie Aviat left relatively little, and what survives is thanks to the Oblate Sisters writing down her instructions and counsels. The following selections offer a sampling.[45] Salient in these brief texts and sayings is Aviat's emphasis on the Salesian practices of continual awareness of the presence of God, living in the present moment and between the two wills of God, and the exercise of the little virtues, as well as the distinctively Visitandine prayer of simple *remise*, that is, entrustment into the hands of God.[46]

EXCERPTS FROM TWO INSTRUCTIONS GIVEN BY MOTHER AVIAT IN 1872 OR 1873 TO A GROUP OF NOVICES, SEVERAL OF WHOM RECORDED THEM[47]

One must see shining in you the gentleness, the humility, the simplicity—in a word, the virtues indicated in the rule of St. Francis de Sales.

If, for example, you went to the Carmelites, and you did not find fasting and austerity there, you would think, "But I am not among Carmelites." In the same way, one must find here, not the austerities of Carmel, but the charity and the renunciations prescribed by the rule of St. Francis de Sales. That is why I ask you to bring a great attentiveness to bear on everything that our Father [= Louis Brisson] will tell you. We have him with us for the time being, but we will not always have him. That is why you must presently apply yourselves well to doing everything that he has told you.

You will ask me, our Good Mother [= Léonie Aviat] added, what continual union with God is. I will give you an example of it. If you work with someone whom you love well, and she speaks to you, you answer her. You are entirely there for her. You love her conversation. Well! With the good Lord, it is the same thing. If you love Him, you are happy to converse heart to heart with Him. If you find that you are alone, and that the good Lord is inspiring good thoughts within you, you will receive them well. If you do not allow yourself to be troubled, distracted in your actions, and if you do them without being overly hurried, then the good Lord will make Himself felt to your heart. You know that the good Lord is not found among noise and trouble….

And thus, as I was telling you earlier, if a person that you like very much is near you, and is speaking with you, or is remaining silent, you are, nevertheless, happy, for you feel her near you. Well, then, with the good Lord, it is the same thing: if you are well-united to Him in all of your actions, either He will speak to you, or He will make you feel His presence.

This week, then, unite yourselves well to God. You will then be in continual meditation. This continual meditation is nothing but a conversation with God, union with Him in all of our actions. If we do not do this, we are not religious....

FROM AN UNPUBLISHED LETTER OF 1907 OF MOTHER AVIAT[48]

Allow the good God to act, and receive from His hand everything, everything without exception, profiting from each exercise so as to carry out the Rule well. In a word, be the little ball of wax in the hand of obedience....

FROM A SMALL BOOK CONTAINING QUOTES FROM MOTHER AVIAT, INTENDED FOR USE WITHIN THE OBLATE SISTERS[49]

[Whether] here or there, an Oblate Sister must be a little ball of wax in the hand of obedience, to have life in the practice of the *Spiritual Directory* and of the observance, being entirely within the present moment.

May the Savior give you, at every moment, the light and strength to act, the peace that is the happiness of an Oblate Sister, even within overwork, uncertainty, and difficult moments.

Remain very confident and abandoned; it is thus that a little Oblate Sister manages to overcome her personal difficulties and respond well to the desires of the good Lord for her soul.

Everywhere, trials make themselves felt, so that everywhere, through union in prayer and in suffering, we may become more and more friends with the cross, and true Oblate Sisters, accepting, from moment to moment, the will of the good Lord, as well as what He permits.

FROM A DOCUMENT, ENTITLED *OF THE TRUE MEANING OF OUR LIVES AS OBLATE SISTERS*, WHICH WAS LIKELY USED TO INSTRUCT SISTERS IN FORMATION[50]

The life of any religious is supernatural, but particularly that of an Oblate Sister. An Oblate is not an extraordinary creature, but she must always act supernaturally. An Oblate who does not act supernaturally in everything is not an Oblate. This supernatural life is desired and willed within the charity of God. It is of an extreme simplicity. It consists in looking at God, following the Savior, and only acting for Him. This life must be as our holy Founder said, very openly frank, very candid.

The foundation of the Oblate Sisters, so dear to Brisson's heart, was not to be the final work of the Troyes Pentecost. After cofounding, with Jane Frances de Chantal (1572–1641), the Visitation Order in 1610, Francis de Sales had wanted to found a comparable congregation of priests animated by the Salesian spirit; however, he was unable to realize this project before his death. Jane and the Visitation Order kept alive this aspiration, which was taken up by Fr. Raymond Bonal (1600–1653), a priest of the Diocese of Rodez, who in 1632 founded the Priests of Holy Mary, a very small congregation that did not survive the French Revolution.[51] While Chappuis and Brisson were well aware of this history,[52] they also knew that the initiative for their project of founding the Oblates had come not from themselves, but from the Lord, who had revealed to Sister Mary de Sales during her novitiate at Fribourg that the congregation's "foundation was one of the fruits of the inner life of the three Persons of the Blessed

Trinity."⁵³ On her arrival in Troyes to become superior of the Visitation, "she understood that this was the place that God had chosen for the accomplishment of His work."⁵⁴

Troyes, like other dioceses throughout France, was confronted by many problems: Jansenism and Gallicanism, widespread religious ignorance and indifference, prevalence of a religion of fear (*pastorale de la peur*) and moral rigorism that repelled the laity and depressed practice of the faith and reception of the sacraments, and neglect of the pastoral care of workers. Troyes was thus a microcosm of nineteenth-century French Catholicism. At the root of these problems was the deficient state of seminary education. Poorly educated and subscribing to the "Sulpician ideal" of the priest shut off from the world, the French clergy was unprepared and unequipped—intellectually, spiritually, and pastorally—to engage the contemporary issues facing the church.⁵⁵

A sharply different view of the priesthood was articulated to Brisson—during the process of seeking papal approbation for the Oblate Constitutions (which was granted in 1887)⁵⁶—by Cardinal Włodzimierz Czacki (1834–88), who had served as papal nuncio to France (1879–82): "How do we reach the world, and attract it to us, to save it? We must jump in with both feet, even if it means getting splashed with mud! Let's make it our responsibility to try to sanctify and cleanse it."⁵⁷ The Oblates were to be a "new breed of priests," who would "go out into the world in search of the lost sheep and bring them back into the fold."⁵⁸ Ministering in the spirit of the Doctor of Divine Love and continuing his work of sanctification, they were to be the instrument through which "the treasure of [the Savior's] charity will be lavished on the earth and given in all its fullness to the world,"⁵⁹ in an era when the gospel of God's love and mercy had been eclipsed by a religion of fear and moral rigorism.

For more than forty years, Brisson was schooled and steeped in Salesian doctrine and spirituality by Mother Chappuis. Inspired to minister as the Doctor of Divine Love did, he was indefatigable in preaching and teaching—by word and by action—that God is loving, "rich in mercy" (Eph 2:4 NRSV), and desirous that all be saved and none be lost. Following Francis de Sales's example, Brisson sought to attract and win hearts, which is possible only by love—the *pastorale de la peur* had no place in his pastoral method and ministry. Likewise, Brisson wanted the Oblates to walk in the Doctor of Divine Love's footsteps by being "apostles of the love of God"[60] and, consequently, apostles of the Salesian spirit. He also wished that those to whom he and the Oblates ministered would become in their own state of life "apostles of the love of God," thereby continuing the evangelizing mission of the apostles and the saving work of the Savior.[61]

When, as a recently ordained priest, Brisson was assigned to the Visitation boarding school, Mother Chappuis was not in Troyes, but serving as superior of the Second Visitation Monastery, on the rue de Vaugirard, in Paris (1838–44). In 1842, the young priest from Troyes went to Paris to visit Chappuis, who immediately recognized him as the one chosen by God to realize the project revealed to her by the Lord.[62] From his mature perspective many years later, Brisson recounts, in a retreat conference to his confreres in 1885, these events and how the Oblates came to be founded.

CONFERENCE, NO. 6, OBLATE RETREAT OF 1885[63]

Every religious order is linked to a notion distinctly its own. For some orders, it is poverty; for others, zeal for the salvation of souls; others practice painful mortifications; others devote themselves to a special ministry, such as the care of the sick. What, then, is our aim? For we have an aim that is distinctly our own. If we did not, we would have no reason for being (raison d'être). We would be no more than a group of individuals doing exactly the same things as others do, and would, as a consequence, have no special reason to exist, nor be in any way successful. It would be better to combine our forces, instead of dispersing them, and to join with others to obtain better results.

Let's return to our origins, to our creation. Teaching based in history has, above all others, an immense advantage: it specifies with great precision the goal and the means to attain it.

The Good Mother. Why did God choose a woman?[64] When does the history of our foundation begin? This foundation dates a long way back. In order to find the first thought of it, the first inspiration, we must go to a little Swiss village. With regard to the early years in the life of the Good Mother, I will pass over these in silence, for at that time she did not yet understand what God was asking of her; she had not received any positive revelations. But why was it that God chose a woman to bring about the foundation? And why wasn't a man chosen? I know nothing about that. Let this be the first answer. As long as the foundation was not definitively established, it was possible to have doubts. But now I can say to you what Jesus said to the Jews: "If you do not believe in the words I say, believe at least because of the deeds that I do [John 10:38]." Yes, you can doubt, our Lord was saying; you can deny the truth, and no doubt your heart is evil enough to deny the truth. In the end, however, the deeds I have done will compel you to believe. *Propter opera ipsa credite*, "Believe Me because of the works themselves" [John 14:11]. I am here to tell you the same thing: Do not look at the person, look at what this person has accomplished.

The Novice at Fribourg and Bishop Yenni. One day, in the novitiate in Fribourg, Sister Mary de Sales Chappuis received some great lights from the good God; she already caught a glimpse of the foundation of the Oblate Fathers. God enabled her to see that this foundation was one of the fruits of the inner life of the three Persons of the Blessed Trinity, and especially of the Father in relation to the Word. These were sublime things. She reported everything to her Superior, following what was prescribed by the Rule. Her Superior, a very remarkable and saintly woman in her own right, did not trust her own judgment; she consulted Bishop Yenni,[65] who had been educated in Rome, the source of doctrine. The saintly and learned bishop gathered around himself a group of the most distinguished priests, who had all been educated at the German College in Rome. These priests spent the greater part of their time not playing cards but studying, having serious conferences about theological and canonical questions, thus buttressing the learning that they had acquired at such a good school. The Mother Superior at Fribourg thus had recourse to the authority and learning of this bishop, who quickly understood and appreciated the value of the nun being submitted to him for examination. On his advice, the Superior said to Sister Mary de Sales: "You must write down and submit to me everything that God communicates to you."

The Notebook of Fribourg. Under obedience, Sister Mary de Sales began to write. A first piece of writing, now in my possession, gives to the Mother Superior an account of some divine operations, of the part which the Sister is to play in them, and of the ensuing consequences. This first notebook provides us a complete overview of the work to be accomplished. God reveals to this soul that He has, in His charity, a particular view of salvation for the world, [and] that a great number of graces and spiritual favors remain in a state of preparation by His divine charity and are at the disposal of the world. She saw this very clearly, and, with even greater clarity, she put it into words. The bishop, to whose examination the Mother Superior submitted everything, studied this question in depth....

This, then, is the context within which Mother Mary de Sales came onto the scene. This is how judgment was passed on her, on her first communications with God. The notebook containing her manifestation of conscience speaks of the communications that she received from the divine Persons, and particularly what God still intends to give to the world. This notebook states:

Behold, I am being called to be an apostle and to contribute to the work that God will establish in order to communicate His graces and to expand the diffusion of His divine charity. The Savior will bring to the fore merits not yet employed. The treasure of His charity will be lavished on the earth and given in all its fullness to the world.

This is what God told this novice in Fribourg. This is what the Mother Superior and the bishop accepted. No one said to her: "Good Sister, this is all well and good, but be good enough to let it remain there. Just limit yourself to mental prayer of the usual kind." She was not told: "Take another road, strike a different note."

Thus, she continued. From time to time, the bishop came to visit her, and he would then say to the Mother Superior: "Let her say and do what she wishes." Often he would say: "You have a saint there. The good God is making use of her and will continue to do so in the future. Let her act; help her."

These are, I believe, well-authorized communications, my friends. There is nothing dangerous in them, nothing contrary to the teachings of the Church. These revelations are supported by doctors in the sacred sciences who are in direct contact with the Holy See.

The Good Mother, nonetheless, did not wish to immediately busy herself exteriorly with this work and to make use of "the effects of the effect." You must understand what she meant by this expression. The "effects" refer to what takes place in the godhead and was being communicated to the Good Mother. These are the contacts (*rapports*) with the three divine Persons: that is the first effect. The second effect—resulting from the first—is the communication that God makes to the faithful called to profit from these things.

At Troyes. The Good Mother came to Troyes....On her arrival, she understood that this was the place that God had chosen for the accomplishment of His work, that in Troyes God had laid the first stone, and that there the effects of the blessed Trinity were to become manifest. "Here," she said on her arrival, "is the place of my abiding rest." She experienced this feeling very strongly. By this time, she already had, in her communications with God, something more positive and with greater clarity....

The Announcement of the Work at Paris. I was sent to the Visitation Monastery of Troyes while the Good Mother was in Paris. A year later, in 1842, I went to Paris to visit her. She told me, "You have been chosen by the good God to help me a great deal in the work that I have to do. The time has come when the good God is going to start His work. And when it will begin, when it was about to begin, there will be a sign."....

The Good Mother's Entreaties. The Good Mother returned to Troyes, and there she speaks to me in more explicit terms: "I have begun," she said, "but my mission is accomplished. At the present time, I have nothing more to say to anyone, nothing more to begin. The enterprise will be accomplished soon."...

I can tell you that I hesitated a long time before believing all that she told me. "God will give you an understanding of this during the celebration of Mass," she assured me. During Mass, I had some enlightenment; after Mass, she would ask me: "Have you received anything?" "I do not know," I would answer, "this is not always clear for me." But she would go on, nonetheless, sure as she was of God's promises....

Her Communications. If I had written down everything that she told me, whole books would not have sufficed to record it, but I did not write anything. Perhaps I was wrong, but nothing can be done about it now. To make reparation for my fault, I must in conscience declare today that, through her mediation, God wanted to entrust us with a mission. I repeat, the things that she told me were the most sublime, the purest kind of doctrine, the most precise description of what took place within the godhead. All this, as communicated by the Good Mother de Sales, is to come to fruition today....

The Words of Pope Leo XIII. Three years ago, I recounted these things to our Holy Father the Pope [= Leo XIII]. Then the Pope, in deep meditation, in a recollection that seemed to make him oblivious to everything, was silent for several moments, during which it seemed that his whole being had been annihilated, or at least withdrawn and totally absorbed in God. Then he said: "All that you do, you, in your apostolates, it is the will of God that you should do it, and all those who have worked with you have personally done what God wanted of them. What you are doing now, God wills it; and God wants it, not only of you, but of all those who work with you. What is left for you to obtain? The approbation of the Holy Roman Catholic and Apostolic Church? I, the Pope, give it to you, and what is more, I am giving you a mission: Go to France! You will also go elsewhere. Spread your works. I love them!"

"Be men of sacrifice," the Pope said, "you must be religious *usque ad effusionem sanguinis*, 'even to the shedding of blood.' And thus the Pope will be with you!..." You would have to see how the Pope's stature was rising and rising. In truth, I say, it was the good God who was speaking....

Faith in Our Mission....Our task, then, is all mapped out....I believe that now there is no longer room for doubt. In the sight of God, I make this declaration: Were I covered with all the sins committed in the world, I would be less ashamed to appear before God at the Last Judgment than if I should fail to put into practice what Mother Mary de Sales told me. I can certainly bring before God the stains of my life, but the failure to believe in these things, that I cannot do. We are not dealing here with an impression that comes and goes; this dominates my entire life. Over fifty years, I have had the time to look at things with a cool head and from a distance sufficiently removed to allow for a correct judgment....

For a long time, Brisson steadfastly resisted Mother Chappuis's entreaties about founding the Oblates, until the Lord appeared to him, revealing that "he was no longer the master in his own house, that he must surrender."[66] Brisson later described this apparition several times,[67] but the most complete and detailed account (given in the third person) is found in chapter 32 of his *Life of the Venerable Mother*

Mary de Sales Chappuis. This event took place one day during Lent 1845, in the upstairs parlor of the Troyes Visitation monastery.

LIFE OF THE VENERABLE MOTHER MARY DE SALES CHAPPUIS, CHAPTER 32[68]

The Good Mother had sent for the young chaplain [Brisson] and told him in a kind of authoritative manner that he ought not to resist God any longer, but obey Him. She did so by stressing the motives of God's will and the necessity of submitting to His supreme authority. Her words wounded the young confessor, who looked upon this solemn injunction as a restraint on his freedom. "Reverend Mother," he said to her, "I shall never do what you want from me." "But if God is leading you?" she said. "Well, Mother, since you go that far, I declare to you that nothing will ever lead me to do it, and, even if I were to see a dead man resurrected from the dead, I would never give in." After this remark, the Good Mother left the parlor without saying a word, and the young confessor found himself alone, discontented and irritated by the violence that she wished to do him.

He began to consider what he would have to do to put an end to all these incidents, which were disturbing his peace, and which were making his existence bitter and intolerable. Just as he raised his eyes, he saw through the grill of the parlor, about two meters from the grill and one meter from the door leading to the boarders' quarters (this door is on the right for anyone who is outside and looking into the parlor), Our Lord Jesus Christ. Our Lord was dressed in a tunic of wool similar in color to the fleece of sheep, and He wore a mantle of whiter wool. He seemed to be between twenty-five and thirty years of age. His beard and hair were chestnut blond, His countenance was open, but His glance toward the young priest was rather severe. He appeared without any rays of glory, as He was at Nazareth. His features were regular and perfectly harmonious. His height was not above average, and in His bearing there was an expression of simplicity and ineffable dignity. He was God with us, and God who became one of us.

The apparition lasted some time, during which the young priest was able to carefully take in all that he beheld.... Nothing escaped him, and it was after this minute examination that his gaze was arrested anew by the Savior's glance, and he saw in the expression on His face and in His gesture what was His will. Our Lord was commanding him to do what Mother Mary de Sales was telling him. The Savior's visit had found the young priest agitated; it left him calm, without any physical emotion, in a state of deep recollection and in the most perfect consciousness of what he had seen.

The apparition then just disappeared; [the young chaplain] did not wish it to be prolonged any longer: that was how God wanted it. He adored, he loved what the Savior had just done; he wanted only what Christ wanted. After several minutes of this recollected adoration, the door alongside the infirmary opened and the Good Mother returned. She did not say a single word to the young confessor, and he said not a word to her. The Good Mother's demeanor indicated that everything was finished, and she left immediately.

MAJOR THEMES ANIMATING THE OBLATE-SALESIAN TRADITION

1. St. Francis de Sales, Patron and Model

Of all the religious congregations founded as part of the nineteenth-century Salesian Pentecost, the Oblate Sisters and Oblates were most closely linked to the Visitation Order. Indeed, the Troyes Visitation was the cradle and nursery of both Oblate congregations. As Brisson's account of their origin attests, the Oblate Sisters were the realization of Francis's "first idea" of the Visitation as "a non-cloistered congregation."[69] Thus, the Oblate Sisters were the counterpart of, or the complement to, the Visitation: "although different from the Visitation by its exterior apostolate, [the Oblate Sisters] would, nevertheless, practice the *Spiritual Directory*, and approximate as much as possible the Visitandine spirit and interior life."[70]

As already stated, the founding of the Oblates fulfilled Francis's unrealized desire, kept alive in the Visitation, to found a congregation of priests to continue his pastoral ministry. The Oblates were not simply "under the patronage of St. Francis de Sales, but also completely under the direction of his thought, his doctrine, his manner of acting and seeing."[71] The Oblate vocation was to "do what [Francis de Sales] did, and…identify as much as possible with his person."[72] To be an Oblate was thus an experience of lifelong learning from Francis de Sales through constant study of his biography and writings, as well as of interior conformation to the saint through the practice of the *Spiritual Directory*, with a view to replicating Francis's messaging and pastoral method in a world that stood in acute need of these. Brisson elaborates this essential theme in a chapter instruction of January 25, 1893, which was intended to help his confreres prepare for the Feast of St. Francis de Sales.[73]

Chapter Instruction of January 25, 1893[74]

On Sunday, we will celebrate the Feast of St. Francis de Sales. It is necessary that each of us prepare carefully for this solemnity, which will bring us very special graces. We have more reason than others to prepare well for this feast and these graces, since we can say, without any self-aggrandizement, that we are truly the children of St. Francis de Sales.…

There are several religious congregations for which St. Francis de Sales is the patron and which have taken his name. They are more important than we;…the good God blesses them greatly. But St. Francis de Sales is only their patron. They have placed themselves under his protection; they desire to enter his spirit, but their special goal is not ours, namely, to reproduce as completely as possible the interior and exterior life of St. Francis de Sales. Theirs is a patronage rather than the real continuation of his work and of his life. I cannot recall who it was that asked Father de Mayerhoffen:[75] "What do you do in order to call yourselves Oblates of St. Francis de Sales? In what way do you seek to imitate him?"…I believe that it was the Vicar General at Annecy.…"We practice the [Spiritual] Directory that St. Francis de Sales practiced," Father de Mayerhoffen replied, "and we try, by means of it, to resemble him in everything." "I understand, then," replied the Vicar General, "that you are achieving something special. You are continuing his work."

We have, therefore, a right to very special protection from St. Francis de Sales insofar as we are his children, his sons. St. Jane de Chantal testified to me of this.[76] The Good Mother very often gave me assurances of this. We are the true sons of St. Francis de Sales.

We, therefore, more than others must prepare ourselves for his feast, and the best means to do this is by trying to imitate him. In every imitation of an image or a portrait, two things are necessary: the features and the color. The features distinguish and delineate the shape of the face and the body; the color achieves the resemblance because it completes the particular and personal existence—the physiognomy of the subject. It is necessary, my friends, that we reproduce our holy Founder from this double point of view.…

St. Francis de Sales tells us that St. Francis of Assisi received the stigmata as a result of contemplating Jesus crucified, and as a result of meditating upon Him lovingly.[77] Likewise, let us contemplate St. Francis de Sales. Let's imitate him, let's work, and let's faithfully practice, like him, the *Spiritual Directory*, and we shall celebrate a beautiful feast of St. Francis de Sales. Each solemnity of the Church brings us special and distinctive graces. The gifts of the Holy Spirit are of many varied forms, *multiformis Spiritus*. May the Holy Spirit, therefore, communicate to us on this feast day love and zeal for our ministry, fidelity to the *Directory*, taking thoughts, intentions, and affections from it. Note well that we shall desire absolutely nothing else but that.

The Oblate vocation is a specification of the Christian baptismal vocation: the Oblate follows Christ by imitating Francis de Sales, who, in the estimation of his contemporaries, was a "true image [*vraie image*] of the Son of God."[78] Closing the circle, Mother Chappuis believed that "through [the Oblates], the Savior…will be seen walking again upon the earth."[79] Chappuis and Brisson maintained that the short text known as the *Spiritual Directory of St. Francis de Sales* (referenced in several texts above) was indispensable to the Oblates fulfilling "their special goal…to reproduce as completely as possible the interior and exterior life of St. Francis de Sales,"[80] which set them apart from other religious congregations associated with the saint.

Composed for the Visitation Order toward the end of Francis's life, "[the] *Spiritual Directory* represents a distillation into a brief and compact form the fruits of Francis's many years of experience and wisdom in living the Christian life and in guiding and directing others in that same endeavor. It provides a privileged access to the style and method of this great spiritual master."[81] In rebuilding the Troyes Visitation in the aftermath of the French Revolution and persistent Jansenist tendencies, Chappuis had found in the *Spiritual Directory* an extraordinarily effective resource for restoring the authentic Salesian spirit to the community.[82] Brisson later adopted the *Spiritual Directory* for use by the Oblate Sisters and Oblates, which he considered as essential to their life and identity.

The *Spiritual Directory*'s purpose was eminently practical: to maintain a sense of God's presence throughout the day and to infuse ordinary activities with a spirit of prayer and communion with God.[83] The core article of the *Spiritual Directory*, the Direction of Intention, exemplifies the wide applicability and appeal of its approach. Not simply one among other articles, the Direction of Intention is the "very essence" of the *Spiritual Directory*, for it "is interwoven with every other article."[84] It "does not concern any action in particular," but "provides the attitude and approach that one should bring toward *every* action, even 'matters which are small and seemingly insignificant.'"[85] The text of the Direction of Intention, as practiced by the Oblates, here follows.

The Direction of Intention[86]

The Oblates who wish to thrive and advance in the way of Our Lord should, at the beginning of their actions, both exterior and interior, ask for His grace and offer to His divine goodness, all the good they will do. In this way, they will be prepared to bear with peace and serenity all the pain and suffering they will encounter as coming from the fatherly hand of our good God and Savior. His most holy intention is to have them merit by such means in order to reward them afterwards out of the abundance of His love.

They should not neglect this practice in matters which are small and seemingly insignificant, nor even if they are engaged in those things which are agreeable and in complete conformity with their own will and needs, such as drinking, eating, resting, recreating and similar actions. By following the advice of the Apostle, everything they do will be done in God's name to please Him alone [1 Cor 10:31; Col 3:17].

2. Pastoral Renewal of the Priesthood

The founding of the Oblates launched a new religious congregation, as well as a pastoral renewal of the priesthood. At a time when God's love and mercy had been supplanted by a religion of fear and moral rigorism, Chappuis and Brisson were inspired to retrieve the spirituality and pastoral style of Francis de Sales, the Doctor of Divine Love. The living image of the Savior, Francis was the standard against which the new congregation and the priesthood were to measure themselves.

In his priestly and episcopal ministry, Francis imaged the Son of God by enfleshing "the two favorite and well-beloved virtues which shone forth in the sacred person of our Lord, and which He singularly recommended to us,...'Learn of Me,' He says, 'for I am gentle and humble of heart'" [Matt 11:29].[87] Francis's appropriation of the heart of Jesus was a phenomenon known in the Christian spiritual tradition as an "exchange of hearts."[88]

Another description of this process is found in Brisson's biography of Chappuis: self-effacement that made space for the Savior to act. In her mystical experiences, Chappuis learned "what the Savior wished to do for the world, and how He wished to employ the Oblates to effect this new Redemption."[89] Subsequently, she insisted, "to respond to their vocation," the Oblates "must strive to efface themselves and leave place for the Savior in themselves and in their ministries; they must identify themselves with Him and assume His divine inclinations,"[90] following the Pauline injunction to have the mind of Jesus Christ (cf. Phil 2:5). Rather than seeking to control or restrict God's mercy, the Oblate priest was called to cooperate with the Savior to bring about a "new Redemption," whereby divine love, mercy, and graces would be profusely poured out on the world. This was a sublime vocation that was to be approached with the most profound humility and sense of unworthiness, which Brisson sought to inculcate in the first Oblates in this chapter instruction.

Chapter Instruction of December 19, 1894[91]

The priesthood is certainly the first dignity among Christians, in this sense: that the priest is chosen by God, elected to consecrate the body and blood of Jesus Christ, to remit sins, and to bless the people. The bishop tells the priest whom he is going to ordain that he must pay careful attention, that he must fully understand his obligations, that he imitate the Victim of the sacrifice that he will offer to God: *Imitamini quod tractatis*, "Imitate the mystery you celebrate."

This admonition by the bishop contains all the priest's obligations. It is essential that the priest be well instructed in them, and that he be fully aware of what he does when he celebrates Mass, when he baptizes, when he hears confessions, when he instructs. Let him render a strict account of himself, and let him bring perfect dispositions. It is something so important, so great, that the entire life of a man who would consecrate all his thoughts without exception and all his efforts to this preparation would not suffice for it. He would never succeed in being worthy of the holy functions that the priest has to fulfill. One becomes accustomed to everything, my friends, if one is not careful, to celebrating Mass, to hearing confessions, to preaching: one is less and less impressed with everything.

Two obligations rise up before us that are very great and very important: to know what we are doing, and to do it worthily. It is necessary to know fully, it is necessary to understand, that we are doing something holy, to imbibe it, to speak of it. We must not do as certain preachers do, who, when speaking of the grandeurs of the priesthood to the faithful or to religious (male or female) say things so beautiful, so uplifting, so admirable, that they seem to want to have these things applied personally to themselves. The priest is very great, of course, but in his own eyes, he must be *servus servorum*, the servant of the servants. Yes, indeed, we are well aware of our grandeur and the eminent dignity of our functions, but only to better recognize our personal unworthiness, our incapacity. Let us not identify the priesthood with ourselves. Let us not take for our little person the praise that the priesthood deserves. Let us give an account, with regard to the sublime state to which we are called, of how much we fall short.

Some good priests give beautiful sermons about the above. They tell the truth, of course, but they ought to distinguish a little more clearly between the thing and the man. The thing is a thousand times beyond all human imagination, but the man is much below the degree of virtue and holiness that he ought to have. He should recognize this and not exalt himself too much.

I refer here to a sermon preached last Sunday to some nuns, and in a way that none of us must ever preach about the priesthood. The preacher made of the priest an extraordinary ideal. This ideal has been realized many times, undoubtedly: St. Vincent de Paul,[92] St. Francis de Sales. That's fine, they were at the summit; but we—are we at the summit? If we truly heed the injunction made by the bishop in the admonition in the Pontifical[93] to be fully aware of what we are doing, and the manner in which we do it, we will only have to lower our head. The grandeur of the priesthood and its lofty dignity shows us at once the immense distance which exists between the thing and the person, between the sublimity of the function and the unworthiness of the minister.

...We are the successors of the seventy-two disciples [cf. Luke 10:1–24]. They aided the Apostles in their ministry; they had received—like the Apostles—the graces and powers of priestly ordination. We also have that grace of the Apostles and of the Disciples; it is the same because it has not diminished, as the Jansenists contend.[94] No, certainly. The disciples had the same weaknesses as we, the same temptations, the same difficulties and discouragements, the same powerlessness...we must hold fast to this conviction....

Doesn't St. Francis de Sales tell us that in the confessional one must venerate the priest as an angel of God who has received from Him the mandate to come to purify us?[95] All that is true. But this does not mean, however, that we are really an angel of God, alas, no! When we measure ourselves, and when we then try to measure an angel of God, we see clearly that we do not have the same stature. In the instruction that we give to the faithful, let's really understand the dignity of the priesthood, of course, but let's be very careful not to put ourselves forward and appear to say: "This is what I am, I who speak to you!"

Imitamini quod tractatis, "Imitate the mystery you celebrate." Imitate our Lord Jesus Christ, Whom you touch, Whom you handle—this is the second obligation of the priest, to do worthily what we do, by imitating and reproducing our Lord. We touch and handle the Word of God, at Holy Mass, at Holy Communion. There is a very great distance between Him and us, and, nevertheless, He submits to our orders, He obeys us....We also go to Him. It is only by repeated and constant effort that we will succeed in imitating our Lord. If our Lord came on earth, it was not only to preach doctrine, it was also to give an example. Let us also give an example. It is essential that we priests be filled with that spirit.

163

When we preach, when we catechize, let us truly recall that we are the providers of the divine Word and that it is He whom we must give to souls. When we are truly imbued with this thought, when we have truly meditated on the instruction in the Pontifical, we shall then understand how far the word that we give the faithful is from being what it ought to be....

Let us carefully consider the distance that exists between us and the things we do, and our ministry—when motivated by humility—will be extremely efficacious. Nothing touches the faithful like the humility of the priest. When one is truly little, when one puts himself in his place, when one really understands the distance that exists between himself and the sublime functions with which he is occupied, one achieves some good for souls, one gains their confidence; one gives them God....

From the outset, the pastoral renewal of the priesthood envisioned by the founding of the Oblates was intended to have an impact beyond the congregation, specifically a third order of priests devoted to living and ministering according to the teachings of St. Francis de Sales.[96] This independently came about when the Parisian diocesan priest Fr. Henri Chaumont (1838–96), another major figure in the Salesian Pentecost, founded in 1876 the Society of the Priests of St. Francis de Sales, whose purpose was to instill in the diocesan clergy the spirit of Francis de Sales. Within a few years, this group numbered in its ranks the elite of the French clergy. In 2020, it had approximately one thousand members, spread over five continents, who are dedicated to the ministry of spiritual direction or accompaniment.

The Oblates also spread the Salesian spirit among diocesan priests. The *Spiritual Directory of St. Francis de Sales* was useful not only for internal Oblate formation, but also for disseminating and popularizing Francis's practical spirituality to a wider public. *The Spiritual Directory of St. Francis de Sales Adapted to the Use of Priests* was published in French (1896), German (1905), and English (1906) editions, and *The Directory or Spiritual Guide for Persons in the World* was first published in 1899.[97] Both the Oblate and diocesan priest editions of the *Directory* included a supplement with, among other things, counsels on the manner of celebrating the sacrament of penance and on preaching that were excerpted from Francis's *Advice to Confessors* and his famous letter on preaching to André Frémyot (1573–1641), the brother of Mother de Chantal and archbishop of Bourges, that is sometimes referred to as the *Treatise on Preaching*.[98]

Chappuis and Brisson also encouraged the Oblates to incorporate the *Spiritual Directory* into their preaching and various ministries. Brisson himself modeled this approach in his catechetical instruction at the *œuvres ouvrières*. His teaching was essentially that of the *Spiritual Directory*, particularly those parts distilling Francis de Sales's instructions in the *Introduction to the Devout Life* (1609). This method is clearly observable in Brisson's "teaching on prayer, especially the preparation of the day, meditation, spiritual recollection and ejaculatory prayer, and the Direction of Intention, which is the very centerpiece and heart of the *Spiritual Directory*."[99] Brisson adapts, or "contemporizes," these elements of Salesian spirituality in a practical way to fit the everyday needs of the young women workers in the often challenging social and work environments in which they found themselves.[100]

3. The Sacredness of Work

French Catholicism's pathological obsession with sin, eternal damnation, and the small number of the saved presented the laity with a grim picture of the afterlife. Its understanding of this life was no less severe. Idleness was a sin, but work was regarded as a penance, the punishment for original sin.[101] As a result, most of the French clergy was unsympathetic to the working class and found it difficult to relate to workers. The situation was exacerbated by the fact that most priests came from rural backgrounds and had a marked preference for agrarian society, coupled with a deep suspicion of the urban environment.[102]

Acutely aware of the gulf between the clergy and the working class, Chappuis and Brisson sought to bring about a basic shift in how priestly ministry was exercised by recovering the pastoral style of Francis de Sales, who "received all comers with the same expression of quiet friendliness, and never turned anyone away, whatever his station in life."[103] Thus, the new Salesian model of the priest did not shy away from openness to and interaction with all, especially the working class. In Brisson's words, "The thought of the Good Mother was that the Oblates, brought into existence at this time,...have a role to play in that great question of work and workers. They are to exercise a healthy influence,...and to usefully serve holy Church in these times, we have to be in contact with workers."[104]

Complementing their emphasis on the priest's approachability and accessibility to all, Chappuis and Brisson, also following the lead of Francis de Sales, had a sacramental view of the world that was the foundation for their development of a spirituality of work that insists on its sacred nature as a participation in God's creative activity and presence in the world: "We are made in the image of God, who sanctified and glorified work, especially in creating the universe. We most resemble the Creator by our human activity. When the Creator works in, with and through us, then we become collaborators and co-creators with God, thereby reflecting God's presence and continued activity in the world."[105] Brisson develops these themes in this chapter instruction.

Conference no. 7, Retreat of 1888[106]

This morning I wish to say a word to you about work. I have no weighty considerations to make to you on work; I am not going to delve into history nor Sacred Scripture for good and excellent thoughts in regard to work. I shall limit myself to a few ideas from the Gospel, St. Francis de Sales, and the Good Mother.

"My Father works until now, and I work," said our Lord Jesus Christ [John 5:17]. "My Father works": He works even until now...; He makes light, He makes worlds, He kneads clay and fashions man out of it. "And I work": I am with you; I speak to you in parables; I teach you. I do, as it seems, nothing else but evangelize the Jewish people, and yet at this moment, I am one with My Father in work—in material as well as supernatural work. It is I who operate the world.

We profess for work, which is specifically attributed to God the Father, an especially religious bent. We have learned that what God does merits our respect, our gratitude. When we work, when we set our hands to these material things that God has created, we return praise and honor to God, and we cause creatures to render this homage to the Creator, in their own secret and wonderful language. We look upon creatures as the property of God, we treat them with respect as holy and divine. Work makes us sharers in the divine action, and, consequently, in the holiness and grace that emanates from God the Father and that communicates itself not only through the ordinary means of the Redemption, but by the special channel of work—by contact with material things that are for our use. With us, work is a thing of awe, of blessedness. By work, we cooperate with God and with the Word. Now cooperation in the action of God is sanctifying. There is in it, we might say, something analogous to what occurs in the Sacraments or at least in the Sacramentals.[107] Work with our hands is our way of honoring God the Father.

In God, there are three Persons, three co-equal Persons. No one of the three is inferior to the others. God forbid that I should belittle the work of Redemption, without which all men would be eternally miserable and reprobate. In this sense, the work of Redemption infinitely surpasses the work of Creation. If in God there is no differentiation, there is for us an immense difference between these two acts. But in that it comes from God, all work is excellent, and St. Francis de Sales and the Good Mother Mary de Sales desire that all that emanates from God be received with very great respect, with deep gratitude and love. By steeping ourselves in this doctrine, it will come to pass that our work of each day, whatever it may be—whether manual or intellectual—will take on a character so elevated, so complete in its union with God that we will treat all things as holy and sacred and as requiring our attention, our care, and our devotion. And in their turn, these things will bring us grace, the grace of God the Father. Let us make use of these material things for the honor of God the Father—*cum gratiarum actione*, with thanksgiving [cf. 1 Tim 4:3–4]. Let us use them, and turn them to our service as blessed things....

God's creations carry within them their graces. As a matter of practice, then, preserve a deep respect for the material things that obedience and religious poverty put in your hands. In the use that we make of these things, there is a thanksgiving and praise that leap towards God, and which God hears, although our bodily ears hear them not. May the beating of our hearts, and the prayer that bursts forth from these hearts, be in union with that prayer of all creation that we hear not. We shall offer, then, to God not only the sacrifice of the morning and the evening, but a perpetual sacrifice, the complete holocaust of our entire life, and all our works.

Moreover, work not only brings us closer to God, but also "brings us closer to all of those who work. It makes us appreciate the toil, trials and effort that especially marked the workers in a highly industrialized city like Troyes."[108] These ideas, as well as the initiatives undertaken on behalf of workers by Chappuis and Brisson, were part of developing Catholic social thought about the dignity of labor and of the church's pastoral outreach to the working class during the nineteenth century.[109] This process culminated in Pope Leo XIII's encyclical *Rerum Novarum*, On the Condition of Labor (1891), the first of the great encyclicals of modern Catholic social teaching.

4. Reimprinting the Gospel

One of the most daunting problems facing the church in the aftermath of the French Revolution, especially its policy of de-Christianization, was widespread ignorance, even among educated Catholics, of the most basic tenets of faith and particularly of Sacred Scripture.[110] The situation among the clergy was no more encouraging. The great majority of seminarians lacked academic aptitude, there was a vast "gap between the standards expected in the secular schools and universities and...in the seminaries," and those ordained priests were deficient even "in the academic subjects in their own professional sphere, ecclesiastical history, canon law, and biblical criticism."[111] This state of affairs was the context for the importance and urgency that Chappuis and Brisson gave to their distinctive imperative, "to reimprint the Gospel" (*réimprimer l'Evangile*).

Chappuis and Brisson's description of what it meant to reimprint the gospel was effectively synonymous with *lectio divina*. Akin to this ancient Christian practice, Chappuis and Brisson conceived of reimprinting the gospel as a highly active and dynamic process of slow, thoughtful reading, in-depth knowledge and understanding (aided by resources such as Scripture commentaries), prayerful rumination, interior assimilation and appropriation, and adaptation to the needs of the present-day world and the souls encountered in ministry. The prototype for reimprinting the gospel was Francis de Sales, whose sustained practice of *lectio divina*[112] made him, in the eyes of his contemporaries, "'the Gospel speaking [*l'Evangile parlant*],' because it was completely integrated into his life."[113] In a retreat conference in 1882, Brisson instructs his Oblate confreres in what reimprinting the gospel specifically entails on their part.

Conference no. 10, Retreat of 1882[114]

The Good Mother often said that it was necessary "to re-imprint the Gospel." By this expression, my friends, she meant that the Gospel must be given a very broad meaning. The Gospel needs to be re-imprinted in our heart and in the world.

In order to re-imprint the Gospel, we must know it. It is impossible to print what we do not know. If we had lost the Gospel according to St. John and you were charged with re-imprinting it, the beginning would go all by itself because you know it by heart. But what about the rest? You must know it, therefore, in order to re-imprint it. In our studies, we learned a few verses each day; in that way we retained something of the Gospel. It is essential that you know the Gospel. Our Rule obliges us to read the New Testament daily. We are supposed to read a chapter per day. Let's be very faithful to this, and let's read it with attention and care so as to understand and retain it.

Bossuet[115] was asked which was the best commentary on the Gospel. He did not reply. "Which is the one you use?" they then asked. "A second reading?" He then answered, "a third, a fourth." You also see how skillfully he worked his knowledge of the Gospel into his sermons.

We must, therefore, in order to re-imprint the Gospel, read it first and read it carefully. This should not be a distracted reading, not one that is simply pious, but a reading made with great attention, great relish, as if you were hearing it from the mouth of Our Lord Himself. You must then strive to carefully penetrate the meaning.

I recommend, nevertheless, that you make use of a few of the more renowned commentators. A good commentator provides the key to how we should understand and interpret the Scriptures. In our courses on Sacred Scripture, we were given the method of interpreting Scripture in its literal, spiritual, and accommodated sense. We must know about these matters....

Nourish yourselves with the Scriptures; read them slowly, three, four or five verses at a time; then pause, allow them to sink in, and ask God for understanding of them. You have read the Scriptures so many times, and it seems that that has produced nothing; pray, and you will be surprised at all that you find in the words of Sacred Scripture. Those who look for silver or gold are obliged to painfully dig through the earth's crust formed by other baser metals; they have to leap over rocks, they have to sift the mud of streams, and it is only in this way that they find the silver-bearing lair, the flakes of gold which are worth a hundred times, a thousand times more than the trouble they cost....

If, until now, the Gospels have said nothing to your heart, this is because you have not yet opened the mine. Make use of prayer, and God will give you the key. Remove the obstacles, and you will find an immense mine full of enlightenment, consolations, and material for your instructions. You will never say anything to souls without Sacred Scripture.

The Good Mother loved the Gospels.[116] During retreats, she used to re-read the Gospel according to St. John. She found in it the good God, the light. She reflected at length on it, and she had some very profound theological intuitions. Fr. Chevalier[117] said to me several times: "What she says, we are unable to say; we are unable to plumb these matters, unenlightened as we are."

It is not sufficient to read the Gospels in order to understand them, we must also put them into practice. The Gospel is the express story of the Word of God appearing on earth among humankind. It is the Gospel thus understood that we are supposed to make a new edition of among people, by prayer, by work, by the evangelization of nations, by sacrifice.

Reimprinting the gospel was of a piece with another key attribute of the Salesian model of the priest: dedication to ongoing intellectual growth and lifelong learning. In a sermon of March 4, 1898, for the occasion of the religious profession of two novices, Brisson takes love of learning as his theme, admonishing his confreres that, as spiritual sons of Francis de Sales, they were to resemble him in every way—in charity, gentleness, and learning.

My sons, we are the spiritual children of St. Francis de Sales. Children ought to resemble their father....St. Francis de Sales is a Doctor of the Church, and in order to become a Doctor of the Church, one must have learning that is beyond the ordinary, that is superior to common learning....I desire that the Oblates of St. Francis de Sales become learned men....I desire that we become learned like St. Francis de Sales....You must be learned, not only in theology, but in all knowledge.... The Fathers of the Church say that learning draws us closer to God, makes us participants in His eternal glory....Thus, all human knowledge will be a way to heaven....We will be true Oblates when we employ our knowledge in a spirit of faith, which will show us God through intelligence, learning, and insight, drawing us to Him through this human awareness. Thus, we will be able to make the good God loved, make Him better known, along with His wondrous powers. Our labor will then…be one with the Savior, who is our sustenance, our aid, our travelling companion, and, finally, our magnificent reward when we will see Him, and when we will love Him on the great day of blessed eternity.[118]

Brisson's exhortation echoed Francis de Sales's of 1603–5 to the priests of his diocese: "I implore you to apply yourselves seriously to study, because knowledge, to a priest, is the eighth sacrament of the hierarchy of the Church."[119] Sacraments are intended to benefit the people of God. Knowledge as the eighth sacrament of the hierarchy of the church was not knowledge for knowledge's sake, but for the sake and benefit of the pastoral ministry. No one modeled this principle more clearly than Francis de Sales himself: one of the best educated and learned men of his age,[120] he put this education and learning completely in the service of the pastoral ministry to build up and accompany the people of God on their earthly pilgrimage to heaven.

5. The "Way"

As did Thérèse of Lisieux (1873–97), Chappuis also used the term *the Way*, in a manner that bears comparison with the youngest doctor of the church.[121] Unfortunately, this part of Chappuis's legacy was misunderstood in some quarters after her death, and here Brisson aims to explain the meaning of her Way clearly and accessibly, while establishing its unimpeachable orthodoxy.

Conference no. 9, Retreat of 1900[122]

In reading the *Life of the Good Mother*,[123] notice, my friends, how very often it speaks of "the Way": "One is in the Way. One must enter the Way. The good God asks us to sustain ourselves in the Way." What are we to understand by this word, "the Way"?

This expression has struck all those who have read the *Life of the Good Mother*. Diverse appraisals and different judgments have been formulated about this word. Detractors have seen in this a kind of mystery which tended to the annihilation of human action and which led inevitably to quietism. This critique appeared in an article which did cause something of a stir.[124] It was successfully refuted by Fr. Fragnières, a doctor of theology and a professor at the Major Seminary in Fribourg. A Jesuit father, the Reverend Fr. Hagen, Director of the Observatory of Washington, replied no less successfully to these attacks.[125] You have recently read, in the *Annales Salésiennes*,[126] the work of Fr. Hagen, who is very solid and unassailable.

He [= Fr. Hagen] seems to have a good understanding of the Good Mother and the method of "the Way." He is in contact with various Visitation monasteries in America. He has understood, digested, and practiced these things. We ought to have complete confidence in what he says about the doctrine. I shall say the same thing about Fr. Fragnières. But I do not know if each has completely understood everything that is contained in this idea of "the Way." Fr. Fragnières sees in it, above all, the charity, goodness, and mercy of God.[127] Fr. Tissot, the former superior of the Missionaries [of St. Francis de Sales] of Annecy said the same thing.[128] He compared "the Way" to devotion to the Sacred Heart. He saw in it a new devotional food, a form of special devotion. All these interpretations are good, of course. However, I am going to say that there is in "the Way" what there is in a reflecting prism, a ray of light. Look at it diametrically before you, it appears blue. Tilt it to the right, there is a nuance of green; tilt it to the left and it appears violet. It changes color depending upon the angle in which you position your eye. "The Way" is a little like that, it seems to me. It is all that these worthy and devout authors have said it is, but it is still something more. This depends on the perspective, the point of view from which one sees it.

We Oblates, how are we supposed to understand and explain—in a practical manner—the Good Mother's "Way"?

We must, of course, see the charity, the infinite mercy of the Savior in it; also new graces, intimate graces. Yes, but I desire that we see in it, above all, the correspondence that God demands by these intimate graces. Let us consider, especially, fidelity to following our Lord. *Ego sum Via.* "I am the Way," He tells us. *Nemo venit ad Patrem nisi per me.* "No one comes to the Father except through Me" [John 14:6]. "The Way" is fidelity to walking with Jesus, to reproducing Him and to imitating Him in everything. "The Way" is loving obedience to all our obligations; it is correspondence to grace; it is fidelity to the *Directory*; to the Direction of Intention. As our Constitutions indicate, those who wish to advance and make progress in the Way of our Lord will find that it is also the most loving and faithful practice possible of our vows of poverty, chastity, and obedience. "The Way," for us, is, therefore, the Rule. "The Way" is the ensemble, the totality, of our life conformed to the life of our Savior.

There you have "the Way" as the Good Mother understood it from the first and before all. It is thus something clear, positive, practical. We realize it by devotion and by following the Savior; we profess to be faithful to and love the person of the Savior; we live in union of heart and action with Him. That is "the Way."

POSTSCRIPT

Chappuis died on October 7, 1875, and was buried in the cemetery within the cloister of the Troyes Visitation. On July 27, 1897, she was declared Venerable, and her cause for beatification was introduced at Rome. On May 17, 1901, her tomb was opened in the presence of a delegate from the Vatican Congregation of Rites, a number of bishops, and other ecclesiastical dignitaries, and her body was found to be incorrupt. It was subsequently reinterred in a vault in the Oratory of Jesus the Redeemer inside the Troyes monastery.[129]

Brisson died in his family's home in Plancy (France) on February 2, 1908, and was buried in his parents' tomb. On April 11, 1961, his remains were entombed in the crypt chapel of St. Gilles in the motherhouse of the Oblate Sisters in Troyes. His cause for beatification was opened on February 11, 1938. On December 19, 2009, Pope Benedict XVI (1927– , r. 2005–13) declared that Brisson practiced the theological, cardinal, and related virtues to a heroic degree and declared him Venerable. Brisson was beatified on September 22, 2012. His feast day is October 12.[130]

Aviat died on January 10, 1914, in Perugia (Italy), where she was buried. Her body was later transferred to Troyes, where, on April 11, 1961, it was entombed in the crypt chapel of St. Gilles in the motherhouse of the Oblate Sisters. On April 9, 1957, Pope Pius XII (1876–1939, r. 1939–58) himself signed the document introducing her cause for beatification. On December 1, 1978, Pope St. John Paul II (1920–2005, r. 1978–2005) confirmed her life of heroic virtue and declared her Venerable. The same pope beatified Aviat on September 27, 1992, and canonized her on November 25, 2001. Her feast day is January 10.[131]

V

CAROLINE CARRÉ DE MALBERG, HENRI CHAUMONT, AND THE SOCIETY OF THE DAUGHTERS OF ST. FRANCIS DE SALES

Suzanne C. Toczyski

It was marvelous to see all three of us holding council to discuss the most timely and practical ways to set the world on fire with devotion to our patron saint.

—Fr. Henri Chaumont[1]

Founded in 1872 by Mme Caroline Carré de Malberg and Fr. Henri Chaumont, the Society of the Daughters of St. Francis de Sales came into existence as a formal means by which ordinary laywomen might consecrate themselves to lives of holiness and virtue. Fed by the Salesian Pentecost that was already taking hold across Europe, and embracing the teachings of St. Francis de Sales, especially as they were laid out in the *Introduction to the Devout Life*, the Society encouraged its members to pursue personal sanctification by practicing the "little virtues" that the saint identified as key to uniting their will to the will of God. Encouraging its members to seek out and nurture spiritual friendships with like-minded individuals (another Salesian principle), the association also promoted an apostolic mission of evangelization. The work of the Society of the Daughters of St. Francis de Sales continues to the present day, with communities found throughout the world.

The older of the two founders of the Society of the Daughters of St. Francis de Sales, Caroline Carré, née Colchen, was born in Metz, France, on April 8, 1829, and received an early introduction to the works of the saint in part because the *Introduction to the Devout Life* was her mother Élisabeth-Charlotte's favorite book. At the age of twelve, Caroline was enrolled at a local boarding school run by religious of the Visitation Order; under the sisters' care, Caroline's knowledge and appreciation of Salesian spirituality and spiritual direction took firm root. Leaving the school in 1846, Caroline returned home and, three years later, in 1849, married her cousin Paul Carré.

Paul's military career obliged the couple to move frequently, making any long-term spiritual direction very difficult for Caroline to establish. In the interim, her school mentors—the abbés Jégou and Spitz and the religious of the Visitation—encouraged Mme Carré to be faithful to the teachings of St. Francis de Sales by focusing her energy on what they called her *devoirs d'état*, the everyday duties of familial life. This was in keeping with the saint's dictum that attention to the little virtues (especially humility, gentleness, patience, and kindness) even in matters as ostensibly trivial as household obligations, can lead one to holiness: "My object is to teach [the principles of the devout life] to those who are living in towns, at court, in their own households, and whose calling obliges them to a social life," he wrote.[2] In her relationship with Paul, Caroline would have ample opportunity to be challenged in all of these areas, but most especially in terms of patience.

The couple moved to Paris in 1862. In addition to their frequent social obligations, which took them all over the city, Paul Carré's temperament made him a difficult man to live with. Moreover, like many Frenchmen of his generation, Paul was not a frequently practicing Catholic, yet he was not hostile to religion; he promised to begin attending Mass again before their first child was born and kept that promise even though the baby died after just a few days. Years of careful zeal and constant prayer on the part of his wife would eventually bring the recalcitrant military man back to wholehearted participation in the church by the time of his retirement in 1879, and by the time of her death, Paul Carré fully embraced his wife's life of holiness.

Throughout her life, Caroline Carré felt special devotion to the Holy Spirit, to the Sacred Heart of Jesus, and to the Virgin Mary, and held a particular place in her heart for Sts. Francis de Sales, Jane de Chantal, and Mary Magdalene. Passionate about her familial duties and frequenting the sacraments (particularly daily communion, which was unusual at the time but eminently Salesian[3]), Mme Carré worked constantly to unite her own will to the will of God, taming her personal pride and desire for control in order to better serve as a model for kindred souls seeking sanctification in a politically turbulent time. It was a personally tumultuous time as well, and three of the couple's four children died before 1864. Indeed, it was Caroline's entry into the confessional of diocesan priest Fr. Henri Chaumont precisely during a period of intense grief that spurred the formation of the Society of the Daughters of St. Francis de Sales.

Nine years younger than Mme Carré, Henri Chaumont's vocation to the priesthood revealed itself early in his life. As a young child, Henri loved to read stories from the *Annals of the Propagation of the Faith*, and at a very young age proclaimed his desire to be a Christian missionary. On the evening of his first communion, at age twelve, Henri was introduced to Msgr. Louis Gaston de Ségur, who would become a tremendous mentor to the young man. At the Seminary of Issy, Chaumont read a collection of St. Francis de Sales's letters, a "revelation" to him;[4] later, at the Seminary of Saint-Sulpice, he listened as the biography of St. Francis de Sales was read aloud during mealtimes. Chaumont would undertake a study of the saint's works that lasted throughout his lifetime, appreciating in particular "the gentle yet strong manner which allowed [St. Francis de Sales] to lead the worldly to perfection, even those bound by the bonds of marriage."[5] Deciding early on to assimilate to the best of his ability the methods of the saint in the area of spiritual direction, Chaumont focused upon the *Introduction to the Devout Life*; over the course of his life, he would distill from the writings of the saint a series of treatises composed entirely of quotations addressing individual Christian virtues, a work culminating in his *Spiritual Directions of Saint Francis de Sales*.[6]

While still at Saint-Sulpice, Chaumont began to conceive of an association that would allow him to bring his practical program of sanctification based on Salesian spirituality to the world. After his ordination to the priesthood in 1864, Fr. Chaumont was assigned to the parish of St. Marcel-de-l'Hôpital in a relatively poor neighborhood of Paris; there, he was able to put to practice St. Francis de Sales's teachings—most notably, the notion that everyone, rich and poor, male and female, can pursue a life of holiness. It was during his tenure at St. Marcel that Fr. Chaumont, having sketched out a Rule of Life based on the *Introduction to the Devout Life*,[7] first offered this plan for a life of perfection to his female directees, women whose social statuses ranged from simple postal worker to countess. The Rule is imbued with the spirit of St. Francis de Sales, covering specific topics such as dilection, humility, love of God, meditation, consolation, and spiritual friendship. Although the early groups formed by Fr. Chaumont would eventually disperse, some of the women active during his ministry at St. Marcel would one day come to join the Society of the Daughters of St. Francis de Sales.

The archive of the Daughters of St. Francis de Sales in Paris possesses a copy of the Rule developed by Fr. Chaumont and written in the hand of one of the early Daughters, Mlle Stiltz, who chose the name Sister Mary of Jesus and who would serve as Mother of the Society after the death of Mme Carré; a more extensive version of the Rule was published in book form in 1896. The rule offers guidelines for personal sanctification as well as for sanctification of one's neighbor.

Rule of the Daughters of St. Francis de Sales, Written by Fr. Chaumont and Copied in the Hand of Mlle Stiltz

a Perfectio legis, dilectio[8]

I. Goal of the Association

1. The individuals who make up this association propose, with the grace of God, to strive, by a spirit of Christian simplicity, for evangelical *holiness*, in

order to procure for Our Lord places of refuge in his affections, for afflicted souls the succor of fraternal charity, [and] for themselves, the shortest and most sure means of salvation.

2. They place this resolution under the special patronage of St. Francis de Sales and St. Jane de Chantal.

3. In order to attain the goal for which they are striving, they will employ the following means, which are related either to their personal sanctification, or to the sanctification of their neighbor.

II. *Rules Pertaining to Personal Sanctification*

A. Rules pertaining to the interior life

1. The daughters of St. Francis de Sales will not forget that the principle, the life, and the goal of the Christian soul is the absolute love of Our Lord Jesus Christ.

2. They will seek among ten thousand not only a confessor, but a holy director, for whom they will always have a reverent respect, the simplicity of a child, a complete obedience.

3. In order to give solid bases to the piety to which they aspire, they will make every effort to renounce all sin and the lightest voluntary imperfection, in such a way that they can say, like their saintly patron, "If I saw in my heart the slightest fiber that was not entirely steeped in the love of my God, I would tear it out in an instant."

4. Every day, they will renew in themselves for a few moments the feelings of the most profound humility.

5. It would be responding to one of the dearest desires of Our Lord to add to these dispositions love and the practice of three religious virtues:

perfect chastity, uncompromising obedience, evangelical poverty.

6. Understanding that God communicates with us in a very special way through the sacraments, the daughters of St. Francis de Sales will make it their duty to confess frequently, and an extraordinary honor and delight to take communion as often as they are permitted to do so.

7. In order to show themselves faithful to the spirit of perfection which must fill them with life, they will make every effort to grow every day in the precious virtues of a firm and simple faith, in absolute confidence, in limitless charity.

8. They will fulfill precisely the exercises of piety which follow:
   a. All the ordinary duties of Christian life;
   b. A little meditation every day;
   c. Insofar as possible, daily communion and attendance at holy Mass;
   d. The personal examen and the general examen;
   e. Visits to the Blessed Sacrament;
   f. The rosary and a pious reading;
   g. At least once a week a visit to the poor or afflicted;
   h. Regular meetings as a group to take stock of their progress, every month, if possible;
   i. Every year a full retreat and an annual review of conscience.

9. Finally, in order to be filled all the more with the spirit of sanctity in simplicity, they will make it a law to read the holy Gospel every year; and they will faithfully practice its principles and counsels.

B. Rules pertaining to the exterior life

1. The daughters of St. Francis de Sales will openly declare their adherence to all questions of dogma, morality, and discipline, not only to all decisions

expressed by Rome, but even to [Rome's] simplest desires and instructions. They will be recognized by their most constant respect, submission, love, and devotion to the Sovereign Pontiff.

2. They will apply themselves in all conscientiousness to accomplishing their household duties.

3. They will make every effort to live in peace with everyone, preferring to be, following the language of their Saintly Patron, robbed rather than robber, bruised rather than bruiser, anvil rather than hammer.

4. They will also remember in all their social relationships that the most delicate approach is simplicity.

5. Finally, they will allow the simplicity of their souls to be reflected, as much as possible, by the simplicity of their exterior life, their clothes, their food, and their furnishings.

III. Rules Pertaining to the Sanctification of One's Neighbor

1. Since Our Lord wanted to make love of neighbor a precept similar to the great precept of the love of God, the Daughters of St. Francis de Sales will practice as best they can the recommendations of the Lord on this point.

2. They will have for each other a most holy and cordial friendship; they will come together as one heart and one soul; and they will exercise together the charitable duty of fraternal correction....

3. They will apply themselves, as much as God will allow them, to the sanctification of souls. Whoever has a counsel to ask of them, a sense of discouragement to master, a sadness to console, will find them entirely devoted [to the problem at hand]. They will humbly but forcefully exhort

souls who have grown away from God to take up
once again the practice of Christian life; indifferent
souls to fervor; pious souls to very serious
advancement in the interior life. Oh! how happy
Our Lord would be, if they all became his zealous
auxiliaries working with souls.[9]

The remaining pages of the Rule describe the organization of the association, including details on how members are to be chosen, what they will do to prepare for entry into the society, and where and when the group is to have regular meetings.

In 1868, an illness left Fr. Chaumont partially paralyzed, during which time a cerebral fever caused his loved ones to fear for his life. Vowing, during a brief lucid moment in the midst of his fever, to make a pilgrimage to Annecy, the spiritual home of St. Francis de Sales, should he survive, Chaumont's recovery began on the saint's feast day. Six months later, he commenced his pilgrimage, stopping en route to visit Mother Mary de Sales Chappuis and Fr. Louis Brisson in Troyes, and Msgr. Mermillod in Geneva. While in Troyes, Chaumont wrote that "it was marvelous to see all three of us [Chaumont, Brisson, and Mother Chappuis] holding council to discuss the most timely and practical ways to set the world on fire with devotion to our patron saint."[10] In addition, Mother Chappuis recommended publication of Chaumont's Rule. But it was at Annecy that his project became clearer, as he was able to frame it in terms of sharing with women of worldly society already inclined toward piety rules for spiritual perfection extracted from the *Introduction to the Devout Life*, that they might join together to form a spiritual family not unlike that of the women of the Gospels, or that of the early church.[11]

Reassigned to the parish of St. Clotilde in the seventh arrondissement of Paris, Fr. Chaumont's parish population would radically alter in nature: rather than working with the *chiffonniers* (or ragmen) of St. Marcel, he would now be ministering to the upper class, particularly those who frequented the worldly *salons* of the time. One such salon was organized by none other than Mme Carré; unlike those devoted to social visits only, Mme Carré's salon was intended to help women "perfect themselves through the all-inclusive practice of familial duties and social relationships."[12] Fr. Chaumont would later say that her salon was "filled with the perfume of the Holy Spirit," calling it "a center of Christian life…and an apostolic flame with a limitless power of influence."[13] Subsequent to their first meeting in the confessional in June 1869, Mme Carré would, after some hesitation, seek regular spiritual direction from Fr. Chaumont; he, for his part, was convinced from the start that she was to be his partner in forming the Salesian society he had for so long envisioned. Their conversations about this project were well underway by November 1869; shortly thereafter, however, political upheaval would ensue in the capital, delaying the long-desired implementation of the project.

Two major sources of turmoil shook the city of Paris in 1870 and 1871. While the Franco-Prussian War of 1870 would bring men back to the church seeking reconciliation before going into battle, the city was traumatized by the possibility of a German invasion. Mme Carré acquiesced to her husband's wishes and fled the city before the Siege of Paris (September 1870–January 1871), burning all of her spiritual letters before her departure, while Fr. Chaumont remained for a time in the city, ministering to injured soldiers in local hospitals in addition to his regular parish duties. However, in the midst of the siege, and with the capital of the newly proclaimed Third Republic having been moved to the city of Tours, another source of turmoil revealed itself as the Paris National Guard attempted to wrest control of the city from representatives of the national government of France remaining in Paris. Guardsmen, calling themselves *Communards*, proclaimed themselves in charge of the city, declaring war on the church as well, as they associated religious authorities in Paris with the constitutional monarchists. Over the course of *la Semaine sanglante* ("Bloody Week," May 21–28, 1871), the archbishop of Paris, Msgr. George Darboy, was executed along with a number of Catholic clergy.[14] Fr. Chaumont escaped the carnage by fleeing the city disguised as a ticket inspector on the train to Orléans. Making his way to Versailles and then on to Saint-Denis, Fr. Chaumont reentered the city on May 27, just as government troops defeated the Communards. Mme Carré would not return definitively until October 1871, making it possible for their projected association to commence at last.

Between January and June 1872, Fr. Chaumont sent three women, one after another, to Mme Carré in the hopes that they would become spiritual friends or sisters, following the model suggested by St. Francis de Sales, and thus form the kernel of a new spiritual society designed to foster "the evangelical perfection of souls"[15] by following the rule Fr. Chaumont had written for them based on the *Introduction*. As later noted by Fr. Chaumont's biographer Msgr. Laveille, the essential goal of the society was to create an association that would "make known...to laywomen inclined to piety the rules of the perfected life set forth by Saint Francis de Sales, and in so doing, make known the code of brief and simple rules excerpted from the *Introduction to the Devout Life*."[16] The women were to focus upon their *devoirs d'état*, their interior life, and charitable works, cultivating humility, abnegation, generosity, and spiritual friendships while remaining in the secular world at large.[17] In a letter dated August 17, 1872, Fr. Chaumont wrote to Mme Carré and her sisters in Christ, encouraging them to practice charity above all; it is the spiritual virtue most clearly foregrounded by St. Francis de Sales, particularly in his *Treatise on the Love of God*.

Letter of Fr. Chaumont to Mme Carré and Her Sisters

August 17, 1872
My child,

May the Spirit of Our Lord be with your dear little spiritual family. Now, the fruits of this Divine Spirit are peace and joy. Savor, all of you, the happiness of loving God in unison, forming but one heart and one soul. There must be no cloud in the sky of charity; whatever excuse one may invoke, I will rule against the one of you three who makes [such a cloud] appear and congratulate the one who clears it away. In the name of holy obedience, I desire that no one rest in the evening before making peace with the sister who might have been for her a subject of pain, voluntary or not. I will pardon all in all of you, with one exception: the neglect of charity.[18]

Particular attention was paid to the duties of the future Mother of the association. These would later be recounted by Mlle Stiltz in her deposition at Mme Carré's beatification proceedings, in the words of the first Mother herself.

Duties of the Mother of the Association, according to Caroline Carré

My first thought, as soon as I awaken, will be for God. I will rise when the bells ring five o'clock, I will dress modestly and quickly, and will make my bed. At five-thirty, prayer and orison; at six o'clock, holy Mass, in one of the chapels where we can attend Mass at that time.

All of my mornings, until one o'clock in the afternoon, will be spent at home, and I will submit myself precisely to the rule. The afternoon's freedom will be used for my good-bye visits and preparations for departure.

I will go to confession every Thursday. When I write, I will remain in the chamber next to the meeting room. It is there that I will receive visits from our sisters.

Unless there is a special reason for it, these visits must not last longer than a half-hour and will not impede the exact observation of the rule.

I will never chat at the entry door; I will receive everyone with an amiable face on which the charity of Our Lord which resides in my heart will be reflected. In every circumstance, my tone will be gentle, my words always maternal, carefully setting aside anything which might suggest any other authority than that of the charity and goodness so recommended by Our Lord.

I will take care, on every occasion, to be a good example for my sisters, according to the duty which my charge imposes on me. I will receive with humility and gratitude all fraternal corrections given to me by sister Margaret-Mary. I will never apologize at the time of a fraternal correction, whatever my reasons might be. If the glory of God requires it, I will do so a few moments later, a quarter of an hour, for example; otherwise, I will put it off until evening.

I will wait an hour before opening my letters, making an exception only for those from my husband and son. I will only dine in the city after having asked the permission of my Father; it will be so for all outings, except those that are authorized. My evening outings must never last beyond nine-thirty. The hour of my return from afternoon outings will be set by sister Margaret-Mary, and I will force myself to observe it precisely.

I will spend no money without permission; I will neither give nor receive anything without permission.

In the house, I will wear a black cape and bonnet. I will go up and down the stairs unhurriedly; I will only speak in the staircase when it is necessary. I will always keep my veil lowered in the street.[19]

During another pilgrimage to Annecy in August 1872, Fr. Chaumont prayed that members of the society would be "capable of bearing valiantly the gentle and easy yoke of our Savior."[20] In a letter dated August 19, 1872, Fr. Chaumont exhorts the women to study and imitate St. Jane de Chantal as a model of humility, dilection, charity, and fidelity to grace.

Letter of Fr. Chaumont to the Daughters

August 19, 1872
My dear Daughters,

I wish you all the blessings of the good God and all the powerful protection of St. Jane de Chantal, whose feast we are about to celebrate. Yes, I would very much like, and this, wholeheartedly, that [resting] in her hands, you both renew the promises you have already made to our dear Lord and Savior Jesus. She will guard them in your soul until she hands them over, on January 29, into the hands of her "very unique Father." Next month, if it pleases the good God, I will go and place your two hearts at the foot of their glorious tomb, at Annecy. You will give me, between now and then, all your messages for them.

Oh! how I would like to see you both already so similar to that great soul, so humble and so full of dilection! Every thought she had of her profound poverty did not stop in any way the burgeoning of her charity for the good God, and all the love with which she was consumed took away nothing from the energy of her profound humility. Tested as few souls were,[21] she learned to remain gentle, amiable, full of thoughtfulness for those who confided their least troubles to her; raised to the most admirable degrees of union with Our Lord, she learned to speak the language that was necessary to the poorest souls to attract them with ineffable violence to the strong and consuming love of God. Oh! What a model she offers for you to study and imitate! She had in perfection what is lacking a little in one and the other of you; may she who does not yet know to give way to humility imitate her in this regard; may she who does not yet dare to love enough imitate her in the holy ardors of her dilection for Jesus, and all will be well.

And yet, I also want to recommend to you the virtue which so marvelously helped St. Chantal to become what she was: her perfect fidelity to grace. Oh! My dear Daughters, what a great and useful science it is to know how to become more flexible under the blessed action of the grace of God! What wise prudence it is to let Our Lord do in us and with us, with Him and for Him, all that He wants, as much as He wants, as He wants! That was the great secret of St. Jane de Chantal in order to advance with giant steps in Christian perfections and that is what most helped St. Francis de Sales in the work of spiritual direction of his "eldest daughter."

I ask that this good saint give you, my dear Daughters, as a souvenir of her feast and as the best guarantee of perseverance in your good resolutions, a holy, simple, and constant spiritual suppleness.

May she bless you and her "true Father" also, and better still, Mary, their Mother in Heaven, ours on earth, and especially Our Lord, in whom I am your humbly and entirely devoted spiritual father,

L'Abbé Henri Chaumont[22]

A scant week later, in a letter dated August 25, 1872, Mme Carré wrote to Fr. Chaumont to express her acceptance of suffering, and her faith in their patrons, St. Francis de Sales and St. Jane de Chantal.

Letter of Mme Carré to Fr. Chaumont

August 25, 1872
In the midst of this ordeal, my Father, Our Lord accords me a grace that seems to me very great, that of loving suffering and to attach myself to it as if it were truly my path. If I were left the choice between Calvary and Tabor, I would run a thousand times to the first before thinking of the second....

I cannot wait to know that you are in Annecy, resting near our dear St. Francis de Sales, and drawing your inspiration for the future for all that he would like to tell you. If you would please, when consecrating me to him and to St. Chantal, ask in a very particular way that my soul become entirely devoted until death to the glory of God and to the good of souls. For the other needs of my soul, you know them better than I do, my Father, and St. Francis de Sales will refuse you nothing.[23]

The society held its first official (albeit secret) meeting on October 15, 1872, at the Maison de la Petite Œuvre (which translates roughly as House of Small Works [of Charity]) located in the rue Cassette in Paris; placed on a table before them was an oak box containing the Rule of Fr. Chaumont, while on the box they set a statue of St. Francis de Sales. Each of the four women chose a new name; Mme Carré would now be known as Sister Jane de Chantal, after the spiritual friend of the saint with whom he established the Visitation Order. As a profession of their desire to become members of the society, each recited an *Acte de Protestation* chosen by Fr. Chaumont from the *Introduction to the Devout Life*.[24] The nascent association would attract the attention and prayers of other movers and shakers of the Salesian Pentecost, including Msgr. de Ségur, Mother Chappuis, Fr. Louis Brisson and others, although Chaumont believed himself unworthy of leading the society, as he explained in a letter to Mme Carré.

Letter of Fr. Chaumont to Mme Carré

October 11, 1872

God be praised, my dear daughter! We can have at our disposal, the souls of the good God, the house about which I spoke to you. We will have there, for you and for each of those with whom the Savior Jesus will unite with you, a small cell whose modesty will recall in no small measure the great poverty of the house of the Gallery....

It is with an extreme and strong gentleness[25] that Our Lord is preparing me for this special direction of your souls; never have I sensed so strongly my profound unworthiness and incompetence, but never have I understood more clearly that the good God will do all that I neither could nor would know how to do alone. Let us embrace humility, my dear daughter; let us pray a good deal and let us hope for all. You see, here we are like Abraham leaving everything and going straight ahead, without knowing where the Lord wanted to lead him. O God, what does it matter that this divine Father and Master has not told us clearly yet where precisely he is leading us, so long as we cannot doubt that it is truly he who leads us? Now, I would not be able to doubt it, even though I might want to, unless I no longer recognized the obvious truth. I must make a confession that will show you to what a poor spiritual father you have been entrusted. The great fear that I have of mixing personal expectations into all this has on several occasions inspired in me the thought not to speak, even with you two, of these things except by always formulating doubts about the future; but in my prayers, today, I sensed a kind of remorse of this behavior; I reproach myself for it as being offensive to a grace which seems to speak so clearly to me, and I will do penance for it.

Oh! my daughter, pray that I have more practical faith. I would be less useless if I dared to do all that God wishes, and if I did not forget that it is in trampling on human wisdom that one performs the work of wisdom according to God. No doubt that my souls [i.e., the Daughters] would be better off if I didn't hesitate to believe in their wholly good will; I am wrong, I know it, and I am saying so, so that you might ask our Lord, in the name of the interests of his glory, to change me. You must not fear, my child, when you see me fall into some negligence, to warn me of it. If I do not have the humility to receive as I should this charitable reprimand, you will make it a subject of mortification....

There you have it, my child, in what hands the good God places his work: the poorest of his servants under the direction of the poorest of his ministers! O God! my Jesus, there is the true reason for our trust! Are we sufficiently nothing so that you might be all? And if, one day, some good should occur, will you fear being eclipsed by such hopeless collaborators? O God! you have chosen well: there are, in all this, enough troubles to make your extreme mercy explode.

Let's get to work, therefore, my dear daughter, and let it be with great courage, wholeheartedly, without accounting for useless complications! Let us go blindly where God is leading us. Mary, Star of the Sea, will enlighten us and direct us. It seems to me, if I am not deceiving myself, that many souls who do not know us, are waiting for us and yearning for those God will send to them. God, who has accomplished everything up until now, and in such a marvelously providential manner, will lead us safe and sound, if we become and remain, humble, confident, and generous.

Farewell, my dear daughter, till Tuesday! May Jesus bless you, you and your dear sister, and all those he reserves for you as companions.

L'Abbé H. Chaumont[26]

The association began to grow as Mme Carré recruited a very select group of friends to consider joining her and her sisters. In a letter to Mlle de Parieu dated October 22, 1872, Mme Carré confides to her friend the secret project, which came to full fruition during Fr. Chaumont's pilgrimage to Annecy.

Letter of Mme Carré to Mlle de Parieu

October 22, 1872

I am writing to you today with a *great secret*, my dear child. It has to do with…a project that developed on the tombs of saint Francis de Sales and saint Jane de Chantal, and that will result, we hope, in the glory of God and the benefit of souls. It is not necessary to name for you in detail all those in whom God inspired it: your heart will tell you enough.

Now, the project involves forming an association of people *still* living in the secular world, under the title of Daughters of Saint Francis de Sales. It goes without saying that the good saint will be their special patron. They intend, with the grace of God and in the spirit of Christian *simplicity*, to move in the direction of evangelical *holiness*. To attain this goal, they will keep in mind that the principle, the life, and the goal of the Christian soul is absolute union with Our Lord Jesus Christ. They will try to renounce their least faults and their slightest willful imperfections. Every day, they will renew in themselves a state of profound humility. In response to the love of Our Lord, they will add to these dispositions love and the related practice of three religious virtues. They will try to grow daily in the precious virtues of a firm and simple faith, absolute confidence, and charity without limits. They will carry out, every day, exercises of Christian piety, and attend holy Mass, holy Communion, &, &.

The Daughters of St. Francis de Sales will practice, as best they can, the precept of charity to one's neighbor. They will have for one another the most holy and the most cordial friendship; they will truly be of one heart and one soul together; they will exercise the charitable duty of fraternal correction, and, if some feeling of jealousy were to enter the heart of one of them, she would confess it as soon as possible before all. They will busy themselves, in the measure that God allows them, with the sanctification of souls.

This association has no official status; it has been placed under the unofficial direction of a priest, chosen as spiritual father. Every pious person can belong, provided that she has solid faith and has been accepted by the director and all the individuals in the association.

The Daughters of St. Francis de Sales will make no formal vows. On the day that they are received, they will pronounce the Profession contained in the twentieth chapter of the *Introduction to the Devout Life*; they will meet once a week.

After the opening prayer, the spiritual father will explain one of the points of the rule; a question related to spiritual direction will be treated, and each will state, humbly and simply, any of her own infractions that fall outside of the rule and will do the penance given to her. They will end with a pious speech.

Do you think, dear child, that your soul might reap some good in welcoming such an association? Is there anything that frightens you in the overview I have just given of the principal points of the rule? Would you like to be a part of it? Answer *simply*, either to the director, whom it is unnecessary for me to name for you, or to me, before next *Tuesday*, if possible. We have only had two meetings so far. Only God knows what future he has in store for this association; for the moment, its true goal is the advancement and sanctification of our souls.

It is formally forbidden for us to speak, except each to her director, a word about this association. You can imagine who authorized me to speak to you about it.

Goodbye, dear child, I leave you to your reflections. May Jesus and Mary inspire you. In them, I remain, more than ever, solidly attached and devoted to you.

C. Carré[27]

To achieve the goals of the society, Fr. Chaumont proposed an educational program of weekly instruction, each focused on a different Christian virtue or practice. He also prepared what he called *probations* for the Daughters, consisting of thirty-day guided meditations on individual virtues, to be followed by thirty days of free meditation, then thirty days of practical application of the virtue in daily life. Each aspirant was accompanied on her spiritual journey by a longstanding member of the Society called a "probatrice" (a word invented by the founders). Fr. Chaumont continued to serve as spiritual director to each member of the group; Sr. Jane de Chantal was elected Mother and was to support the spiritual director in his work, encouraging members of the Society to serve God, follow the examples of the Virgin Mary and the saints, and maintain their openness to their spiritual director. In fact, Marian devotion grew markedly over the course of the nineteenth century, placing the Mother of God squarely at the center of popular devotional practices in France. In a letter to the Daughters dated March 16, 1873, Fr. Chaumont encourages them to imitate the Virgin Mary, whose visit to her cousin Elizabeth inspired the establishment of the Order of the Visitation by St. Jane de Chantal and St. Francis de Sales; the latter's preaching often cited Mary as a model to be followed.[28]

Letter of Fr. Chaumont to the Daughters

March 16, 1873
My dear Daughters,

Our Lord wants to make use of me today for another care than the consolation of edifying myself in your midst; I will lead a rich man of this world to his final resting place; pray for his soul.

I hope that the very pious and zealous M. Gérard will go to see you and will offer you some good words of encouragement. Be very thankful for the interest he is taking in you and take advantage of the wise counsel he will give you. If the good God enables to come, you could beg him to explain what I would have—the method for the prayer of union. I am thrilled that he might give you this useful explanation for me, for he is a man of prayer. If he can't come, you will consult amongst yourselves, piously and amiably, about prayer or any other good thing.

And I, who was so happy to speak to you about the very Holy Virgin, will I then not say anything? Yes indeed, and I am going to let my pen flow freely on this topic, as if I were simply speaking in person with you.

Now, note, it is not the incomparable grandeur of Mary that I want to exalt: do you not know, as I do, that her throne yields only to the throne of God himself? I do not want to speak to you of her admirable virtues either; each of you knows very well that the virtue most necessary to her is found in Mary, to a very lovely degree of perfection. What will be of more benefit to you, no doubt, will be to present her to you as the accomplished model of this particular good for which you are aiming: to work, given the means that the good Lord offers to you, for the salvation and edification of souls.

No one would be able to describe for you, my dear Daughters, the zeal of the very holy Virgin for this great and holy cause. What was she doing, pray tell, in the shadow of the tabernacle of the Lord, reading and meditating, and savoring, and commenting on the holy Scriptures, if not concerning herself, but with a more than angelic ardor, with the redemption of the world? It is to this end that, according to the opinion of several Fathers of the Church, her desires hastened the Incarnation of the Son of God.

Later, as soon as she had the joy of pressing to her heart her God become her Son, see how she was pleased to make him known and loved by all, by poor shepherds, first of all, and then by kings also. Who will question that, in Egypt, in Nazareth, during the public life of Jesus, Mary enjoyed making him known, loved, adored by all the upstanding souls that she encountered?

But where she appears more directly as your model is during her long sojourn still on earth after her Jesus rose from the dead. Oh! how admirable were her humility and her zeal! She is the Queen of the Apostles, the glory of the Church, the model of sanctity, and yet here she remains among the ranks of the humblest Christians. To others the honor of the priesthood and its divine powers; to others the official mission of guides and savers of souls; to Mary the care, less apparent and yet so useful, of good example, gentle insinuations, maternal exhortations to bring still hesitant souls to the good, and to push generous souls toward perfection. Thus, her very humility became in her hands a powerful means of zeal, like an arm with two blades that nothing can resist, like a charm whose secret virtue triumphs without struggle over all obstacles.

Pious traditions show her to us continuously occupied with everything that concerned the glory of God through the salvation of souls, true refuge of sinners, true consoler of the afflicted, true help of Christians, most wise counselor, entirely devoted friend, so good and charitable toward all souls that have the joy and honor of knowing her, such that each, seeing her so entirely affectionate, believed herself to be the most loved, though she loved them all as much as each deserved to be. Oh! how easy and comforting did the ministry of the Apostles become to souls prepared by Mary, or encouraged by Mary, or uplifted by Mary!

But why place yourselves at such a distance from the one who is your model, my dear Daughters? Is it that, even now, this is not the particular role of our Mother of heaven? Does she not still fulfill the same very humble, but so effective mission toward souls? Has she not been for us, as well as for the first Christians, counselor, consoler, help, maternal providence?

Well! that is what you will also become, in your lowly fashion, if you are faithful to the graces of the good God. You will not remain strangers to [other] souls; you will not refuse to enlighten them, to support them, to make them better; you will consider yourselves infinitely honored to be particularly chosen by the good God to exercise humbly, but effectively, like Mary, by Mary, with Mary, this gentle service of souls.

Oh! may God make you receptive to this word, my very dear Daughters! The sky of the very near future is full of clouds; great storms seem yet to be brewing.[29] What will God do with us during these terrible times? Whatever he likes, and whatever it might be, may he be blessed! But when the storm has passed, when the sky has become calm once more, when you find each other again, if the storm has carried me on high, and if you are looking for God's will for you, here it is, clearly: pursue humbly but firmly what you have begun.

Sanctify yourselves at the school of the Gospel and the works of St. Francis de Sales. Aim modestly, but straight ahead, toward perfection, by the solid virtues of humility, mortification, a life of faith, charity, charity above all, charity, I tell you, which is the perfection of all things.

And, as you sanctify yourself in this way, be docile instruments in the hands of divine mercy, and you will see marvels. O God! Shall I flatter you, my dear Daughters? God forbid, for I say precisely that you will only do good if you remain docile instruments, and the honor of what is done comes, not to the instrument but to the artist. But I repeat that you will see marvels of grace, that the good Lord will give you remarkable virtue to attract souls, to do them great good; that never will your zeal lie idle; that your influence will go on spreading, as our saint says, like a drop of fragrant oil that each day gains a bit of ground, until it has invaded an entire section of the fabric on which it has fallen.

And, as a sign that this will be from God, to numerous tests like those that have been announced to you recently, the gentle goodness of your Savior will join interior consolations so great, joys so powerful, a happiness so celestial, that you will have no doubt that God is there present in all things.

Courage, therefore, my dear Daughters, and to work straight away. Go quickly to the holy labor of your sanctification, in order soon to become useful to souls. The good God is waiting for you; he is anxious for you to be able to do that which he has reserved for you; strike with redoubled blows and without pity on your own will; crush your pride without mercy; may there be no languishing hearts among you, no sleeping souls! Hold close the bonds of your mutual charity. Love one another, my very dear daughters! Poor patients placed by Providence in the same hospital, bear your mutual infirmities. You are all such very poor souls; but you are thus, and it is as such that you must love one another. I declare intruders among you those who, now or later, enter without this nuptial robe of charity; I cry in betrayal against those who, having entered in sheep's skin, reveal themselves later to be devouring beasts; I bless a thousand and a thousand times in the good God those who will be faithful to the urgent recommendations of the Savior with regard to charity.

May the very holy Virgin obtain for you, my dear Daughters, the imitation of her modest and fruitful apostolate! And, since the good God calls you to do, in a special and entirely providential manner, the same type of good as his divine Mother, may he give you, as he gave her, the humility that attracts his graces, the charity that nourishes them, the zeal that makes them produce thirty, sixty and one hundred times over. May Jesus be blessed! Amen![30]

The Virgin Mary was also the focus of the *probation* prepared by Fr. Chaumont for the Daughters entitled *Être Marie*, or "Being Mary." Ideally, the Daughters would so absorb their model as to become, in essence, one with her. The following excerpt from this *probation* is based on notes taken during the conferences offered by Chaumont at the novitiate over the course of 1883 and 1884 (ten years after the above letter was written) and is corrected by him in red ink in the original. It is likely that this first draft was created by Mother Mary Gertrude, one of the first Daughters of St. Francis de Sales, a dear friend of Mme Carré and an especially gifted writer. In essence, the *probation* calls the Daughters to participate in the suffering and radical mission of Jesus through Mary; in this way, they may be incorporated into the mission of Mary, who was incorporated directly into the mission of Jesus.

Excerpt from the *Probation* "Being Mary" Prepared for the Daughters by Fr. Chaumont

TENTH MEDITATION

Mary help of Jesus during his public life

1. The exterior action of Mary

If Mary cooperated in a very powerful way in the mission of the Savior, her exterior action is barely perceptible. It seems that we only hear her, that we only glimpse her just enough to know that she is there. Mary appears for the first time at Cana; her humble and discreet prayer moves forward just a little the hour of Jesus' manifestation and ends with his first miracle. During the apostolic travels of the Savior, she helps the holy women, to the extent that she can, to meet the material needs of Jesus and his apostles.

The exterior role of Mary becomes important once again only at the foot of the Cross, when the Savior, associating his holy Mother to his sacrifice and his Redemption, establishes her as mother of Christians, their mediator and their advocate.

2.   Hidden action of the very holy Virgin

The true character of Mary's mission during the public life of Jesus is that of prayer and sacrifice. While Jesus evangelizes the crowds, Mary raises up to heaven the most ardent supplications for the success of the Savior's mission. And at the same time, she immolates herself with heroic generosity, not only does she accept, with all the power of her will, all the anguish and heartbreak that are the consequence of her Son's suffering, but she also offers herself unceasingly to the celestial Father as a victim entirely devoted to the salvation of her brothers.

In this way she attracts to souls the fertile grace that causes the word of Jesus to bear fruit.

O Mary, obtain for me this intimate and calm union with Jesus that alone gives one the strength to sacrifice oneself in silence.

ELEVENTH MEDITATION

Mary help of Jesus after the Resurrection

1.   Mary help of Jesus at the Last Supper

Jesus wants Mary to already begin her role of Mother and Queen of the apostolic association and of all Christians at the Last Supper where she withdrew, after the Ascension, with the Apostles, the disciples, and the holy women. She helps to maintain their courage, she teaches them to pray, she gives them an example of holy contemplation with which they must prepare themselves for the coming of the Holy Spirit.

These men, still weak in faith, remained in the Cenacle, as much perhaps by "fear of the Jews" as by the desire to obey the orders of the divine Master. Without the fortifying presence of she whose noble features reminded them of the absent Lord, would they have known how to "persevere" in union until the day of Pentecost, and proceed calmly to the election of a new apostle?

2.   Mary help of Jesus on the day of Pentecost
At the hour when then Holy Spirit came to consecrate the Church definitively, it was necessary that this nascent Church find, to receive it, the heart and arms of a Mother; Mary, as on the day of the Annunciation, surrenders herself entirely to the interventions of the Holy Spirit; and this divine Spirit forms in her the "Mother of the Living" with the same complacence that he had formerly put toward making of the humble virgin of Israel the mother of the Redeemer. "Streams of the river," as the King-Prophet says, "gladden this city of God" (Ps 46:5), which receives him with delight.

O Mary, sustain my feeble courage as you sustained that of the Apostles and the first Christians, help me to surrender, like you, entirely to the interventions of the Spirit of Jesus, whose supple and blind instrument I want to be.

TWELFTH MEDITATION

Mary help of Jesus in the holy Church, from Pentecost to the Assumption

1. Mary is the mother of the emerging Church

A new maternity was given to Mary on the day of Pentecost. A new love was kindled in her heart, and she is entirely given over to the mission for which she has been left here on earth. "Like a generous milk, the irresistible word of this universal mother gives to the first children of the Church the vigor that makes them triumph from the assaults of evil."[31] They are to seek unceasingly in her maternal heart consolation and support; and it is beside her that Saint Stephen draws on the courage to open the noble profession of the martyrs.

2. Mary is an apostle in the midst of the apostles

The Holy Spirit filled Mary with apostolic grace. The tongue of fire that rested on her did not bestow on her the mission to teach by means of apostolic preaching, she limits herself to speak privately with the Apostles; she enlivens their zeal, she consoles them and encourages them in their labors; she reveals to them secrets from the Heart of Jesus as only she was given the privilege of knowing them.

Her soul filled with memories of the Man-God, Mary affirms in faith and love the newly baptized that the Apostles send her, telling them stories of the marvelous humility, gentleness, and generous charity of their Redeemer.

3. Mary is a practical model for the first faithful

For the apostles, it is an invaluable help to be able to introduce Mary to their neophytes, as the perfect type of the virtues they must henceforth practice. When the first faithful see Mary plunged in meditation and adoration before the Host consecrated by saint John, they understand with what respect full of love they must surround the Very Blessed Sacrament. When they contemplate her, always modest and gentle in her incomparable dignity, they sense their harshness transform in the light that radiates from her pure virtue.

O Mary, support your child as you supported the first Christians, and keep her humble and faithful on the path that you traveled before her.[32]

In the 1870s and '80s, the Daughters' meeting place would move from the rue Cassette to the rue de Breteuil, where it was rebaptized the Maison du Bon-Dieu, or "House of the Good God" (a name that would be maintained over time as the center was relocated more than once); it was a great blessing to them all when permission was given for the Society to establish a tabernacle with the Blessed Sacrament in the chapel of their center. Both Fr. Chaumont and Mme Carré continued to recruit women to the society. In a letter to Mme Carré dated November 7, 1873, Fr. Chaumont explains the qualities necessary to postulants to the Society, written just as the current Daughters are about to enter into their yearly retreat. He first speaks directly to Mme Carré, then expands the scope of his letter.

Letter of Fr. Chaumont to Mme Carré and the Daughters

November 7, 1873

My dear child, it is with great care and concern that you are going to see the new companions whom our Lord has given you to love and serve commence their retreat. While the Mother of the aspirants will, as best she can, facilitate for them the meditation exercises that they will have to do, together you will all pray that our sweet Savior excite them to acquire his spirit of perfection and simplicity. You must tell them, repeating to them incessantly and without fear of being mistaken, that Jesus needs and will continue to need pious souls, vigorously tempered with faith, with a confidence that no difficulty or contradiction must weary, with unlimited charity, I will go so far as to say, with inordinate charity, for, as far as our good God is concerned, our love must know no limits, and with regard to our neighbor, one must pay no heed to rumors or false accusations.[33]

Tell them that, once they have acquired what is asked of them according to the little rule, they will be capable of doing a lot of good; this is true and I know it. And you who are the elders, give to the new members perfect examples [of conduct]; let there not be among you any half-virtues or feeble efforts! You have received so much from Our Lord that you must return a great deal to him. The precious virtue of humility has required that you be hospitable; you have welcomed it with joy: let nothing bring it sorrow; let nothing harm it! May the one among you who might believe she is something remember that she is less than others who recognize their nothingness, and who are thus in the truth. Honor also, and even more, if it is possible, the queen of virtues, charity. Oh! you all love each other well, don't you? But you must keep at it; and your charity, passing through the crucible of little tests that your mutual spiritual poverty gives it, must become stronger daily. The entire future of this little endeavor that you have started lies in that. Oh! tell your dear sisters, my child, all lies in that: if you love each other perfectly, if you mutually support each other, if the difficulties or joys of one become the difficulties or joys of all, you will do each other great good, you will do good all around yourselves, each in her sphere, and our Lord will not be able to refuse you anything.

He is reserving for you more than an ordinary grace: once you are loving and charitable, in accordance with his perfection, he wants to give you an altogether special outpouring of his divine Spirit. The Spirit of Jesus! It is he who perfected the apostles, it is he who enlivened the saints, it is he who is going to prepare, patiently but surely, souls destined to bear, when the time comes, the supreme combats of hell against God. Woe, in those days, which we will no doubt not see, but for which we are preparing others, woe for those whose faith is weak, whose Gospel is diminished, whose humility is false; only those with true faith in the Spirit, true charity in the heart, those souls who have been formed by the Spirit of Jesus will remain standing. Oh! How I pray the very holy Virgin to acquire for you all a sympathetic understanding of these things. If you pray to her, she will help you to understand them so well that you will not know how to thank her enough for such a benefit, which you will owe to her maternal intercession.

It is to you that I was writing, my child, and here, unable to separate you from your sisters, I have taken it upon myself to speak to you all together. It is therefore all of you together whom I ask Jesus to bless, and to the prayers of all that I commend.

—*The least of his priests*[34]

Sr. Jane de Chantal continued to serve as Mother to the group even during a very difficult period of five years during which her husband was relocated to Rouen; pending her return, she monitored the Daughters' "progress in Salesian formation"[35] while devoting herself to the reading of works by her namesake, St. Jane de Chantal, at the suggestion of her spiritual director Fr. Chaumont. Her own personal spiritual work continued, as evidenced by notes recorded during a retreat made while Mme Carré was in exile in Rouen (1874–79) in preparation for the Feast of the Immaculate Conception.

Retreat Notes Recorded by Mme Carré, December 1–8, 1874

Our good God will ask me for an account of the manner in which I receive the sacraments, which I benefit from, and also the way I fulfill my household duties. They are a daily cross, my household duties; but one is condemned to hell if one does not fulfill them well, and the good God will judge me severely on this matter. He will also ask for an account of my duties of vocation or perfection, and of certain stages of his grace, which he doesn't bestow on so many others. There is something formidable in all of these thoughts; if I only considered my sins, there would be reason to fear discouragement; but the good God is full of mercy; I must not fear but have the courage to judge myself here on earth....

As for voluntary sins, one must pay serious attention to them, for God gives of himself without reserve only to those who give of themselves without reserve. The soul that deliberately retains and willfully tolerates wrongdoing is not giving of herself without reserve, and Jesus cannot communicate to her the secrets of his divine Heart.

On the final page of her retreat notes, she writes,

> In all of my relations with my husband, I will work to acquire gentleness, patience, kindheartedness, the supernatural spirit that will cause me to benefit so greatly from my difficulties, and that will help me so powerfully to subjugate my wretched pride, in order to die completely to myself.[36]

Indeed, Mme Carré believed her husband to be an instrument for her perfection in patience and humility; she devoted herself to his happiness, admired and respected him, and, conforming to the spirituality of suffering so predominant in her time,[37] offered herself as "a victim for the sanctification of his soul."[38] Imperious and demanding, tending to fits of anger and displays of intellectual superiority, Paul Carré often manifested his irritation and displeasure by mocking his wife's spiritual goals and criticizing her, even in front of their servants; at times he struck her.[39] To his credit, Paul did not stand in the way of the formation of the Society of the Daughters of St. Francis de Sales; he would eventually come to recognize his wife's remarkable gifts and praise her as a saint after her death. Yet again, in the spirit of the time, his behavior toward his wife led Sr. Jane de Chantal to impose severe mortifications upon herself, far more severe, in fact, than any St. Francis de Sales would have approved. Testimony by Mlle Stiltz given during the beatification proceedings (1906) describes the physical mortification to which Mme Carré, like many pious Catholics of her era, regularly had recourse, not only for her own sanctification, but for the salvation of the soul of her husband.

Testimony by Mlle Stiltz at the Beatification Proceedings of Mme Carré (1906)

Here is her rule of penance which must date from 1872, I think (she had it in Luchon, where I saw the instruments, and since then, I saw very frequently that she used them): "Sundays, no leaning; Monday, two iron bracelets two hours every morning; Tuesday, something that annoys, for example, a little iron cross, for an indeterminate time; Wednesday, cilice in the morning, Thursday, an iron bracelet, three hours; Friday, horsehair cuffs in the morning; two iron bracelets on the feet in the afternoon if one does not go out; otherwise they are put on the arm; every fifteen days, the hairshirt; Saturday, horsehair belt, two hours; Wednesday and Friday when possible, the scourge: Thursday evening, before going to bed, a quarter of an hour on the ground, in memory of the passion of Our Lord, kissing the ground often, making an act of love when one has committed an error; stretch out on the ground, arms extended in a cross, twice a day; sleep on the floor every fifteen days; Fridays, get up in the night for a quarter hour of prayer."[40]

Moreover, Mme Carré was no stranger to other forms of suffering. In Paris, she would see three of her four children die before the age of four; the fourth, Paul, predeceased his parents in 1885, at the age of twenty-nine. Mme Carré herself was taxed with severe migraines throughout her life; like St. Francis de Sales, she also experienced the temptation of despair.[41] One might imagine that her personal suffering would diminish her focus on pursuing a life of holiness, and yet, as her fellow Daughter Mlle Stiltz noted, following St. Francis de Sales, "She did not seek the God of consolations, but the consolations of God."[42] At the end of a letter dated August 18, 1878, written during one of her holidays in Lorry, Sr. Jane de Chantal appends the signature, "Sr. Jane of the Thorns of Jesus."

Letter of Mme Carré to Fr. Chaumont

August 18, 1878
The worst of the storm took place in the woods, before the statue of the most holy Virgin whom we so love to venerate, close to my mother and the children who were playing. It took a harsh effort on my part to compose myself physically, and, in the midst of the sighs and tears of my soul, I sang some words of a canticle, to protest against the sadness that overwhelmed me, and as an act of obedience.

Sister Jane of the Thorns of Jesus[43]

Her biographer Laveille explains, "In one of her conversations with Our Lord, she seemed to see a heart surrounded by thorns, and she came to believe that her Savior wanted the heart of his servant surrounded, like his own, by this painful crown." Elsewhere, she explained, "Why would I not take the name that suits me better than any other? Have I not been, am I not, for Jesus, like a crown of thorns? It is right that, before those who know me best, I bear the name that I deserve."[44]

In 1880, the Society received a letter of blessing from the archbishop of Paris, and, in an extraordinary development given the lay membership of the group, in 1911, twenty years after the death of Mme Caroline Carré, the Society of the Daughters of St. Francis de Sales would see its constitution receive the official approval of the Holy See. Shortly after receiving the blessing of the archbishop, Sr. Jane de Chantal wrote to Sr. Mary of Jesus (who would replace her as Mother of the association after Mme Carré's death), offering advice on the act of perfecting oneself. In it, Sr. Jane de Chantal notes that she too has her cross to bear yet is grateful for the suffering Christ allows her.

Letter of Sr. Jane de Chantal to Sr. Mary of Jesus

August 11, 1882
What better wish might I make for you, my child, than that of becoming, in every sense of the word, "Jesus' little one," for, in truth, the more I think about this path, which is truly yours, the more I find it *beautiful, grand,* and *all encompassing.* May you arrive one day at the full realization of faith that it requires! It is your daily work which will lead you there, my child, and I promise you, on the day of the Assumption, to fervently redouble [my efforts] to entreat Our Lord, by his holy and Immaculate Mother, to give you the grace necessary to reach perfect submission to the Holy Spirit....

The assurance that you give me that Our Lord is showing you more and more the abyss of your wretchedness, has once again been proof to me of the very intimate union of our souls. I confess to you, my child, that it is one of the most pressing graces I ask of Jesus. Would you like me to tell you the whole truth? Well! I ask this grace as a consolation. For to know oneself, to know one's inexhaustible depth of weakness and wretchedness, to have it unceasingly before one's eyes, to be penetrated by it, seems to me indispensable so that Our Lord can give us all that we need to have to become his instruments.

Only, one must be logical when making a prayer like this and expect the consequence. It is necessary for us to be crushed, yes, crushed in every way. But then Jesus makes us love this kind of trial, so crucifying for the heart, the intelligence, the soul, and the body. Ah! My child, I insist. While I am at it, must I tell you everything? Yes, since I am conversing with my *own soul*. Well! Jesus makes me or made me so apt for this crucifying life, I feel so much in my element, and it is an indispensable grace for me that he support me in such a persistent way, that, if Jesus takes me out of it one day by some consolation such as those which He alone knows how to give to my soul, my first movement is to drink avidly of this consolation like a poor, parched soul; then, very quickly, little suited to this treatment, I feel as if out of my element, I seek suffering, which can no longer exist when Jesus is manifest, and, as soon as Jesus gives [that suffering] back to me, I experience a feeling of well-being and of gratitude, all the while following Jesus with the eyes of my heart, that All who draws away [from me], and whose apparition has been so brief but so fortifying.

That is my life, my child. May this simple overture, which is only for you, make you understand, more still than in the past, the necessity of praying very much in order to acquire for us humility, which is the indispensable basis of all the virtues.

Several years later Fr. Chaumont wrote to Mme Carré, to clarify the role of the Daughters as "an instrument God has placed into the hands of the priest-directors."

Letter of Fr. Chaumont
to Mme Carré

February 22, 1888

Masters of the spiritual life make serious direction one of the primary means of formation for souls of good will. Now, the Society of the Daughters of Saint Francis de Sales is essentially an instrument that God has placed in the hands of the priest directors. To be honest, it has no other reason for existing; it will be useful only to the extent that it will be a docile instrument, and it will do an incalculable good if it is perfectly faithful to the will of God over it. I ask and command you in a paternal fashion, my child, never to allow into the Society a soul who is not yet perfectly earnest about this design of Our Lord over the work, or who would not be absolutely determined to enter into this project and to serve him with all her power. And if ever, God forbid! one of the members of the council were to stray from this spirit, you would have the duty to enlighten her charitably, to correct her affectionately; and, if she remained obstinate in her personal or prideful views, you would have to, of necessity, exclude her from this privileged circle, and perhaps from the society, this soul who has strayed outside the will of God.[45]

From the time of its formation in 1872, the association grew rapidly, counting thirteen members by January 1873, over two thousand in 1896 (just five years after Mme Carré's death), and more than four thousand by 1900. Groups would be formed in provinces around France, from Aurillac and Bréménil to Dijon, Lyon, Nevers, Orléans, and Toulouse. Eventually, Sr. Mary-Anna would establish the Society of the Daughters of St. Francis de Sales in England while Delphine Madill would bring the Society to the United States. At present, groups in the United States range from Delaware to Florida, to Michigan, Missouri, and Minnesota; they can also be found in more than twenty countries around the world. Gaëtan Bernoville attributes the success of the Society to its eminently Salesian inspiration and to the "modernity" of the Salesian vision.[46]

During her lifetime, Mme Carré also worked to establish several offshoots of the Society, including the Société des Dames chrétiennes (for the wives of military personnel compelled to live very worldly lives), the Société des institutrices chrétiennes (for Christian elementary school teachers whose personal sanctification was a balm to the secularization of the French school system), and, most importantly and most enduringly, the Society of Priests of St. Francis de Sales, a group of clergy recruited and trained by Fr. Chaumont to serve the needs of the Daughters in terms of spiritual direction and the sacraments. To that end, Fr. Chaumont developed a program of formation for these priests that included spiritual exercises and meditations. The Society of the Sons of St. Francis de Sales was established in 1876; Mme Carré and Fr. Chaumont also considered creating a society for servants; this project, however, did not materialize.[47]

Both Mme Carré and Fr. Chaumont recognized as well the need for spiritual intervention on behalf of women around the world in need of evangelization and spiritual support. Recalling his early desire to become a missionary, Fr. Chaumont enlisted the women of Paris in a kind of prayer crusade for the conversion of women in faraway lands; he also enjoined Parisians to raise funds to provide dowries for Christian marriages abroad, the transmission of which was facilitated by the group. Named the Œuvre de Marie-Immaculée, or Charitable Works of Immaculate Mary, it grew to a remarkable 300,000 participants by 1900. A still more ambitious project consisted of the formation of the Salesian Catéchistes-Missionnaires (Catechist-Missionaries, known today as the Salésiennes Missionnaires de Marie Immaculée, or Salesian Missionaries of Mary Immaculate), women who enlisted to go abroad to serve the needs of local populations, first in India, then in China and Africa. Suffering from cancer at the time of the departure of the first Catechist-Missionaries in 1889, Sr. Jane de Chantal received moving letters from her missionary Daughters, describing their living conditions, the Hindu ceremonies they witnessed, and their efforts to learn the local language and to provide medical assistance to the indigent populations of their service area. Shortly before their departure, Mme Carré wrote to the first four women who left for India to serve as Catechist-Missionaries:

Letter of Mme Carré to the First Catechist-Missionaries

October 8, 1889
My beloved Daughters,

One more heartfelt message carrying to all four of you my good-bye, or rather, "until we see each other again" when and where Jesus wills. All the thoughts and all the sentiments of my heart are bursting forth with such vigor, my very dear Daughters, that it is impossible to express them to you. Jesus and his Holy Mother see them, and that is enough, and you have faith in them....The most pressing need, my dear Daughters, is that of once again exciting your souls to the most complete and absolute confidence toward the divine and paternal Heart of Jesus and that of his Immaculate Mother. Whatever happens, *Sursum corda!*[48] Confidence, filial abandon! Have recourse to them unceasingly, let yourself sink into them more and more. The more your nature inclines you to fear or suffer, the more you will sing out a note of confidence. Ah! who then will be the children of Jesus given by Him to his Mother if not you?...It is in mutual union, is it not, that we are going to work to strengthen this blind confidence, to the point of folly if necessary, in the intimacy of the soul, without removing any aspect of the exterior prudence which we must always maintain.

My dear daughters, the greatest graces of my life have always arrived after great acts of confidence and abandon, and it will be thus for you.

Ally dear humility to this virtue of loving abandon, of loving *Fiat*. They cannot be separated from one another; the one attracts the other.

Go now, leave joyously, guided by the Star of the sea, always visible for souls who have surrendered themselves.

I embrace all four of you with my most true maternal heart, after having kissed your feet respectfully, and having let fall there the tear which Jesus would like to use to bless you again.

> Your Mother, who will not leave you.
> *Sr. Jane de Chantal*[49]

Catechist-Missionaries were also sent to China beginning in 1890.

Madame Caroline-Barbe Colchen Carré de Malberg succumbed to cancer on January 28, 1891, at the age of sixty-one. Shortly after her death, Mlle Stiltz recorded a speech made by Fr. Chaumont after the death of Mme Carré, declaring the spiritual merits of Mme Carré; she later submitted the speech to the body examining Mme Carré's cause, which went forward almost immediately.

Speech Made by Fr. Chaumont after the Death of Mme Carré, Cited by Mlle Stiltz in Her Deposition for Mme Carré's Cause

Your Mother has died without my being able to attest to a difference between her and saint Jane de Chantal....

As a simple Christian, she had: 1. a great natural energy, preferring by choice things that cost her the most; 2. a grace infused with love and adherence to the will of the good God; 3. the spirit of obedience, but out of reason, not out of attraction. A very dominating nature, if it had not been broken, all her confessors would have been dominated by it. But, at the end of her life, her obedience left nothing to be desired. It was, in her, like a second nature to obey.

As a Daughter of Saint Francis de Sales, your First Mother fulfilled her state perfectly. She sensed her unworthiness for working with souls, believing herself always to be an abominable creature. It was a feeling of humility: she had a need to sanctify herself, in order to help others to sanctify themselves. It would be very difficult to find a more perfect example, more given over to the Holy Spirit, and entering more into the divine plan, drawing near, although still in the world, to love and the practice of the virtues of perfection. Her supernatural spirit vis-à-vis the Priest was perfect: she was, in that sense, all that one could hope for, and in an absolutely marvelous way.

When I recall what I was at that moment [when the Association was begun], I say to myself more and more, "It must be that your Mother was already a saint, without whom the society would not have been founded."[50]

Mme Carré's cause for beatification was ratified by Pius X, and she was declared Venerable by Pope Francis on May 10, 2014. Fr. Henri Chaumont died in 1896, having witnessed the constant growth of the Society he so ardently championed until his final days, confident that women around the world would continue to live by the dictum *Live Jesus!*[51]

TIMELINE FOR FRANCIS DE SALES, JANE DE CHANTAL, AND THE SALESIAN PENTECOST

Year	Lives of Francis de Sales and Jane de Chantal	The Salesian Pentecost	Contemporary Events
1534–1540			Ignatius of Loyola establishes the Jesuits.
1545			Council of Trent opens.
1562			Beginning of the French Wars of Religion.
1563			Council of Trent closes.
1567	August 21: Birth of Francis de Sales in Thorens.		July 24: Mary Stuart abdicates the Scottish throne in favor of her infant son James VI (later James I of England).
1571			October 7: The Holy League defeats the Turkish armada at Lepanto.
1572	January 23: Birth of Jane Frances Frémyot (Mother de Chantal) in Dijon, France.		August 24: St. Bartholomew Day Massacre of French Calvinists (Huguenots) in Paris and the French provinces.
1573	October: Francis attends elementary school in the town of La Roche.		

Year	Lives of Francis de Sales and Jane de Chantal	The Salesian Pentecost	Contemporary Events
1575	October: Francis and cousins begin school at Collège Chappuys in Annecy.		
1578	September 20: Francis receives tonsure. September 25: Francis enrolls in humanities at the Jesuit Collège de Clermont in Paris.		
1579			December 15: Claude de Granier succeeds Angelo Giustiniani as bishop of Geneva.
1580			August 30: Death of Savoy's Duke Emmanuel Philibert (1528–1580); Charles Emmanuel I (1562–1630) becomes duke. Michel Eyquem de Montaigne publishes the first edition of his *Essais*.
1581			April 24: Birth of Vincent de Paul, Pouy, Gascony (France). December 1: Jesuit Edmund Campion is executed in London.
1582	Francis begins to frequent the course of letters and liberal arts.		October 4/15: Death of Teresa of Avila, reformer of Carmel.
1584	Francis begins course of philosophy and studies theology (until 1588); he frequents Gilbert Génébrard's lectures on the Song of Songs.		November 3: Death of Charles Borromeo, archbishop of Milan.
1586	December: Francis experiences a grave spiritual crisis through January 1587.		

Year	Lives of Francis de Sales and Jane de Chantal	The Salesian Pentecost	Contemporary Events
1588	Spring: Francis completes his licentiate and master of arts at the College of Clermont.		May 12: Henry de Guise enters Paris and is acclaimed king on this *Day of the Barricades*.
1588	December 26: After a brief stay in Savoy, Francis departs for Padua to study law.		August 8: Defeat of the "invincible" Spanish Armada by the English.
1589	Francis draws up the Rule of Padua.		Death of Catherine de' Medici; assassination of Henri III; Henry de Navarre becomes Henry IV of France, installing the Bourbon dynasty.
1590	Repeat of Francis's crisis of faith experienced in Paris, continues into 1591.		
1591	September 5: Francis is awarded doctorate in civil and canon law from the Sacro Collegio Giurista of the University of Padua.		
1592	November 24: Francis passes his bar exam and is registered as an attorney for the Senate of Savoy in Chambéry. December 28: Jane Frances Frémyot marries the Baron Christophe de Rabutin-Chantal.		January 30: Florentine Ippolito Aldobrandini (1536–1605) is elected pope and reigns as Clement VIII (1592–1605); he favors France over Spain.
1593	May 7: Francis is nominated provost of the Cathedral Chapter of Geneva. December 18: Francis is ordained to priesthood.		July 25: Henry IV abjures Protestantism.
1594	September 14: Francis and his cousin Louis begin their preaching mission in the Chablais region of Savoy.		December: Jesuits are expelled from France; the crown seizes their assets.
1595	January 25: Francis begins writing and editing the *Controversies*.		May 26: Death of Philip Neri, founder of the Oratory, in Rome.

Year	Lives of Francis de Sales and Jane de Chantal	The Salesian Pentecost	Contemporary Events
1600	*Defense of the Standard of the Holy Cross.*		August: Henry IV invades Savoy; gains control of Tuscany by marrying Maria de' Medici.
1601	October: Death of the Baron de Chantal, husband of Jane de Chantal.		January 17: Peace between France and Savoy (Treaty of Lyons).
1602	January 22: Francis visits Paris to represent the interests of the Diocese of Geneva.		
1602	September 17: Death of Claude de Granier, bishop of Geneva, in Annecy. December 8: Francis's episcopal ordination in Thorens		December 21–22: Duke Charles Emmanuel I of Savoy leads his army in a surprise attack against Geneva and is repelled (Escalade).
1603			March 24: Death of Elizabeth I (Tudor dynasty), Queen of England; she is succeeded by James I (Stuart dynasty). July 12: Treaty of Saint-Julien between Geneva and Savoy ends all Savoyard claims.
1604	Bishop de Sales has a vision that convinces him that at some future point, God wants him to establish a religious order. March 5: Lenten series begins at Dijon, where Francis first meets Baroness Jane Frances Frémyot Rabutin de Chantal.		October 15: Foundation of the Carmel of the Incarnation in Paris, which is the first monastery of Teresian Reform in France.
1606	Foundation of the Florimontane Academy.		

Year	Lives of Francis de Sales and Jane de Chantal	The Salesian Pentecost	Contemporary Events
1607			May 14: Virginia Company merchants establish first English colony in America at Jamestown.
1609	Publication of the *Introduction to the Devout Life*.		August 21: Galileo Galilei demonstrates his eight-power telescope to the nobles and doge of the Serene Republic of Venice in the belltower of San Marco.
1610	June 6: Foundation of the Visitation, with Jane de Chantal, Jacqueline Favre, Charlotte Bréchard, and Anne Coste.		May 14: Assassination of Henry IV; reign of Louis XIII (1610–1643). Honoré d'Urfé (member of the Florimontane Academy) publishes *Astrée*. Galileo Galilei is appointed mathematician and philosopher to the Court of the Grand Duke of Tuscany, Cosimo II. November 1: Paul V canonizes Charles Borromeo and Frances of Rome.
1611	June 16: Jane de Chantal professes her first vows.		Pierre de Bérulle founds the Oratory in Paris. Authorized (King James) Version of the Bible is published in England.
1613	Francis composes the Constitutions for the Sisters of the Visitation of Holy Mary.		
1615	January 28: Francis sends Jane de Chantal, Jacqueline Favre, and two others to open the first Visitandine community in France, at Lyons; community begins on February 2.		Assembly of the Clergy in France adopts the decrees of the Council of Trent (1545–1563).

Year	Lives of Francis de Sales and Jane de Chantal	The Salesian Pentecost	Contemporary Events
1616	Publication of the *Treatise on the Love of God*.		February 26: Galileo Galilei meets with Cardinal Robert Bellarmine to discuss Copernican theory, and they part on good terms. April 23: Death of William Shakespeare in Stratford-upon-Avon (England).
1616–1619	Following the foundation in Lyons (1615), further expansion of the Visitation Order in France, with Mother de Chantal founding monasteries in Moulins (1616), Grenoble (1618), Bourges (1618), and Paris (1619). When Francis de Sales died in 1622, there were thirteen monasteries, and at the death of Mother de Chantal in 1641, there were eighty-six foundations.		
1617	November 29: First "Last Will and Testament" of Francis de Sales.		Savoy goes to war against Spain; the Duke of Savoy gives up claims to Monferrato and Mantua in exchange for the return of Vercelli to Savoy.
1618	October 9–16: Pope Paul V approves the new constitutions of the Visitation, and erects the community as a religious Order.		May 23: The Defenestration of Prague and the beginning of the Thirty Years War. (Savoy immediately joins war against the Habsburgs.)

Year	Lives of Francis de Sales and Jane de Chantal	The Salesian Pentecost	Contemporary Events
1618–1619	November 1618–September 1619: Francis de Sales is in Paris for the marriage of the Prince of Piedmont with Christine of France and for the foundation of the first Paris Visitation monastery. Vincent de Paul is introduced to Francis, who subsequently appoints him as ecclesiastical superior of the first Paris Visitation.		
1620			November 11: Settlement of Plymouth in New England by English separatists from Netherlands.
1621			September 17: Jesuit theologian and cardinal Robert Bellarmine dies in Rome.
1622	November 6: Francis dictates his second "Last Will and Testament." December 28: Bishop Francis de Sales dies in Lyons.		March 12: Canonization of Ignatius Loyola, Francis Xavier, Isidore of Madrid, Teresa of Jesus, and Philip Neri.
1623	January 24: Translation of Bishop de Sales's mortal remains and funeral in Annecy.		
1625			Foundation of the Congregation of the Mission (Vincentians) by Vincent de Paul.
1626			Pope Urban VIII gives pontifical recognition to the Visitation of Holy Mary.
1627	Beatification process of Francis de Sales begins.		July 22: Celse-Bénigne de Rabutin-Chantal dies in combat at Ile de Ré.

Year	Lives of Francis de Sales and Jane de Chantal	The Salesian Pentecost	Contemporary Events
1629	Mother de Chantal publishes Francis de Sales's conferences, the *Entretiens Spirituels*, in Lyons.		End of the French Wars of Religion. October 2: Death of Cardinal Pierre de Bérulle.
1631	Foundation of the Visitation Monastery of Troyes.		
1632	Reintroduction of Francis's cause of beatification, suspended because of the plague of 1629.		
1633			Foundation of the Company of the Daughters of Charity by Vincent de Paul and Louise de Marillac.
1641	December 12: Death of Mother Jane Frances de Chantal.		
1642			Foundation of the Society of the Priests of Saint Sulpice by Jean-Jacques Olier.
1647	Birth of Margaret Mary Alacoque, Burgundy, France.		
1653			Condemnation of Jansenism.
1656	Pope Alexander VII personally reintroduces the process of beatification, suspended due to procedural difficulties.		
1660			September 27: Death of Vincent de Paul.
1661	December 28: Alexander VII beatifies Francis de Sales.		
1665	April 19: Pope Alexander VII canonizes Francis de Sales.		

Year	Lives of Francis de Sales and Jane de Chantal	The Salesian Pentecost	Contemporary Events
1672	Jacques Harel, Minim friar, publishes Francis de Sales's collected evangelization leaflets from his mission in the Chablais (1594–1598), under the title *Controversies*. November 6: Margaret Mary Alacoque professes her first vows.		
1673–1675	Margaret Mary Alacoque's visions of the Sacred Heart, Visitation Monastery at Paray-le-Monial, France.		
1687			Condemnation of Quietism.
1690	Death of Sr. Margaret Mary Alacoque.		
1715–1772			Publication of the *Encyclopedia* by Denis Diderot, Jean le Rond d'Alembert, and others, spreading Enlightenment ideas.
1732			Foundation of the Redemptorist Order, by Alphonsus Liguori, Naples.
1733			Publication of Voltaire's *Letters on the English*.
1737			Canonization of Vincent de Paul by Pope Clement XII.
1740			Publication of David Hume's *A Treatise of Human Nature*.
1754			Publication of Jean-Jacques Rousseau's *Discourse on Inequality*.
1762			Publication of Jean-Jacques Rousseau's *The Social Contract*.

Year	Lives of Francis de Sales and Jane de Chantal	The Salesian Pentecost	Contemporary Events
1764			Publication of Voltaire's *Philosophical Dictionary*.
1767	August 21: Clement XIII canonizes Mother de Chantal, on Francis's two hundredth birthday.		
1769			Birth of Napoleon Bonaparte, Corsica.
1773			Suppression of the Jesuit Order by the Holy See.
1775–1783			American Revolution.
1781			Publication of Immanuel Kant's *Critique of Pure Reason*.
1786			Birth of John Vianney, Ars, France.
1789–1799			French Revolution.
1790		Birth of Pierre-Marie Mermier, Chaumont, Savoy.	
1791			France embraces a Constitutional Monarchy.
1792			Proclamation of the French Republic.
1793		Birth of Marie-Thérèse Chappuis, Soyhières, Switzerland.	Execution of Louis XVI.
1793–1794			Reign of Terror.
1795–1799			The Directory.
1798			Imprisonment of Pope Pius VI.
1799			Napoleon Bonaparte serves as First Consul of France (through 1804).

Year	Lives of Francis de Sales and Jane de Chantal	The Salesian Pentecost	Contemporary Events
1801			Concordat between Napoleon and Pope Pius VII.
1811		Birth of Joseph Cafasso, Castelnuovo d'Asti, Sardinia.	
1814		Marie-Thérèse Chappuis enters the Visitation Monastery in Fribourg, Switzerland.	Restoration of the Jesuits by Pope Pius VII. May 24: Establishment of the Feast of Mary Help of Christians by Pope Pius VII.
1814–1815			Congress of Vienna. Restoration in Italian peninsula. New map of Europe. Louis XVIII and the Bourbon Restoration.
1815		June 23: Birth of John Bosco, Becchi, Piedmont.	Defeat of Napoleon at Waterloo.
1816		Marie-Thérèse Chappuis professes her first vows and becomes Sr. Mary de Sales.	Foundation of the Marianist Sisters by William Joseph Chaminade, Bordeaux, France.
1817		Birth of Louis Brisson, Plancy, France.	Foundation of the Marianists by William Joseph Chaminade, Bordeaux, France.
1820		Birth of Louis Gaston de Ségur, Paris, France.	
1821			Death of Napoleon Bonaparte, St. Helena.
1824		Birth of Gaspard Mermillod, Carouge, Switzerland.	
1829		Birth of Caroline Colchen, Metz, France.	

Year	Lives of Francis de Sales and Jane de Chantal	The Salesian Pentecost	Contemporary Events
1830			Abdication of Charles X of France. July Monarchy, followed by the establishment of the Constitutional Monarchy in France under Louis Philippe I.
1833			Foundation of the lay Society of St. Vincent de Paul by Frederic Ozanam.
1835		Seminarian Louis Brisson meets Mother Mary de Sales Chappuis for the first time.	
1837		Birth of Maria Mazzarello, Mornese, Piedmont.	
1838		Foundation of the Missionaries of St. Francis de Sales (Fransalians) by Pierre-Marie Mermier at Annecy, Savoy. Congregation of Sister of the Cross of Chavanod founded by Pierre Mermier and Claudine Echernier. Birth of Henri Chaumont, Paris, France.	
1840		Louis Brisson is ordained to the priesthood and becomes confessor and professor at the Visitation Monastery's boarding school in Troyes.	
1841		Caroline Colchen enters a boarding school run by the Order of the Visitation.	

Year	Lives of Francis de Sales and Jane de Chantal	The Salesian Pentecost	Contemporary Events
1842		Birth of Dominic Savio.	
1843		Fr. Brisson is appointed confessor of the Visitation Monastery at Troyes. Mother Mary de Sales Chappuis predicts his future founding of the Oblates.	
1844		Birth of Léonie Aviat, Sézanne, France.	
1845		Fr. Louis Brisson receives an apparition of our Lord in the parlor of the Visitation Monastery at Troyes.	
1846			Apparition of the Virgin Mary at La Salette, France.
1848			Revolution of 1848. Proclamation of the Second Republic.
1849		Caroline Colchen marries Paul Carré.	
1852		Mme Carré gives birth to Eugénie, who dies after four days.	Beginning of the Second French Empire under Napoleon III (through 1870).
1854	St. Francis de Sales is named Patron of the Deaf and Hearing Impaired in an apostolic brief issued by Pope Pius IX.		Proclamation of the dogma of the Immaculate Conception by Pope Pius IX.
1855		Mme Carré gives birth to a son, Paul.	
1857		Death of Dominic Savio.	

Year	Lives of Francis de Sales and Jane de Chantal	The Salesian Pentecost	Contemporary Events
1858			Daughter of Charity Catherine Labouré receives visions of the Virgin Mary revealing the "Miraculous Medal," rue du Bac, Paris. Apparitions of Our Lady at Lourdes, southwest France.
1859		Establishment of the St. Francis de Sales Association for the Defense and Preservation of the Faith. Foundation in Turin of the Salesians of Don Bosco (Society of St. Francis de Sales). Mme Carré gives birth to Léon. Henri Chaumont enters the Seminary at Issy.	Death of John Vianney, the curé d'Ars.
1860		Henri Chaumont transfers to the Seminary at Saint-Sulpice, where he studies the works of St. Francis de Sales. Death of Joseph Cafasso, Turin.	
1862		Death of Pierre Mermier. Henri Chaumont is ordained a deacon.	
1863		Léon Carré dies at age three.	
1864		Henri Chaumont is ordained to the priesthood and is named the vicar of the Church of Saint-Marcel-de-l'Hôpital in Paris.	

Year	Lives of Francis de Sales and Jane de Chantal	The Salesian Pentecost	Contemporary Events
1867		Fr. Henri Chaumont begins to outline the Rule of the future Daughters of St. Francis de Sales.	
1868		Consecration of Don Bosco's Church of Mary Help of Christians, Turin-Valdocco. Fr. Henri Chaumont's illness and subsequent pilgrimage to Annecy.	
1869		Fr. Henri Chaumont hears Caroline Carré's confession at the Church of St. Clotilde, Paris, and immediately recognizes her as a potential partner in his desire to create a lay organization under the patronage of St. Francis de Sales.	
1869–1870			First Vatican Council.
1870			Franco-Prussian War. Declaration of the Third French Republic.
1871		Foundation of the Oblate Sisters of St. Francis de Sales, with Léonie Aviat (Sr. Frances de Sales) as superior.	Paris Commune (April–May). Unification of Italy with capital transferred to Rome; King Victor Emmanuel and government enter the city.

Year	Lives of Francis de Sales and Jane de Chantal	The Salesian Pentecost	Contemporary Events
1872		Foundation of the Daughters of Mary, Help of Christians (Salesian Sisters), Mornese, Piedmont. Foundation of the Society of St. Francis de Sales, including the Daughters of St. Francis de Sales, Paris, France.	
1873		October 12: Bishop Ravinet presents the Oblate religious habit to Frs. Brisson, Gilbert, Rollin, Lambert, Lambey, and Perrot. The nascent Daughters of St. Francis de Sales have their first meeting at the Maison de la Petite Oeuvre.	
1874		Mme Carré is elected Mother Superior for Life of the Daughters of St. Francis de Sales. She begins an extended period of "exile" in Rouen, away from her community, and also visits Mother Chappuis during this year.	

Year	Lives of Francis de Sales and Jane de Chantal	The Salesian Pentecost	Contemporary Events
1875		Death of Mother Mary de Sales Chappuis. Foundation of the Oblates of St Francis de Sales at Troyes with the *Decretum Laudis* or official papal decree of approbation of December 21, 1875, issued by Pope Pius IX. First mission expedition of Salesians to America. Foundation of the Priests of St. Francis de Sales by Fr. Henri Chaumont.	Construction begins on the Basilica of the Sacred Heart, Paris.
1876		The first Oblate Fathers (Brisson, Gilbert, Rollin, Lambert, Lambey, and Perrot) profess their first vows. Union of Salesian Lay Cooperators is founded in Turin.	
1877	July 7: Pius IX declares Francis de Sales a doctor of the universal church, with the official announcement following on November 16.		
1879		Mme Carré returns from Rouen to Paris.	
1880		Mme Carré is diagnosed with cancer.	

Timeline

Year	Lives of Francis de Sales and Jane de Chantal	The Salesian Pentecost	Contemporary Events
1881		Pope Leo XIII meets with Fr. Brisson and asks him (i.e., the Oblates) to help with the mission work of the church. Death of Archbishop Louis Gaston de Ségur. Death of Maria Mazzarello.	
1882		The Congregation of the Oblates of St. Francis de Sales is placed under the jurisdiction of the Congregation for the Propagation of the Faith. September 2: Fr. John Simon, Fr. Jouaux, and Brother Giraud become the first three Oblate Missionaries (in South Africa)	
1885		Mme Carré's son Paul dies following an accident.	
1887		December 7: The Oblate Constitutions are approved by Rome *ad experimendum* for a period of ten years.	
1888		Death of Don Bosco.	
1889		Establishment of the Salesian Missionaries of Mary Immaculate; their first mission is to India.	

NINETEENTH-CENTURY SALESIAN PENTECOST

Year	Lives of Francis de Sales and Jane de Chantal	The Salesian Pentecost	Contemporary Events
1891		Death of Mme Caroline Carré de Malberg.	Publication of *Rerum Novarum* by Pope Leo XIII, the first of the Catholic social encyclicals, written in the context of industrialization.
1892		Death of Cardinal Gaspard Mermillod.	
1893		Fr. Joseph Marechaux becomes the first Oblate to work in the United States.	
1893–1914			Modernist Crisis in the Catholic Church.
1896		Death of Fr. Henri Chaumont.	
1897		July 27: Final approval of the Constitutions of the Oblates of St. Francis de Sales. July 27: Mother Mary de Sales Chappuis is declared Venerable and her cause for beatification is introduced. December 8: Oblates are granted Final Approbation as a religious congregation.	
1898		Foundation of the Sons of St. Francis de Sales.	
1908		Death of Fr. Louis Brisson.	
1909		Formal introduction of the cause for the beatification of Mme Carré under Pope Pius X.	

Timeline

Year	Lives of Francis de Sales and Jane de Chantal	The Salesian Pentecost	Contemporary Events
1911		The Constitutions of the Oblate Sisters are given final approval by Rome. The Constitutions of the Daughters of St. Francis de Sales are approved by the Holy See.	
1914		Death of Léonie Aviat (Mother Frances de Sales).	Completion of the Basilica of the Sacred Heart, Paris.
1914–1918			The "Great War" (World War I)
1919			Consecration of the Basilica of the Sacred Heart, Paris.
1920	St. Margaret Mary Alacoque is canonized by Pope Benedict XV.		
1923	January 26: Pius XI proclaims Francis de Sales heavenly patron of journalists and Catholic writers.		
1929		Beatification of Don Bosco.	
1934		Canonization of Don Bosco.	
1938		The cause for the beatification of Fr. Louis Brisson is introduced.	
1939–1945			World War II.
1947		Canonization of Joseph Cafasso.	
1951		Canonization of Maria Mazzarello.	
1954		Canonization of Dominic Savio.	

Year	Lives of Francis de Sales and Jane de Chantal	The Salesian Pentecost	Contemporary Events
1957		The cause for the beatification of Mother Léonie Frances de Sales Aviat is introduced.	
1986	Pope John Paul II visits Lyons and Annecy to pay special tribute to St. Francis de Sales and the entire Salesian Family.		
1992		Mother Léonie Frances de Sales Aviat is beatified by Pope John Paul II.	
2001		Blessed Léonie Frances de Sales Aviat is canonized by Pope John Paul II.	
2012		Fr. Louis Brisson is beatified with Cardinal Angelo Amato, SDB, presiding on behalf of Pope Benedict XVI.	
2014		May 9: Caroline Colchen Carré de Malberg is declared Venerable by Pope Francis.	

NOTES

1. INTRODUCTION: THE NINETEENTH-CENTURY SALESIAN PENTECOST

1. Cited in the testimony of Mlle Stiltz in the *Meten. Beatificationis et Canonizationis Servae Dei Carolae Barbarae Colchen Carré de Malberg Fundatricia Societatis Filiarum S. Francisci Salesii, Positio super Introductione Causae* (Rome: Ex Typographia Polyglotta: S. C. de Propaganda Fide, 1906), 156.

2. *The long nineteenth century* is a term coined for the period between the years 1789 and 1914 by Russian literary critic and author Ilya Ehrenburg and British Marxist historian and author Eric Hobsbawm. It refers to the period beginning with the French Revolution, which sought to establish universal and egalitarian citizenship, until the outbreak of World War I, after which the long enduring European power balance of the century was eliminated. In terms of the history of the Catholic Church, Jesuit historian John O'Malley has proposed that the death of Pope Pius XII in 1958 is the terminus of the era in which papal centralization was achieved in opposition to the increasingly centralized nation states and revolutionary movements. That era begins with the emergence of secular and often antireligious ideas within nations and ends with new thinking entering the church after the election of Pope John XIII (1881–1963) and Vatican II. See John W. O'Malley, SJ, *What Happened at Vatican II?* (Cambridge, MA: Harvard University Press, 2010).

3. In this book we will follow the convention of citing those persons who have been canonized or beatified with the English versions of their names. Thus, Saints François de Sales, Jeanne de Chantal, and Marguerite-Marie Alacoque will be referred to as Francis de Sales, Jane de Chantal, and Margaret Mary Alacoque. In addition, English language versions will be given to other figures whose names are commonly translated within the religious communities to which they belonged. An example is Marie de Sales Chappuis, who is commonly known among Oblates of Saint Francis de Sales as Mary de Sales

Chappuis. Other less familiar figures will retain the form of their names in their original languages. For example: Henri Chaumont and Maria Mazzarello.

4. The phrase was coined by Henri l'Honoré, OSFS, in "Ramifications de la famille salésienne," *L'Unidivers Salésien: Saint François de Sales hier et aujourd'hui*, textes réunites et publiés par Hélène Bordes et Jacques Hennequin (Paris: Université de Metz, 1994), 459–71.

5. An alternate version of the divine gift of the Holy Spirit is found in John 20:19.

6. Nancy Davenport, "The Cult of Philomena in Nineteenth Century France: Art and Ideology," *Religion and the Arts* 2, no. 2 (1998): 123–48.

7. On the profile of Catholic reformation saints, see R. Po-Chia Hsia, *The World of Catholic Renewal 1540–1770* (Cambridge: Cambridge University Press, 1998), 122–37. While Francis was not primarily a wonder-worker saint, he was deemed responsible after his death for the healing of the infamous possessed prioress of the Ursulines of Loudun, Jeanne des Anges. See the account by her exorcist Jean-Joseph Surin, *Into the Dark Night and Back: The Mystical Writings of Jean-Joseph Surin*, ed. Moshe Sluovsky, trans. Patricia M. Ranum, Jesuit Studies 19 (London: Brill, 2019), esp. 453–55.

8. The critical edition of Francis de Sales's work is *Oeuvres de Saint François de Sales*, édition complète par les soins des Religieuses de la Monastère de la Visitation, XXVII vol. (Annecy: J. Nierat, 1892–1964). This is referred to as the Annecy edition and afterward here is referred to as *OEA*. Additionally, see *Saint François de Sales, Oeuvres*, textes présentés et annotés par André Ravier, Bibliotheque de la Pléiade (Éditions Gallimard, 1969). This latter contains critical treatments of de Sales's major published works and is known as the Pléiade edition.

9. Francis was known as the Doctor of Divine Love from the time of his beatification. The title was reprised in the twentieth century by Pope St. Paul VI and Pope St. John Paul II and continues to be used today.

10. Religious emblems can be seen as "visual exegesis" that express the "ingenuity and theological subtlety" of the mysteries of Sacred Scripture itself. Agnes Guideroni, "Exegetical Immersion: The Festivities on the Occasion of Francis de Sales' Canonization (1665–1667)," in *Imago Exegetica: Visual Images as Exegetical Instruments, 1400–1700*, ed. Walter S. Melion et al, Intersections: Interdisciplinary Studies in Early Modern Culture 33 (Boston: Brill, 2014), 855–84.

11. Francis's canonization was vigorously promoted by Jane de Chantal's secretary, Mère de Chaugy. On the latter's travails and insistent work, see Marie-

Notes

Patricia Burns, VHM, *Françoise-Madeleine de Chaugy: dans l'ombre et la lumère de la canonisation de François de Sales* (Annecy: Académie Salésienne, 2002), and Ernestine Lecouturier, *Françoise-Madeleine de Chaugy et la tradition salésienne au XVIIe siècle* (Paris: Bloud et Gay, 1933). Mère de Chaugy was also responsible for writing a crucial memoir of Jane for the Visitation communities. See Sainte Jeanne-Françoise Frémyot de Chantal, *Sa vie et ses oeuvres, Édition authentique publiée par les soins des religieuses du monastère de la Visitation Sainte Marie d'Annecy* (Paris: Plon, 1875). The eight-volume set of *Sa vie et ses oeuvres* by the Annecy Visitandines is generally referred to as the Plon edition. Vol. 1 is *Mémoire sur la vie et les vertus de Sainte Jeanne de Chantal par le Mère Françoise-Madeleine de Chaugy.* Jane's own deposition for the canonization of her mentor is found in volume 3 of that collection and has been translated into English by Elisabeth Stopp, *Saint Francis de Sales: A Testimony by St. Chantal* (London: Faber and Faber, 1967).

12. On the Missionaries, see Francis Moget, MSFS, *The Missionaries of Saint Francis de Sales of Annecy* (Bangalore, India: SFS Publications, 1985). Also see Adrien Duval, *Monsieur Mermier 1790–1862: Founder of Two Religious Congregations*, trans. Vincent Kerns (Bangalore, India: SFS Publications, 1985).

13. The anastatic reprint of Don Bosco's published works (he published from 1884 into the late 1880s) is in thirty-eight volumes: Giovanni Bosco, *Opere edite, Ristampa anastatica*, vols. 1–37, *Prima Serie: Libri e Opuscoli*, Centro Studi Don Bosco, Universita Pontificia Salesiana (Roma: LAS, 1976–77); and *Opere edite, Ristampa anastatica*, vol. 38, *Seconda Serie: Contributi su giornali e periodici*, Studi Don Bosco, Università Pontificia Salesiana (Rome: LAS, 1987). Critical editions of Bosco's unpublished works continue to be issued.

14. Domenico Agasso, *Maria Mazarello: The Spirit of Joy*, trans. Louise Passaro (Boston: Pauline Books and Media, 1996).

15. For a full account of Chaumont's life and ministry, consult Msgr. Laveille, *L'Abbé Henri Chaumont, fondateur de trois sociétés salésiennes (1838–1896)* (Tours: Maison Alfred Mame/Paris: Pierre Téqui, 1919). A recent biography is Daniel Moulinet, *Au Coeur du monde, Henri Chaumont, un prêtre dans l'Esprit de Jésus.* An English language version of this work is trans. Suzanne Gasster-Carrière as *Henri Chaumont: A Priest Living the Spirit of Jesus in the Heart of the World* (Create Space Independent Publishing, 2016).

16. See Msgr. Laveille, *Madame Carré de Malberg (Vénérable Caroline-Barbe Colchen), Fondatrice de la Société des Filles de Saint-François-de-Sales (1828–1891)* (Paris: Téqui, 1925) and Laveille, *L'Abbé Henri Chaumont, La*

Première Mère des Filles de Saint-François de Sales, 3rd ed. (Paris: Au Siège de la Société, 1900).

17. See Louis Brisson, *Vie de la Vénérée Mère Marie de Sales Chappuis de l'ordre de la Visitation Sainte-Marie* (Paris: Chez M. l'Aumonier de la Visitation, 1891) and the *Life of the Venerable Mother Mary de Sales Chappuis of the Order of the Visitation of Holy Mary (1793–1875)*, trans. the Sisters of the Visitation (Brooklyn, 1924).

18. On the Catholic Association and details of its work in Troyes, see Yvon Beaudoin, OMI, *Father Louis Brisson (1817–1908): A Documented Biography*, trans. several De Sales Oblates, ed. Alexander T. Pocetto, OSFS, and Daniel P. Wisniewski, OSFS (Wilmington, DE: Oblates of St. Francis de Sales, 2008), 39–64. See also *Cor ad Cor: Meditations for Every Day of the Year from the Teachings of Father Louis Brisson*, trans. Joseph E. Woods, OSFS (Philadelphia: William T. Cooke Publishing, 1955).

19. Marie-Aimée D'Esmauges, *To Forget Myself Entirely: Léonie Aviat, Mère Françoise de Sales 1844–1914*, trans. Oblate Sisters of Francis de Sales of Childs, Maryland (Wilmington, DE: Litho Print, 1991), 38.

20. This is the era in which the Catholic social teaching tradition first emerged, marked by the 1891 promulgation of Leo XIII's *Rerum Novarum* on the rights and duties of capital and labor.

21. Dirk Koster, OSFS, *Louis Brisson* (Noorden: Bert Post, 2007), chronicles Louis Brisson's peregrinations and his repeated consultations with varied members of the Salesian Pentecost.

22. Koster, *Louis Brisson*, 158.

23. *Annales de l'Oeuvres de Marie Immaculée*, archives of the Société des Filles de Saint François Sales, Paris.

24. Laveille, *L'Abbé Henri Chaumont*, 153.

25. Laveille, *L'Abbé Henri Chaumont*, 151.

26. This unity in diversity is quintessentially Salesian. Francis de Sales wrote, "God draws the wonderful variety of people and things in seasons, generations, centuries, each in its order as they were meant to be. The supreme order of God's activity is the reverse only of confusion, of disorder, NOT of distinction or variety; on the contrary, it makes use of these to constitute beauty… which is made up of every created thing, visible and invisible, all these things, taken together, are called the universe—perhaps because their diversity amounts to unity. It was as though we were saying *unidivers*; that is to say, unique and diverse, uniquely distinct or distinctly unique." *Treatise on the Love of God*, bk. 2, ch. 2. *OEA* IV, *Traité de l'amour de Dieu* I, 93.

Notes

27. For an overview of the entire Salesian tradition, see Wendy M. Wright, *Heart Speaks to Heart: The Salesian Tradition* (Maryknoll, NY: Orbis Press, 2004).

28. On Francis de Sales's approach to evangelization, esp. the use of the Forty Hours devotion, see Jill Fehleison, *Boundaries of Faith: Catholics and Protestants in the Diocese of Geneva* (Kirksville, MO: Truman State University Press, 2010).

29. For de Sales as preacher, see *On the Preacher and Preaching: A Letter by Francis de Sales*, trans. John K. Ryan (Chicago: Henry Regnery Co, 1964). The original 1604 letter to André Frémyot that exhaustively describes de Sales's approach to preaching is found in *OEA* XII, *Lettres* II, 299–325.

30. See Viviane Mellinghoff-Bourgerie, *François de Sales (1567–1622), un homme de lettres spirituelles: Culture—Tradition—Epistolairité* (Geneva: Droz, 1999).

31. On Francis as spiritual guide, see Francis Vincent, *St. François de Sales, Directeur d'âmes: l'éducation de la volonté* (Paris: Beauchesne, 1923) and *Francis de Sales and Jane de Chantal: Letters of Spiritual Direction*, trans. Péronne-Marie Thibert, VHM, ed. Joseph F. Power and Wendy M. Wright (Mahwah, NJ: Paulist Press, 1988).

32. Of the many works on the early Visitation, perhaps the most central are *Visitation et Vistandines aux XVIIe aux XVIIIe siècles (Actes de Colloque d'Annecy, 1999)*, études réunies et presentées par Bernard Dompier et Dominque Julia (Saint-Étienne: Publications de l'Université de Saint-Étienne, 2001); Roger Devos, *L'origine sociale des Vistandines d'Annecy aux XVIIe et XVIIIe siècles* (Annecy: Académie Salésienne, 1973); Marie-Ange Duvignacq-Glessgen, *L'Ordre de la Visitation à Paris aux XVIIe et XVIIIe siècles* (Paris: Cerf, 1994). See also Wendy M. Wright, "The Visitation of Holy Mary: The First Years," in *Religious Orders of the Catholic Reformation: In Honor of John C. Olin on His Seventy-Fifth Birthday*, ed. Richard L. DeMolen (New York: Fordham University Press, 1994), 217–52.

33. De Sales's theological knowledge was wide and deep. On his sources and the way in which he integrated a range of perspectives to arrive at his own synthesis, see Hélène Bordes, "Une pensée forgée dans le crueset de l'humanisme et de la Renaissance," in *François de Sales, prophète de l'Amour* (Epinay-sur-Seine, C.I.F., 1982), 12a–15c. His vision of a world of hearts was especially marked by its leanings toward the thought of Jesuit Luis de Molina (1563–1600) on grace and free will that posited that God intends all persons for salvation, providing sufficient grace for salvation but also free will and the capacity to

choose other than to respond to divine love. He was indebted as well to the medieval Franciscans, especially Duns Scotus (d. 1308), on the incarnation, the Immaculate Conception, the linkage between creation, incarnation, and redemption, and *haecceitas*, or "thisness."

34. On Francis as scriptural exegete, see especially Terence McGoldrick, "The Living Word: Francis de Sales, A Humanist Biblical Theologian of the Renaissance," in *Love Is the Perfection of the Mind: Salesian Studies Presented to Alexander T. Pocetto OSFS on the Occasion of His 90th Birthday*, ed. Joseph F. Chorpenning, Thomas F. Dailey, and Daniel P. Wisnewski (Center Valley, PA: Salesian Center for Faith and Culture, 2017), 83–102; Anthony R. Ceresko, OSFS, *St. Francis and the Bible* (Bangalore, India: SFS Publications, 2005); and André Ravier, "Saint François de Sales et la Bible," in *Le Grand siècle et le Bible*, ed. Jean-Robert Armogathe (Paris: Beauchesne, 1989), 617–27.

35. On Francis de Sales and the Song of Songs, see André Brix, *François de Sales commente le Cantique des Cantiques* (Crapone: Le Messager, 1965); *The Mystical Exposition of the Canticle of Canticles*, trans. Thomas F. Daily (Center Valley, PA: Allentown College, 1996); and Anthony R. Ceresko, OSFS, "The Interpretation of the Song of Songs in St. Francis de Sales: How a Saint Learned 'the Lessons of Love,'" *Salesianum* 66 (2004): 31–50. Francis's original commentary is found in *OEA XXVI, Opuscules V*, 10–39.

36. Wendy M. Wright, "'That Is What It Is Made For': The Image of the Heart in the Spirituality of Francis de Sales and Jane de Chantal," in *Spiritualities of the Heart: Approaches to Personal Wholeness in Christian Tradition*, ed. Annice Callahan, RSCJ (Mahwah, NJ: Paulist Press, 1990), 143–58.

37. Most scholars accept that the Savoyard held the Molinist position on grace and free will. While this was an important theological perspective in his day, a more nuanced discussion of de Sales on the question of grace and free will and predestination is found in Eunan McDonnell, *The Concept of Freedom in the Writings of St. Francis de Sales* (New York: Peter Lang, 2009), 62–77.

38. Wright, *Heart Speaks to Heart*, 33.

39. There is no one definitive list of the Salesian "little virtues," but gentleness and humility are always among those included. See Vincent, *Francis de Sales and Jane de Chantal: Letters of Spiritual Direction*, 62–69, and Thomas McHugh, "The Distinctive Salesian Virtues: Humility and Gentleness," *Salesian Studies* (October 1963): 45–74. "Little virtues" is commonly used in English to refer to this cluster of virtues so prized by Francis de Sales and Jane de Chantal. The term does not translate back into French well, as it tends to evoke a woman of "little virtue."

40. *Introduction to the Devout Life*, bk. 3, ch. 1. *OEA*, II, *Introduction à la vie dévote*, I, 209–17.

41. See Thomas A. Donlan, *François de Sales and Militant French Catholicism* (St. Andrews, UK: St. Andrews University Press, 2018). Historians have expanded the traditional 1562–1589 dates of the Wars of Religion. See Donlan, "Oasis of Gentleness in a Desert of Militancy: François de Sales's Contribution to French Catholicism," in *Surrender to Christ for Mission: French Spiritual Traditions*, ed. Philip Sheldrake (Collegeville, MN: Liturgical Press, 2018), 90–108.

42. Protestant-raised Henry of Navarre (1553–1610) was, according to Salic law, the rightful successor to the throne of France following the death of Henry III (1551–89). Huguenots (French Calvinists), who were a sizeable, well-placed minority, were pitted against Catholics, who in turn were viciously divided among themselves around the question of succession, moderates vs. the militant and zealous Holy League.

43. Thomas Donlan (n. 41) has argued that de Sales's pastoral approach can be primarily linked to his encounters during the Wars of Religion. But the Savoyard also seems to have reflected his natal land's tendency to seek political, religious, and diplomatic compromises. Duke Emmanuel Philibert of Savoy (1528–80) especially sought peace internally and externally. Although he was faith filled, he felt that unity in his country was paramount and did not threaten or persecute the Protestant minority. He also sought peace with neighboring Calvinist Geneva. See Maria José Savoia, *Emanuele Filiberto di Savoia: un valoroso guerriero, un principe illuminato* (Milan: Rusconi Libri, 1994), 212–17.

44. The frequency of collaboration between men and women in seventeenth- through nineteenth-century France is striking. Vincent de Paul and Louise de Marillac and Jane de Chantal and Francis de Sales are perhaps the most well-known examples. But there were many more. See Mary Christine Morkovsky, CDP, "Women and the French School of Spirituality," in Sheldrake, *Surrender to Christ for Mission*, 109–26.

45. Barbara B. Diefendorf, in her *From Penitence to Charity: Pious Women and the Catholic Reformation in Paris* (New York: Oxford University Press, 2004), demonstrates how among elite Parisian women the penitential mood of the Wars of Religion gradually gave way to a new style of piety focused on charitable social action.

46. On Francis as exponent of mystical theology, see Terence O'Reilly, "The Mystical Theology of Saint Francis de Sales in the *Traité de l'amour de Dieu*," in *Mysticism in the French Tradition: Eruptions from France*, ed. Louise Nelstrop and Bradley B. Onishi (Burlington, VT: Ashgate, 2015): 207–20;

Hélène Michon, *Saint François de Sales, une nouvelle mystique* (Paris: Cerf, 2008); and Wendy M. Wright, "He Opened His Side: Francis de Sales and the Exchange of Divine and Human Hearts," in *Mysticism and Contemporary Life: Essays in Honor of Bernard McGinn*, ed. John J. Markey and J. August Higgins (New York: Crossroad, 2019), 183–204.

47. *Introduction to the Devout Life*, part 3, ch. 23. *OEA*, III, *Introduction à la vie dévote*, vol. 2, 216–17.

48. On the opened heart, see Francis's sermon of 1616 that references the contemporary French custom of displaying the opened heart of a recently deceased ruler, and concludes that at the time when the Lord laid down his life for his friends, he in fact commanded that his side should be opened so that the thoughts of his heart—of special love for his beloved children—might be made visible so that they might see his desire to give them his grace and blessings and to give them his own heart. *OEA*, IX, *Sermons* III, 79–80.

49. On the biography by Jean Goulu, see Elisabeth Stopp, "The First Biography (1624)," in *A Man to Heal Differences: Essays and Talks on St. Francis de Sales* (Philadelphia: St. Joseph's University Press, 1997), 149–53.

50. Th. Schueller, *La femme et le saint: la femme et ses problèmes d'après saint François de Sales* (Paris: Les Éditions Ouvrières, 1970), and Linda Timmermans, *L'accès des femmes à la culture (1598–1715): Un débat d'idées de Saint François de Sales à la Marquise de Lambert* (Paris: Éditions Champion, 1993).

51. These would be the luminaries of the movement referred to as the "French School:" Pierre de Bérulle (1575–1629), Jean-Jacques Olier (1608–57), Jean Eudes (1601–80), and Vincent de Paul, founders, respectively, of the French Oratory, the Sulpicians, the Eudists, and the Congregation of the Missions.

52. Notably the Vincentian family headed by Vincent de Paul (1581–1660) and Louise de Marillac (1591–1660), which included the Congregations of the Missions and the Daughters of Charity.

53. These include the Society of Jesus and the Discalced Carmelites. See also *Religious Orders of the Catholic Reformation*.

54. *OEA* II and III, *Introduction à la vie dévote*. Also see *Encountering Anew the Familiar: Francis de Sales' Introduction to the Devout Life at 400 Years*, ed. Joseph F. Chorpenning (Rome: International Commission for Salesian Studies, 2012).

55. It was not until the late twentieth century that the bishop's own definitive 1619 version was recirculated. It was often highly edited, reformulated, and recast to conform to others' perspectives. See Viviane Mellinghoff-Bourgerie, "Four Centuries of Editions of the Introduction to the Devout Life:

Biographical Lessons," in Chorpenning, *Encountering Anew the Familiar*, 1–22, and William C. Marceau, "Recusant Translations of Saint Francis de Sales," *The Downside Review* 114, no. 396 (1996): 221–33.

56. *OEA* VI, *Traité de l'amour de Dieu* I, 8.

57. *OEA* VI and V, *Traité de l'amour de Dieu* I and II. See William C. Marceau, *Optimism in the Works of St. Francis de Sales*, Toronto Studies in Theology, vol. 41 (Lewiston, NY: Edwin Mellen Press, 1989). De Sales held a Scotist view of the incarnation, positing that God intended the incarnate Word from the beginning out of love for creation and a desire to be in union. It was not an afterthought, or response to the fall of Adam and Eve. The crucifixion is thus not primarily a juridical issue, with infinite justice demanding infinite restitution, but a merciful and loving act of friendship that redeems humankind from the sin that God foretold would result from human free will. See especially his *Treatise on the Love of God*, bk. 2, ch. 4, *OEA* IV, *Traité de l'Amour de Dieu*, vol. I, 99–102.

58. For the incarnation as kiss see Francis's 1621 sermon for the annunciation. *OEA* X, *Sermons* IV, 41–60. An English translation is found in *The Sermons of St. Francis de Sales on Our Lady*, ed. Louis Fiorelli, vol. 2 (Rockville, IL: TAN Publishers, 1985), 135–36.

59. *OEA* IV, *Traité*, II,117.

60. See n. 31.

61. In 1618 the canonical structure of the early Visitation was altered to be more in keeping with the dictates of the Council of Trent. While its distinctive Salesian spirit was retained, it became an enclosed contemplative order. It is often argued that Francis intended to found an apostolic congregation and that his aim was thwarted by the imposition of the decrees of the Council of Trent and that Vincent de Paul's Daughters of Charity later fulfilled his aim. This is not quite accurate. The Daughters of Charity drew their members from the lower working class while the Visitation had upper-class entrants. When the Savoyard diocesan congregation was introduced into France, Denis de Marquemont, archbishop of Lyon, was a stanch supporter of Trent and, given the entrants to the Visitation, found himself unable to support a community that had only annual vows and a mitigated cloister.

62. On the significance of friendship in the Salesian tradition, see Terence McGoldrick, *The Sweet and Gentle Struggle: Francis de Sales on the Necessity of Spiritual Friendship* (Lanham, MD: University Press of America, 1996); Daniel P. Wisniewski, "Chains of Love: The Eternity of Friendship in the Spirituality of St. Francis de Sales," in Chorpenning, *Encountering Anew the Familiar*, 95–110.

63. On their friendship, see Wendy M. Wright, *Bond of Perfection: François de Sales and Jeanne de Chantal* (Mahwah, NJ: Paulist Press, 1985; enhanced edition, Stella Niagara, NY: De Sales Resource Center, 2001). For an English translation of all the extant letters of Francis to Jane, see *From My Heart: Personal Messages and Self-Reflections of Francis de Sales to Jane de Chantal*, trans. Eugene Kelly, OSFS (Stella Niagara, NY: De Sales Resource Center, 2017).

64. Donlan, "Oasis of Gentleness in a Sea of Militancy."

65. The description of the Visitation mystery as a proto-Pentecost comes from René Laurentin. See Joseph F. Chorpenning, "The Dynamics of Divine Love: Francis de Sales's Picturing of the Biblical Mystery of the Visitation," in *Ut Pictura Amor: The Reflexive Imagery of Love in Artistic Theory and Practice, 1500–1700*, ed. Walter S. Melion, Joanna Woodall, and Michael Zell (Boston: Brill 2017), 485–531; and Chorpenning's "Mother of Our Savior and Cooperator in Our Salvation: *Imitatio Mariae* and the Biblical Mystery of the Visitation," *Marian Studies* 53 (2002): 63–85.

66. The idea of Jesus's redemptive activity while he was in the womb is especially associated with the French School of spirituality. For an exploration of this idea, see John Seward, *Redeemer in the Womb: Jesus Living in Mary* (San Francisco: Ignatius Press, 1993).

67. Artistic presentations of the Visitation at the time, known as the double Visitation, often portrayed the husbands Joseph and Zechariah as present at the meeting of Mary and Elizabeth. Francis sees them as part of the radiating circles of visitation that transform the world.

68. Hélène Bordes, "Méditation du Mystère de la Visitation par François de Sales et l'esprit de l'ordre de la Visitation," in *Visitation et Visitandines aux XVIIe et XVIIIe siècles*, Actes du Colloque d'Annecy 1999, études réunies et présentées par Bernard Dompnier et Dominique Julia (Publications de l'Université de Saint-Étienne, 2001), 71.

69. "Paroles consolantes," in *Sa vie et ses oeuvres*, vol. 3, *Oeuvres divers II*, 489. These words of Jane, collected by her sisters, are composed for meditation on successive days of the year as they are numbered, perhaps in imitation of the *L'Année Sainte*, the circulars that traveled between monasteries and recorded the holy lives of deceased Visitandines.

70. *OEA XXV, Opuscles IV*, 133–74. English language versions are *Spiritual Exercises by St. Francis de Sales*, trans. William N. Dougherty, intro. Joseph F. Chorpenning (Toronto: Peregrina Publishing, 1993), and St. Francis de Sales, *Spiritual Conferences*, trans. Ivo Carneiro, 2 vols. (Bangalore, India: SFS Publications, 1998). Francis's talks to the early Visitation about the practice of the

virtues are found in *OEA* VI, *Les Vrays Entretiens Spirituels*. Although the Annecy edition of his works is considered the critical one, these conferences have received a more detailed treatment in the Pléiade *Oeuvres* volume edited by Ravier, 975–1304.

71. See particularly B. Peyrous, "Les messages de Marguerite—Marie à Louis XIV," in *Saint Marguerite-Marie et le message de Paray-le-Monial*, ed. R. Darricau et B. Peyrous (Paris: Editions Desclée, 1993), 269–90, for a discussion of the widespread belief that Louis XIV himself embraced the Sacred Heart devotion.

72. See *L'Unidivers Salésien*, esp. section IV on "Influences et receptions," 333–459. On influential biographies, see Elisabeth Stopp, "The First Biography (1624)," in *A Man to Heal Differences: Essays and Talks on St. Francis de Sales by Elisabeth Stopp* (Philadelphia: Saint Joseph's University Press, 1997), 139–57. Especially influential was *l'Esprit de Saint François de Sales* by Jean-Pierre Camus (1584–1652), friend and fellow bishop of de Sales. An English translation is *The Spirit of St. Francis de Sales*, trans. Carl Franklin Kelley (London: Longmans, 1953). Margaret Mary Alacoque's visions were authenticated by her Jesuit confessor Claude de la Colombière and her story actively promoted by members of the Society of Jesus. The first biographies of the visionary were by Jesuits Jean Croiset, SJ (1656–1737), and Joseph de Gallifet, SJ (1663–1749). See E. Glotin, "Sainte Marguerite-Marie et les Jésuites," in *Sainte Marguerite-Marie et le message de Paray-le-Monial*, sous le responsibilité de R. Darricau-B. Peyrous (Paris: Éditions Desclée, 1993), 323–48.

73. Margaret Mary was canonized in 1920, somewhat beyond the scope of this study.

74. On the authoritative importance of canonization, see Vivienne Mellinghoff-Bourgerie, "François de Sales au XVIIe siècle—entre rayonnement spiritual et autorité canonisée," *Transversalites* XVII (July–September, 2004): 151–84.

75. The earlier accommodations for the Huguenot minority, established by the Edict of Nantes in 1598, were diminished under Henry IV's successor Louis XIII (1601–43) after the former's assassination in 1610. The siege of the Huguenot stronghold at La Rochelle in 1629, under Louis XIII and Richelieu, was a blow to the Protestant cause. That minority was virtually eliminated under Louis XIV, who assumed the crown in 1643 and reigned until 1715.

76. Indeed, the foundation of the Visitation monastery and the Jesuit community in Paray-le-Monial, a region of former Huguenot dominance, and

the site from which the Sacred Heart devotion was to emerge, is an example of the re-Catholicization taking place.

77. Norman Ravitch, *The Catholic Church and the French Nation 1598–1989* (New York: Routledge, 1990), 28–31.

78. It took fifty years for the decrees of the Council of Trent to be implemented in France. In part, this was because of the tumult of the Wars of Religion, in part because of the resistance of the Gallican factions of the French church opposed to Ultramontane efforts.

79. Jansenists tended to align with the Gallican faction at the Parlement of Paris, which threatened the king's absolute power, while any religious enthusiasm like Quietism was viewed with suspicion as having political impact. On Jansenism and the monarchy, see Ravitch, *The Catholic Church and the French Nation*, 12–22.

80. For an analysis of Madame Guyon in the context of the epistemological rupture taking place in the era, see Marie-Florine Bruneau, *Women Mystics Confront the Modern World: Marie de l'Incarnation (1599–1672) and Madame Guyon (1648–1717)* (Albany: State University of New York Press, 1998).

81. Tibor Bartók, "Louis Lallemant and His *Doctrine Spirituelle*: Myth and Facts," in *A Companion to Jesuit Mysticism*, ed. Robert A. Maryks (Boston: Brill, 2017), 112–38.

82. On the controversy surrounding *Abandonment*, see Wendy M. Wright, "Jean-Pierre de Caussade and the Caussadian Corpus," in Maryks, *A Companion to Jesuit Mysticism*, 193–224.

83. Indeed, the reputation of Visitandine Marie de Sales Chappuis, one of the leading lights of the Salesian Pentecost, would be clouded by such suspicions.

84. Ralph Gibson, *A Social History of French Catholicism, 1789–1914* (London: Routledge, 1989), 14–40.

85. Gibson, *Social History of French Catholicism*, 21.

86. The critical sources for Margaret-Mary are *Vie et oeuvres de Marguerite-Marie*, présentations de Professeur R. Darricau (Paris: Fribourg: Editions St. Paul, 1990 and 1991). See also *The Letters of St. Margaret-Mary Alacoque*, trans. Clarence A. Herbst (Rockford, IL: TAN Books, 1954).

87. On the general shift in the Visitation toward emphasizing abandonment, submission to the will of God's good pleasure, love of obedience, suffering, and martyrdom, see Wendy M. Wright, "The Visitation Stream of Salesian Spirituality," in Chorpenning et al., *Love Is the Perfection of the Mind*, 138–58.

Notes

88. This is the underlying claim of French scholar of mysticism Michel de Certeau in his two-volume *The Mystic Fable: The Sixteenth and Seventeenth Centuries*, trans. Michael B. Smith (Chicago: University of Chicago Press, 1992 and 2015).

89. Gibson, *A Social History of French Catholicism*, 14.

90. Clearly, such new ideas challenged the existing religious order, but it is also possible to detect sociological signs that the near universal Catholic practice of the past was already breaking down: a town and countryside dichotomy developed with urban areas and the male population and youth generally resisting attempts to impose a strict Tridentine conformity. The nobility was skeptical and open to secularization while the provincial elite, embracing capitalism, tended to abandon traditional religious culture. See Gibson, *A Social History of French Catholicism*, 3–14.

91. Ulrich L. Lehner, *The Catholic Enlightenment: The Forgotten History of a Global Movement* (New York: Oxford University Press, 2016).

92. Ravitch, *The Catholic Church and the French Nation*, 60–78.

93. Jeffrey D. Burson, "The Catholic Enlightenment in France from the *fin de siècle* Crisis of Consciousness to the Revolution, 1650–1789," in *A Companion to the Catholic Enlightenment in Europe*, ed. Ulrich L. Lerner and Michael Printy (Boston: Brill, 2010), 63–125.

94. By contemporary standards, his approach may not seem quite so pastorally sensitive: the early Redemptorists gained reputations for their thundering sermons, described as being lions in the pulpit yet lambs in the confessional.

95. It has been argued that, in fact, Liguori's theology was quite distinct from Francis's but the influence in spirit cannot be disclaimed. R. Culhane, "St. Alphonsus and St. Francis de Sales: A Contrast in Their Spirituality," *Irish Ecclesiastical Record*, LXIX (5th series), 3 (1947): 782–91.

96. Liguori worked on his great textbook for seminarians, *Moral Theology*, for nearly twenty years. It grew out of the need he perceived to elaborate a system that could steer a middle road between the opposing trends of laxism and rigorism that had been debated by theologians for some time. Early on there was vacillation between welcome reception, suspicion of, and open opposition to Ligouri's moral teaching. See R. Gallagher, CSSR, "The Systemization of Alphonsus' Moral Theology through the Manuals," *Studia Moralia* XXV, no. 2 (1987): 247–77.

97. Those considered "citizens" were males who were French, at least twenty-five years old, paid taxes equal to three days of work, and could not be

defined as servants. This led to outcries. The question of women's rights emerged as especially prominent. Nor did the 1789 Declaration revoke slavery, although the Haitian Revolution would put an end to that institution in at least one French colony only fifteen years later.

98. A detailed study of this period is Nigel Aston, *Religion and Revolution in France 1780–1804* (Washington, DC: Catholic University of America Press, 2000).

99. Ravitch, *The Catholic Church and the French Nation*, 84.

100. Ravitch, *The Catholic Church and the French Nation*, 43–46.

101. Ravitch, *The Catholic Church and the French Nation*, 58–59.

102. See Maryline Masse, "La Visitation et la dévotion au Sacré-Cœur," in *Visitation et Visitandines*, 461–82.

103. See Raymond Jonas, *France and the Cult of the Sacred Heart: An Epic Tale for Modern Times* (Berkeley: University of California Press, 2000). For the dramatic story of the disbanded Lyons Visitation community that fled to Mantua, carrying with them the devotional practices outlined by Margaret Mary Alacoque and the reliquary enshrining St. Francis de Sales's heart, *I Leave You My Heart: A Visitandine Chronicle of the French Revolution; Mother Marie Jéronyme Verot's Letter of 15 May 1794*, trans. Péronne-Marie Thibert (Philadelphia: Saint Joseph's University Press, 1999).

104. Ravitch, *The Catholic Church and the French Nation*, 66–78. A forerunner of liberal and social Catholicism, Lamennais eventually left the church disappointed at its failure to realize its potential.

105. Carol E. Harrison, *Romantic Catholics: France's Post-revolutionary Generation in Search of a Modern Faith* (Ithaca, NY: Cornell University Press, 2014). See as well Raymond L. Sickinger, "Sanctification, Solidarity and Service: The Lay Spirituality of Antoine Frederic Ozanam," in Sheldrake, *Surrender to Christ for Mission*, 143–60, and Sickenger's *Antoine Frédéric Ozanam* (Notre Dame, IN: University of Notre Dame Press, 2017).

106. Among the most well-known of these congregations of French origin were the Religious of the Sacred Heart (f. 1800), Sisters of Providence (f. 1806), Missionary Oblates of Mary Immaculate (f. 1816), The Society of Mary or Marianists (f. 1817), and Marianist Sisters (f. 1816).

107. As indicated above, collaboration between women and men in the work of ecclesial renewal was one of the hallmarks of French Catholicism during the period of the reformations. This would continue to be the case in the long nineteenth century.

108. Thomas A. Kselman, *Miracles and Prophecies in Nineteenth Century France* (New Brunswick, NJ: Rutgers University, 1983).

109. Marian apparitions across the centuries is the focus of Joachim Bouflet and Philippe Boutry, *Un signe dans le ciel: les apparitions de la Vierge* (Paris: Bernard Grasset, 1997). On Lourdes, see Ruth Cranston, *The Miracle of Lourdes* (New York: Image/Doubleday, 1988), as well as Nicolas Perry and Loreto Echeverria, *Under the Heel of Mary* (London: Routledge, 1988).

110. These included the 1571 Battle of Lepanto against the Turkish armada and the 1683 battle against the Turkish armies in Vienna. Don Bosco favored the invocation and dedicated the monumental church he had constructed at Turin to *Maria Auxilium Christianorum*.

111. Whether Catherine de Labouré's account can be described as apparitions or visions is unclear. See Bouflet and Boutry, *Un signe dans le ciel*, 108–15. In the wake of the popularization of the Miraculous Medal, a pious association for young people, the Children of Mary, was established to promote consecration to Mary and the wearing of the medal. On the significance of Marian cults, see Kselman, *Miracles and Prophesies*, 89–94. On the nineteenth-century popularity of devotional medals, consult Eli Heldaas Seland, "19th Century Devotional Medals," in *Instruments of Devotion: The Practices and Objects of Religious Piety from the Late Middle Ages to the 20th Century*, ed. Henning Laugerud and Laura Skinnebach (Denmark: Aarhus University Press, 2007), 157–72.

112. Ravitch, *The Catholic Church and the French Nation*, 80.

113. Kselman, *Miracles and Prophecies*, 106–7, 196–98.

114. Kselman, *Miracles and Prophecies*, 197.

115. The writings of de Sales, especially the *Introduction to the Devout Life*, enjoyed a popularity in the nineteenth century that went beyond the direct influence of the communities specifically named as part of the Salesian Pentecost. Well-known Catholic figures such as Carmelite Thérèse of Lisieux (1873–97) as well as lesser-known but significant persons such as lay woman Élisabeth Leseur that emerge as representative of the era, owe much of their spiritual nurture to vision of de Sales. See Wendy M Wright, "A Salesian Pentecost: Thérèse of Lisieux, Léonie Aviat and Salesian Tradition," *Studies in Spirituality* 12 (2002): 156–77, and *Elizabeth Leseur: Selected Writings*, Classics of Western Spirituality Series, ed. Janet Ruffing (Mahwah, NJ: Paulist Press, 2005).

2. PIERRE-MARIE MERMIER, JOSEPH-MARIE FAVRE, PIERRE-JOSEPH REY, AND THE MISSIONARIES OF ST. FRANCIS DE SALES OF ANNECY

1. I am deeply grateful to Fr. Yves Carron, MSFS, assistant superior general of the Fransalians and Postulator for the Cause of Pierre-Marie Mermier's Beatification, for his invaluable generous help in the preparation of this chapter. This assistance took several forms: providing a PDF of Mermier's extensive, though largely unpublished writings, which were collected and transcribed by Adrien Duval, MSFS, under the title, *Pierre-Marie Mermier: Recueil de Textes, Série I, Le Fondateur* (n.d.) (hereafter *Mermier: Recueil de Textes*); sharing the text of his "Fr. Mermier and the Usefulness of a Body of Missioners in the Diocese of Annecy," Jubilee talk, La Puya, Annecy, France, October 22, 2013 (hereafter Jubilee Talk); and reading, and offering corrections and suggestions for improvement of, an earlier draft of this chapter.

Unless otherwise indicated, all English translations are from the original French texts by the author, who thanks Dr. Suzanne Toczyski for her advice and suggestions for improvement.

2. Adrien Duval, MSFS, *Monsieur Mermier 1790–1862: Founder of Two Religious Congregations*, trans. Vincent Kerns, MSFS (Bangalore: SFS Publications, 1985), 68 (hereafter Duval 1985).

3. John Dormandy, *A History of Savoy: Gatekeeper of the Alps* (London: Fonthill, 2018), 148, 152 (hereafter Dormandy); Duval 1985, 7.

4. Dormandy, 143–67; Duval 1985, 8.

5. Duval 1985, 8, 12–18; Francis Moget, MSFS, *The Missionaries of St. Francis de Sales of Annecy* (Bangalore: SFS Publications, 1985), 12 (hereafter Moget); and Jubilee Talk.

6. Alphonsus Liguori's moral theology aimed to steer a middle course between laxism and Jansenist rigorism by winning back sinners through patience and moderation, rather than repelling them by severity and fear. Founder of the Congregation of the Most Holy Redeemer, Alphonsus wished the Redemptorists "to be lions in the pulpit but lambs in the confessional" (Patrick W. Carey, *Confession: Catholics, Repentance & Forgiveness in America* [New York: Oxford University Press, 2018], 128). While this was an improvement over existing pastoral practice, it fell short of the Salesian principle of all through love, nothing through fear or force (cf. letter of October 14, 1604, to

Notes

Madame de Chantal, in *Œuvres de saint François de Sales*, Édition complète, 27 vols. [Annecy: J. Niérat et al., 1892–1964], 12:352–70, at 359 [hereafter Annecy edition]). In fact, the Redemptorists had the reputation of being "the leading specialists in hellfire preaching," sometimes even being described as "Redempt-terrorists" (Ralph Gibson, "Hellfire and Damnation in Nineteenth-Century France," *Catholic Historical Review* 74 [1988]: 383–402, at 387). They were also considered to be severe and rigorist in their approach: see Louis Châtellier, *The Religion of the Poor: Rural Missions in Europe and the Formation of Modern Catholicism, c. 1500–1800*, trans. Brian Pearce (New York: Cambridge University Press, 1997), 192 (hereafter Châtellier). Recent scholarship has highlighted that after Liguori's death, "the Redemptorists somewhat distorted the heritage of their founder…, and they also forgot much of his message," which contrasted "with the hard-hearted reforms many [Catholic] Enlighteners proposed" (Ulrich L. Lehner, *The Catholic Enlightenment: The Forgotten History of a Global Movement* [New York: Oxford University Press, 2016], 173).

    7. Duval 1985, 5–11; Moget, 12–14.

    8. Duval 1985, 29–31; Moget, 15–18.

    9. Adrien Duval, MSFS, "At the Service of the Mission: Pierre-Marie Mermier," unpublished paper, trans. Ivo Carneiro, MSFS (1987), 4, at https://d2y1pz2y630308.cloudfront.net/19852/documents/2018/7/A.3.%20Fr%20Mermier%20at%20the%20service%20of%20the%20Mission.pdf (accessed November 24, 2021) (hereafter Duval 1987). The classic study of the parish mission in early modern Catholicism is Châtellier.

    10. An innovative method used during the Chablais mission's first phase to reach more people was the series of leaflets on the major points of Catholic doctrine that Francis wrote, possibly printed, and delivered by hand to those whom he was unable to reach by his preaching. Francis later assembled and titled these leaflets *Meditations on the Church* but did not publish them in book form during his lifetime. This collection was first published in 1672, with the title *The Controversies*, analogous to St. Robert Bellarmine's *Controversies of the Christian Faith* (1586–93), which Francis used as a reference in composing the leaflets. See Elisabeth Stopp, "*Meditations on the Church* (1595–96)," in her *A Man to Heal Differences: Essays and Talks on St. Francis de Sales* (Philadelphia: Saint Joseph's University Press, 1997), 51–74 (originally published in *Salesian Studies* 4, no. 4 [Autumn 1967]: 35–69). Unlike the Forty Hours devotion, this initiative had no impact on the mission apostolate of Favre and Mermier.

    11. See Jill R. Fehleison, "Appealing to the Senses: The Forty Hours Celebrations in the Duchy of Chablais, 1597–98," *Sixteenth Century Journal* 36, no.

2 (2005): 375–96 (hereafter Fehleison 2005), and *Boundaries of Faith: Catholics and Protestants in the Diocese of Geneva* (Kirksville, MO: Truman State University Press, 2010), 53–99 (hereafter Fehleison 2010).

12. The original of this letter is preserved in the Fransalian Archives in Rome. For a transcription, see Adrien Duval, MSFS, *Un disciple de Saint François de Sales: Pierre-Marie Mermier, 1790–1862. Pionnier de la "Mission Pastorale" en Savoie* (Annecy: Gardet, 1982), 266–68.

13. *Miserere*, an abbreviation for the penitential Psalm 51 (50) in the Vulgate: *Miserere mei, Deus,* "Have mercy on me, O God."

14. *Parce, Domine* is a penitential antiphon based on Joel 2:17: *Parce, Domine, parce populo tuo: ne in aeternum irascaris nobis,* "Spare, Lord, spare your people: Be not angry with us forever."

15. Among Favre's ceremonies, the Celebration of the Sacred Heart of Jesus stands out for its intricacy and elaborateness. Having quickly demonstrated its efficacy for bringing the faithful to frequent the sacraments of penance and the Eucharist, as well as responding to their desire for a more affective religious experience, the Sacred Heart devotion entered the world of parish missions well before its official approbation by the Holy See (1765). It was indispensable for achieving what Favre and Mermier considered to be one of the primary goals of the parish mission: to free souls from the cold rigorism of Jansenism that instilled fear of God in the faithful and discouraged reception of holy communion. See Châtellier, 119–21; Moget, 77.

16. The acclamation *Vivat Jesus!* is believed to have originated with St. Bernardine of Siena (1380–1444), an ardent promoter of devotion to the Holy Name of Jesus.

17. The "two standards" refers to the meditation invented by St. Ignatius of Loyola (1491–1556) in the *Spiritual Exercises*. It applies "to everyday life the belief, expounded vividly in the Gospel of John, that human existence is a struggle between light and dark, life and death, truth and the lie" (Joseph A. Tetlow, SJ, *The Spiritual Exercises of Ignatius Loyola with Commentary* [New York: Crossroad, 1992], 66). One standard is that of Christ, and the other of Satan. A Salesian version of this theme is found in the tenth meditation (The Election and Choice Which the Soul Makes of a Devout Life) in the *Introduction to the Devout Life*, part 1, ch. 18.

18. The ritual of the procession to the baptismal font, which would have been adorned as magnificently as possible, with the solemn renewal of baptismal promises aimed to bring parishioners to make a break with their past and

to return to God in a kind of new baptism that was almost a sacrament bestowed upon the whole community. See Châtellier, 180–81.

19. While the Mission Cross figured prominently in Favre's ceremonies, traditionally and later in the missions conducted by Mermier and the Fransalians, it was accorded even greater importance. The Mission Cross—a large cross made of wood or stone—would be planted, that is, cemented into place, so that it remained as a permanent reminder of what had been said, promised, and experienced during the mission's days of fervor. Set up in the center of the village or on the top of a hill overlooking it, it was constantly present to everyone's gaze. The Mission Cross also resacralizes the space that had been desacralized by the removal of crosses during the Revolution. See Châtellier, 109; Moget, 152, 163–64. More broadly, during the mission, as Anne Régent-Susini observes, "the landscape [was] made sacred by becoming the theatre of various devotional practices (for example, processions or sermons performed in public spaces)" ("Tears for Fears: Mission Preaching in Seventeenth-Century France—a Double Performance," in *Spoken Word and Social Practice: Orality in Europe (1400–1700)*, ed. Thomas V. Cohen and Lesley K. Twomey [Boston: Brill, 2015], 185–205, at 185).

20. The *Te Deum* (from its incipit, *Te deum laudamus*, "Thee, O God, we praise") is a Latin Christian hymn of praise and thanksgiving, which was composed in the fourth century and is sung on solemnities, feasts, jubilees, and special occasions.

21. For examples of plans for parish missions extending over several weeks, see those for the mission at Abondance, November 1–22, 1840, and for the mission at Montriond, January 6–February 4, 1849, in Duval 1985, 286–89.

22. See Régent-Susini, "Tears for Fears," 185–205. For testimonies about the Fransalians' parish missions, see Duval 1985, 159–67; Moget, 86–87. During the mission, each missioner kept a notebook in which observations about the conduct of the mission were recorded on a daily basis. These observations were the basis for the subsequent evaluation of the effectiveness of each of the mission's components, as well as how each missioner comported himself. See Duval 1985, 147; Moget, 84–85.

23. Duval 1985, 138; Moget, 77. Forty-seven missions were also given during this period, mostly by Jesuits, Capuchins, and Redemptorists.

24. *Mermier: Recueil de Textes*, Text no. 75. Philippe Gaiddon (1803–63) was Mermier's closest confidant and collaborator, serving as Provincial, Assistant General, and second Superior General.

25. Fehleison 2005, 379, and 2010, 61–62.

26. Favre and Mermier had very different personalities: Favre tended to be impatient and idealistic, while Mermier was more level-headed and realistic. Like many human relationships, theirs was also complicated in ways that worked against their combining their efforts to found a single religious congregation. See Duval 1985, 19–49.

27. Moget, 19–23.

28. Quoted in "St. Francis de Sales, A Missionary Leader; Fr. Mermier in His 'I want mission experience,'" Working Paper 2, General Chapter 2007, Missionaries of St. Francis de Sales, 1.1.2. Originally, though no longer available, at: www.fransalians.com (retrieved May 1, 2006).

29. *Mermier: Recueil de Textes*, Text no. 133.

30. Charles Albert, Duke of Savoy and King of Sardinia (1798–1849; r. 1831–49).

31. Quoted in Duval 1985, 69. Cf. Moget, 25.

32. For an illustration and discussion of the *Christ in Glory* fresco and its relevance for the Chablais mission, see Joseph F. Chorpenning, OSFS, "Salesian Gentleness and Humility in Action: St. Francis de Sales's Missionary Apostolate in the Chablais," *ICSS* [= International Commission for Salesian Studies] *Newsletter* 17 (Jan.–Feb. 2006): 3–5, 12, esp. 4 (fig. 2).

33. Duval 1985, 69–79; Moget, 24–26.

34. *Mermier: Recueil de Textes*, Text no. 71.

35. Duval 1987, 15.

36. Due to poor health, Decompoix left India in 1866, after seventeen years in Vizag. From 1867, he ministered as a parish priest in the Fransalian English Mission for the next fifty-one years, dying in 1918 at the age of ninety-three (Moget, 123, 185–87).

37. Duval 1987, 6; Blandine Delahaye, "Le visage du prêtre selon François de Sales (1567–1622) à la lumière de sa *Correspondance*," and Jacques Hennequin, "Aspects du sacerdoce selon François de Sales," in *L'image du prêtre dans la littérature classique (XVIIe–XVIIIe siècles): Actes du colloque organisé par le Centre "Michel Baude—Littérature et spiritualité" de l'Université de Metz, 20-21 novembre 1998*, ed. Danielle Pister (New York: Peter Lang, 2001), 25–46, esp. 33–34, and 47–52, esp. 51–52, respectively.

38. *Mermier: Recueil de Textes*, Text no. 93.

39. Known as the Mellifluous Doctor, St. Bernard of Clairvaux (1090–1153) was a founder of the Cistercian Order and prophetic in denouncing abuses in the church.

40. Theophilus-Sebastian Neyret (1802–62) was ordained a priest in 1826 and made his novitiate as a Fransalian in 1844. He went to India in 1847 as Pro-vicar Apostolic of Visakhapatam and was consecrated bishop of Madras in 1849.

41. Louis de Carrières (1662–1717) was a French Oratorian priest and scripture scholar, whose *La Sainte Bible en français, avec un commentaire littéral inséré dans la traduction* (The Holy Bible in French, with a literal commentary inserted in the translation) was unlike anything published by earlier scholars. Carrières would add a few words of paraphrase here and there to explain difficulties or clear up obscure passages; these brief additions were printed in italics to easily distinguish them from the text itself. During the nineteenth century, Carrières's *Sainte Bible* was reprinted fourteen times, with the commentaries of Giovanni Stefano Menochio (1575–1655), an Italian Jesuit biblical scholar. See the entries on Carrières and Menochio in *The Catholic Encyclopedia*, 1907–12, at https://www.newadvent.org/cathen/.

42. On St. Alphonsus Liguori, see n. 6 above.

43. In addition to being the founder of the Fransalians, Mermier was also the cofounder, with Claudine Echernier, of the Sisters of the Holy Cross of Chavanod, who often worked in tandem with the Missionaries of St. Francis de Sales. Francis de Sales was also the patron of the Sisters of the Holy Cross, whose primary apostolate was to teach rural poor girls. See Duval 1985, 87–94; Moget, 32–35. Current statistics for the Fransalians was kindly provided by Yves Carron, MSFS, in an email of Feb. 29, 2020.

44. Carron, email of Feb. 29, 2020.

45. Yves Carron, MSFS, "Towards the Beatification of the Servant of God Fr. Peter Marie Mermier: What Is Done So Far and What Is Yet to Be Done," *Missionaries of St. Francis de Sales Global Mission Bulletin* 1, no. 1 (June 2020): 23–25.

3. THE FAMILY OF DON BOSCO: SALESIANS, DAUGHTERS OF MARY HELP OF CHRISTIANS, SALESIAN COOPERATORS

1. This passage comes from the critical editions of the *Memoirs of the Oratory of St. Francis de Sales*, prepared and annotated by Aldo Giraudo for the bicentenary of Don Bosco's birth. This is the text we are using for our entire presentation here. See Giovanni Bosco, *Memorie dell'Oratorio di S. Francesco di*

Sales dal 1815 al 1855, Saggio introduttivo e note storiche a cura di Aldo Giraudo (Roma: LAS, 2011), 55.

    2. Giovanni Battista Lemoyne, *Memorie Biografiche di Don Giovanni Bosco*; ediz. extra-comerciale (S. Benigno Canavese: Tipografia Salesiana, 1905), 5:882.

    3. Cf. Pietro Braido, *Don Bosco prete dei giovani nel secolo delle libertà* (Rome: LAS, 2003), 1:378–90.

    4. Buttigliera d'Asti: agricultural center 2.5 km from Castelnuovo; in 1834 it had 2,170 inhabitants.

    5. The function took place in the Easter period. John, who was 11 on August 16, 1826, was presumably admitted to communion at Easter 1827.

    6. Giuseppe Sismondo (1771–1827) had been parish priest of Castelnuovo since 1812. Vicar forane: title given to a parish priest who coordinated the parishes in a vicariate (today we might say a deanery). The Archdiocese of Torino at the time had 463,400 inhabitants; there were 242 parishes divided into 27 vicariates.

    7. Don Bosco should have written *1829*; Fr. Giovanni Calosso, whom John would meet during that Holy Year Mission, only arrived in Morialdo to serve as chaplain in the first months of 1829. There were two Jubilees, or "Holy Years," celebrated during that period: one called by Pope Leo XII for the Holy Year 1825/1826, the other granted as an exception by Pope Pius VIII on June 12, 1829. Here Don Bosco confuses one with the other.

    8. Fr. Giovanni Calosso was born in Chieri in 1760. He earned a doctorate in theology at the University of Torino and had extensive experience as a parish priest and an educator until he was forced to resign during the Napoleonic occupation of Piedmont. After several years of seclusion, he served as parochial assistant in Carignano, for a few years before being transferred to Morialdo in the Spring of 1829, where he worked until his death in 1830. See Aldo Giraudo, *Clero, seminario e società: Aspetti della Restaurazione religiosa a Torino*; Series Centro Studi Don Bosco, Studi Storici, n. 13 (Rome: LAS, 1992), 42–44.

    9. Fr. Calosso offers to give John four *soldi*. The four-*soldi* coin did not amount to very much, but it would have seemed attractive to a farm boy, and, at the market, might have had the buying power of $5 U.S. (2020).

    10. "Donato" was the name of the text used in lower secondary (latinitas) classes (*Donato ossia rudimenti di lingua latina ed italiana* [Turin, Stamperia Reale, 1815]); "Grammar" was the text used in the upper classes (*Nuovo metodo per apprendere agevolmente la lingua latina tratto dal francese...a uso*

delle scuole regie [Turin, Stamperia Reale 1817], 2 vols.). John, who had little schooling, had never heard of either text.

11. *Ember Days* were a series of four days of fasting and penance at the beginning of each season: spring, summer, autumn, and winter. Special liturgies were celebrated in each season, and special recipes were used by Catholic families as well. Ordinations often took place on Ember Saturdays. The days had special significance in rural societies, more than in urban settings. As the Northern Hemisphere began to depend less on agriculture in the 1970s, the observance of Ember Days disappeared in many dioceses. They were never abolished, however.

12. A *biretta* is a square cap with four peaks or "horns," worn by Catholic clergy of all ranks, and by seminarians. The use of the *biretta* by seminarians and priests became extremely uncommon after the 1950s.

13. Giuseppe Cafasso, *Meditazioni per Esercizi Spirituali al Clero*, a cura di Giuseppe Allamano (Turin: Canonica, 1892), 341–42.

14. *Memoirs of the Oratory*, Second decade, unit 13.

15. *Memoirs of the Oratory*, Second decade, unit 14.

16. Giovanni Bonetti, *History of Don Bosco's Early Apostolate*, declared venerable, July 23, 1907; a translation from the work of G. Bonetti, SC, with a preface by His Grace the Archbishop of Westminster (London: Salesian Press, 1908), 18.

17. Waldensians credit King Charles Albert with introducing religious freedom to Italy. He did so in his open letter of February 17, 1848, and confirmed it in the "Fundamental Statute of the Monarchy of Savoy," issued on March 4 of the same year. Shortly afterwards the Waldensians began to function openly in Turin. In 1853 they completed the construction of their "temple" and in 1855 they opened a printing press that was to become the Editrice Claudiana, which is today the foremost Protestant publishing house in Italy.

18. St. John Bosco, "Regulations for the Oratories," quoted in Giovanni Battista Lemoyne, *Memorie biografiche di Don Giovanni Bosco* (S. Benigno Canavese: Tipografia Salesiana, 1903), 3:91.

19. Cf. Pietro Stella, *Don Bosco*, vol. 2, *Religious Outlook and Spirituality*, trans. John Drury (New Rochelle, NY: Salesiana Publishers, 1996), 382.

20. See Stella, *Don Bosco: Religious Outlook and Spirituality*, 2:383–84.

21. The phrase *da mihi animas* is not found in the writings of Francis de Sales. Jean Pierre Camus, a close friend and disciple, used this biblical passage to describe his pastoral spirit (see *Lo spirito di S. Francesco di Sales vescovo e principe di Ginevra*, raccolto da diversi scritti di monsignor Gio. Pietro Camus,

vescovo di Belley [Venice: Remondini, 1758], 129). Don Bosco, through the influence of Fr. Cafasso, chose the phrase as the motto for his priesthood.

22. See Matt 25:21.

23. See Egidio Viganò, "Maria Rinnova la Famiglia Salesiana di Don Bosco," *Atti del Consiglio Generale* 57, no. 289 (January–June 1978): 13–14. For a description of the "Marian atmosphere" in Valdocco taken from sworn depositions made during D. Bosco's beatification process, see Joseph Boenzi, "Reflections on Virtue: Saint John Bosco's Heroic Faith as Reported by Eyewitnesses in his Beatification Process," *Journal of Salesian Studies* 6, no. 2 (Fall 1995): 100–101.

24. Giovanni Cagliero, in Sacra Ritum Congregatione, *Taurinem, Beatificationis et Canonizationis Ven. Servi Dei Joannis Bosco, Sacerdotis Fundatoris Piae Societatis Salesianae necnon Istitui Filiarum Marie Auxliatricis: Positio Super Virtutibus. Pars I. Summarium. Relator: Antonio Vico* (Rome: Agostiniana, 1923), 408 (from this point on, this source will be abbreviated as SUM).

25. S. Giovanni Bosco, *Il Giovane Provveduto per la pratica de' suoi doveri negli Esercizi di Cristiana Pietà per la Recita dell'Uffizio della Beata Vergine e de' principali Vespri dell'anno, coll'aggiunta di una Scelta di Laudi Sacre ecc.* (Turin: Paravia, 1847), 51, quoted in Pietro Stella, *Don Bosco nella Storia della Religiosità Cattolica*, vol. 2, *Mentalità Religiosa e Spiritualità*, 2nd ed., Centro Studi Don Bosco—Studi Storici, no. 4 (Rome: LAS, 1981), 149.

26. S. Giovanni Bosco, *Mese di Maggio*, 19–20, in *The Spiritual Writings of Saint John Bosco*, ed. Joseph Aubry, trans. Joseph Caselli (New Rochelle, NY: Don Bosco Multi-Media, 1984), 173–74.

27. The original letter was dictated, but it bears the signature of Maria Domenica Mazzarello. This translation is found in *I Will Never Forget You: Letters of Maria Domenica Mazzarello*, collected and ed. María Esther Posada, Anna Costa, and Piera Cavaglià. English edition presented by the FMA English-Language Translation Group (Rome: Institute of the Daughters of Mary Help of Christians, 2000), 40–41.

28. Posada et al., *I Will Never Forget You*, 55–59.

29. Mother Mazzarello echoes St. Francis de Sales, who tells Philothea that he has never trusted those who want to reform someone by starting from externals: by changing their looks, their clothing, or their hair. Instead, true conversion begins on the inside, that is, in the heart. And whoever places Jesus as a seal on their heart, will find all their actions follow Jesus's lead. See St. Francis de Sales, *Introduction to the Devout Life*, part III, chapter 23.

Notes

30. These three Sisters were all critically ill. Sisters Ferrettino and Ginepro both died later that year, only a few months after the death of Mother Mazzarello. Sr. Massa died in 1884.

31. Cf. S. Giovanni Bosco, *Costituzioni della Società di San Francesco di Sales [1858]–1875*, testi critici a cura di Francesco Motto. Istituto Storico Salesiano, Fonti, Series 1, no. 1 (Rome: LAS, 1982), 73, version 1875, ch. 1, art. 1; Pietro Stella, *Don Bosco*, vol. 2: *Religious Outlook and Spirituality*, trans. John Drury (New Rochelle, NY: Salesiana Publishers, 1996), 381.

32. Cf. Pietro Stella, *Don Bosco nella Storia della Religiosità Cattolica*, vol. 1, *Vita e Opere*, 2nd ed., Centro Studi Don Bosco—Studi Storici, no. 3 (Rome: LAS, 1979), 212–13.

33. *Bibliofilo Cattolico o Bollettino Salesiano Mensuale*, Turin, 3, no. 5 (Aug. 1877): 2.

34. Paolo Albera, "Esercizi Direttori 1910" (Instructions for the spiritual exercises preceding the eleventh general chapter of the Salesian Society) AMs, 1910. Archivio Salesiano Centrale, Fondo Paolo Albera, B0480137-8, Università Pontificia Salesiana, Rome, copybook 4, insert u1 (unpublished manuscript): "Non si sa definire. Ne abbiamo fissa nella mente la bellissima fisionomia, sappiamo che è il complesso di pietà, di carità, di bontà. Sappiamo che si manifesta in maniere diverse, però tutte veramente seducenti. Definirla però non sappiamo."

35. Paolo Albera, "Tutto per Gesù: Istruzioni per gli Esercizi Spirituali" (All for Jesus: Instructions for the spiritual exercises), 4 notebooks, AMs, 1893. Archivio Salesiano Centrale, Fondo Paolo Albera, B0480111-4, Università Pontificia Salesiana, Roma, 1:93–94 (unpublished manuscript): "E' pure un favore segnalato che ci fece il Signore coll'averci posti sotto la bandiera di quel maestro della mansuetudine che è il Salesio, quasi a dirci che l'arma più atta a combattere i nostri nemici in questi tempi si è la dolcezza—e come per rendere più autorevole l'ammaestramento di questo gran santo, la Chiesa lo dichiarava Dottore della Chiesa. Il grande Pontefice dell'Immacolata quanti segni d'affetto ci ha dati! Non meno ci ama il suo dottissimo successore Leone XIII."

36. Paolo Albera, "Raccolta di Istruzioni predicate dal Sign. D. Albera, Catechista Generale de' Salesiani, in occasione degli Esercizi Spirit[uali]. Tenuti in Foglizzo agli Ascritti Salesiani il Marzo 1894" (Instructions given to Salesian Novices in Foglizzo, March 1894), Ms., 1894 (Archivio Salesiano Centrale, Fondo Paolo Albera, B0480115, Università Pontificia Salesiana, Rome), 119–120 (unpublished manuscript): "E con D. Bosco stesso bisognava che foste state qualche tempo, ed avreste visto quanto gli costava l'esser sempre calmo e dolce.

Si racconta che una volta c'era una donna che disturbava molto l'Oratorio, perché aveva una betola vicino al medesimo. E là radunava tanti poveri giovani ed impediva che andassero alle funzioni; e là si faceva peggio che mangiare e bere. E D. Bosco trovò mezzo di comperare quella casa, e quindi mandare a spasso la donna. La quale quando seppe che la sua bettola doveva chiudersi, andò a trovare D. Bosco, che era in mezzo ad alcuni ragazzi, perché era sempre coi giovani in principio; e gliene disse di tutti i colori. Assicurano quelli che erano vicini a D. Bosco, che prima venne rosso, poi pallido, poi di nuovo rosso e non disse nulla. Solamente quando l'altra si ebbe sfogata bene, D. Bosco disse ai giovani: accompagnatela un poco fino alla porta; e non volle rimproverarla nemmeno della cattiva sua educazione. Cari fratelli, che cosa vuol dire quel cambiar colore? che egli faceva grande sforzo a se medesimo."

4. MARY DE SALES CHAPPUIS, LOUIS BRISSON, LÉONIE FRANCES DE SALES AVIAT, AND THE OBLATE SISTERS AND OBLATES OF ST. FRANCIS DE SALES

1. Unless otherwise indicated, all English translations are from the original French texts by the author, who is grateful to Dr. Suzanne Toczyski for her advice and suggestions for improvement.

2. The official date of founding for the Oblate Sisters is October 11, 1871, when Léonie Aviat and Lucy Canuet professed their first vows. That for the Oblates is December 21, 1875, when, in a *Decretum Laudis*, or official papal decree, Bl. Pope Pius IX (1792–1878, r. 1846–78) granted the congregation its first charter and placed it under the direct and immediate jurisdiction of the Holy See. See "A Salesian/Oblate Chronology," in *The Constitutions, the General Statutes, and the Spiritual Directory of the Oblates of Saint Francis de Sales*, American Centenary Edition (Wilmington, DE: De Sales Publishing, 1991), 266–78, esp. 270–71 (hereafter Salesian/Oblate Chronology).

3. Louis Brisson, *Vie de la vénérée Mère Marie de Sales Chappuis* (Paris: chez M. l'Aumonier de la Visitation, 1891), 9, 35–36, 61–64, 70, 78–79; quotes at 78–79 (hereafter Chappuis Biography). Marie-Thérèse initially entered the Fribourg Visitation in 1811, but only remained a few months, suffering from a severe bout of homesickness. After remaining at home for three painful years, she again entered the monastery, but hesitated at the doorway because she experienced the same repugnance as before. However, her brother and sister,

who had accompanied her, convinced her to try it out for three days and, if she still felt homesick, they would take her home again. Her apprehension immediately dissipated as soon as she heard the monastery door bolted behind her.

4. Chappuis Biography, 86–107. Also see Alexander T. Pocetto, OSFS, "Mary de Sales Chappuis (1793–1875): Apostle of the Salesian Spirit," *Salesianum* 71 (2009): 321–40, esp. 322–23, 325, 327 (hereafter Pocetto 2009). Chappuis's life is best understood in the context of the ecclesial tradition of female mystics-apostles, who "mediate glimpses of God's mysteries intended to expand mankind's knowledge of his plan for salvation history," thus "fulfilling a thoroughly prophetic mission, for the benefit of many people" (Wolfgang Riehle, *The Secret Within: Hermits, Recluses, and Spiritual Outsiders in Medieval England*, trans. Charity Scott-Stokes [Ithaca, NY: Cornell University Press, 2014], 211). This was certainly how Chappuis saw herself: "I am being called to be an apostle and to contribute to the work that God will establish in order to communicate His graces and to expand the diffusion of His divine charity" (Louis Brisson, OSFS, *Chapîtres, Retraites, Instructions et Allocutions*, 7 vols. [Tilburg, The Netherlands: Maison "Ave Maria," 1966–68], 4:126 [hereafter Brisson]). Brisson's retreat conferences, allocutions, and chapter instructions are also available electronically, in unpaginated format, in the millennium edition (2000) of Brisson's *Œuvres*, ed. Roger Balducelli, OSFS, assisted by Jean Gayet, OSFS, and the Oblate Sisters of the Motherhouse in Troyes: www .louisbrisson.org. Due to ease of reference by volume and page, here the Tilburg edition is cited throughout. When there is a discrepancy between the Tilburg edition and the millennium edition, priority is given to the latter in translating the French text. Chappuis was absolutely convinced that this mission was "her very *raison d'être*" and the work to which the Lord had called her, and accordingly "she speaks [of it] with all of the confidence and certainty of an Old Testament prophet" (Pocetto 2009, 338–39).

5. Austin Gough, *Paris and Rome: The Gallican Church and the Ultramontane Campaign 1848–1853* (Oxford: Clarendon Press, 1986), 171 (hereafter Gough). This was the assessment of the papal nuncio in Paris, Archbishop (later Cardinal) Raffaele Fornari (1788–1854, nuncio 1843–50).

6. Pocetto 2009, 327. A radical reform movement within Catholicism that originated in Flanders but whose true home was France, Jansenism espoused positions similar to, and sometimes identical with, those of Calvinism. See Dale K. Van Kley, *Reform Catholicism and the International Suppression of the Jesuits in Enlightenment Europe* (New Haven, CT: Yale University Press, 2018), 32 (hereafter Van Kley); Ulrich L. Lehner, *The Catholic Enlightenment: The Forgotten*

History of a Global Movement (New York: Oxford University Press, 2016), 19–22, 49–53, 170–73 (hereafter Lehner); John W. O'Malley, SJ, *Vatican I: The Council and the Making of the Ultramontane Church* (Cambridge, MA: Harvard University Press, 2018), 32–33.

7. Chappuis Biography, 103; Van Kley, 41.

8. Jacques-Bénigne Bossuet's nephew and namesake, who was bishop of Troyes from 1716 to 1742, was a leading Jansenist, and the liturgical books that he prepared for the diocese were permeated by Jansenist doctrine. See Yvon Beaudoin, OMI, *Father Louis Brisson (1817–1908): A Documented Biography*, trans. several De Sales Oblates and ed. Alexander T. Pocetto, OSFS, and Daniel P. Wisniewski, OSFS (Wilmington, DE: Oblates of St. Francis de Sales, 2008), 21n5, 221 (hereafter Beaudoin); Michael Kwatera, OSB, "Marian Feasts in the Roman, Troyes and Paris Missals and Breviaries and the Critique of Dom Prosper Guéranger" (PhD diss., University of Notre Dame, 1993), 55–66.

9. Beaudoin, 21n5, 25, 221, 268n114. Gallicanism held that the French themselves controlled the church in France, independent of Rome. Gallicans were opposed by Ultramontane Catholics, who looked beyond the Alps to the papacy for guidance. See Lehner, 18–19.

10. Chappuis Biography, 303–12. Also see Beaudoin, 220–21. Bishops Jacques-Louis-David de Séguin des Hons (1826–43) and Pierre-Louis Cœur (1849–60) were well-known Gallicans. A former professor of the Sorbonne and a vigorous defender of Gallican liturgical prerogatives, Cœur was censured by the Holy See for granting a general exemption from the Roman liturgy, which had been restored by his predecessor (Jean-Marie Debelay [1844–48]). See Gough, 169–71; Beaudoin, 21n5.

11. Ralph Gibson, "Hellfire and Damnation in Nineteenth-Century France," *Catholic Historical Review* 74, no. 3 (1988): 383–402, at 385 (hereafter Gibson 1988). Also see his *A Social History of French Catholicism 1789–1914* (New York: Routledge, 1989) (hereafter Gibson 1989); Jean-Louis Quantin, *Le rigorisme chrétien*, Histoire de Christianisme (Paris: Cerf, 2001); and Alexander T. Pocetto, OSFS, "Blessed Louis Brisson (1817–1908), the Laity, and the Social Dimensions of the New Evangelization," *Salesianum* 76 (2014): 121–40, esp. 127–28, 132 (hereafter Pocetto 2014), who examines how Brisson greatly contributed in his ministry to moving away from the religion of fear by consistently focusing on the love of God.

12. Gibson 1988, 385. On the emergence and dominance of rigorism in early modern French Catholicism, see Robin Briggs, *Communities of Belief:*

Cultural and Social Tension in Early Modern France (Oxford: Clarendon Press, 1989).

13. Gibson 1989, 247.

14. Chappuis Biography, 254.

15. Louis Brisson, draft of letter of October 14, 1867, to Fr. Claude Perrot, OSB, in the Archives of the Oblate Generalate in Rome, box 30, Einsiedeln Collection (hereafter Perrot letter). I thank Fr. Barry R. Strong, OSFS, Superior General of the Oblates of St. Francis de Sales, for retrieving and scanning this document.

16. Brisson, 2:152.

17. For example, the aim of the solemn celebration of Francis's beatification that took place in Annecy on April 30, 1662, was "to set ablaze all the hearts of the city's inhabitants in the school of this incomparable Doctor of Divine Love." Barthélémy Magistri, *Cérémonies et resjouissances faites en la ville d'Annessy sur la solennité de la béatification et l'élévation du corps sacré du bienheureux François de Sales, le 30. d'avril 1662* (Annecy: Pierre Delachinal, 1662), 21, quoted in Agnès Guiderdoni, "Exegetical Immersion: The Festivities on the Occasion of Francis de Sales's Canonisation (1665–1667)," in *Imago Exegetica: Visual Images as Exegetical Instruments, 1400-1700*, ed. Walter S. Melion et al., Intersections: Interdisciplinary Studies in Early Modern Culture 33 (Boston: Brill, 2014), 855–84, at 876. Pope Alexander VII signed the brief of Francis's beatification on December 28, 1661, with the formal ceremony following in St. Peter's Basilica on January 8, 1662. Francis's designation as the Doctor of Divine Love is now commonplace in papal documents: see, e.g., Pope St. Paul VI, *Sabaudiae gemma* (Gem of Savoy): *Apostolic Letter Commemorating the 400th Anniversary of the Birth of St. Francis de Sales, Doctor of the Church*, trans. Neil Kilty, OSFS (Hyattsville, MD: Institute of Salesian Studies, 1967), 4, 8; and Pope St. John Paul II, *Letter on the Fourth Centenary of the Episcopal Ordination of St. Francis de Sales* (Nov. 23, 2002), n. 3 (available at https://www.vatican.va/ content/john-paul-ii/en/letters/2002/documents/hf_jp-ii_let_20021209 _francesco-sales.html). Earlier John Paul referenced Francis as the "Doctor of Love" in a homily given in Annecy, Oct. 7, 1986, during his apostolic pilgrimage to France (available at https://www.vatican.va/content/john-paul-ii/fr/ homilies/1986/documents/hf_jp-ii_hom_19861007_annency-francia.html; accessed May 3, 2016).

18. Francis de Sales, *Avertissements aux Confesseurs* (1603 or 1604), in *Œuvres de saint François de Sales*, Édition complète, 27 vols. (Annecy: J. Niérat et al., 1892–1964), 23:279–97, at 284 (hereafter Annecy edition).

19. Francis de Sales, *Treatise on the Love of God*, in Saint François de Sales, *Œuvres*, ed. André Ravier – Roger Devos, Bibliothèque de la Pléiade (Paris: Gallimard, 1969), 433 (book 2, ch. 8) (hereafter *Œuvres*). Francis's teaching stood in stark contrast to that of rigorist proto-Jansenist, militant Catholic preachers of the Wars of Religion (1562–1629), as well as later purveyors of a religion of fear. This contrast was salient, e.g., during Francis's 1602 visit to Paris: "His sermons captivated [his listeners] by their direct and simple pronouncements about God's love for man. In elegant French, [he] would exhort his listeners to recall the sufferings of Christ, His compassion for the unfortunate, and the beauty of the love of God for those whom He has created. This seemed like poetry to the Parisians, who for decades had heard nothing but invective and hellfire" (Orest Ranum, *Paris in the Age of Absolutism: An Essay*, rev. and exp. ed. [1968; University Park: Pennsylvania State University Press, 2002], 174). For an examination of the contrast between Francis and militant Catholicism, see Thomas A. Donlan, *The Reform of Zeal: François de Sales and Militant French Catholicism*, St. Andrews Studies in French History and Culture (St. Andrews, UK: Centre for French History and Culture of the University of St Andrews, 2018).

20. Only Francis de Sales appeared to be equal to the challenge. The moral theology of St. Alphonsus Liguori (1696–1787), who was influenced by Francis, had aimed to steer a middle course between laxism and Jansenist rigorism by winning back sinners through patience and moderation. However, Liguori's message was inconsistent, as he counseled his Redemptorists "to be lions in the pulpit but lambs in the confessional" (Patrick W. Carey, *Confession: Catholics, Repentance & Forgiveness in America* [New York: Oxford University Press, 2018], 128). This fell well short of the Salesian principle of all through love, nothing through fear: see Francis de Sales, letter of October 14, 1604, to Madame de Chantal, in Annecy edition, 12:352–70, at 359. In fact, the Redemptorists had the reputation of being "the leading specialists in hellfire preaching," sometimes even being described as "Redempt-terrorists" (Gibson 1988, 387). It has recently been noted that after Liguori's death, "the Redemptorists somewhat distorted the heritage of their founder…, and they also forgot much of his message" (Lehner, 173). Also see Wendy M. Wright, "The Doctor of Divine Love and Fear of the Lord," in *Saving Fear in Christian Spirituality*, ed. Ann W. Astell (Notre Dame, IN: Notre Dame University Press, 2020), 182–208. Chappuis and Brisson welcomed introduction of Liguori's moral theology to the seminary of Troyes. See Beaudoin, 25, 252, 334; Wendy M. Wright, *Heart Speaks to Heart: The Salesian Tradition*, Traditions of

Notes

Christian Spirituality Series (Maryknoll, NY: Orbis Books, 2004), 144 (hereafter Wright 2004); Pocetto 2009, 337–38.

21. Beaudoin, 3–4 (quote at 4).

22. Jean-Emil Fonteneau, archbishop of Albi, letter of January 6, 1887, to Brisson, printed in the 1891 edition of Brisson's *Life of the Venerable Mother Mary de Sales Chappuis*, vi–vii. The text of this letter is also in Beaudoin, 252–53, with quote at 252.

23. Beaudoin, 334.

24. A priest of the diocese of Nîmes, d'Alzon was the founder of the male religious order, the Augustinians of the Assumption (the Assumptionists). He originated the idea of the Association of St. Francis de Sales as a means to assist by prayer and alms those who defended the faith against Protestantism, which was firmly rooted in some regions in southern and western France, though practically nonexistent in the Department of the Aube. The Association received papal approval in 1855, and by 1859 it was established in seventy-two dioceses in France, Belgium, Italy, Spain, and Canada. See Beaudoin, 39–42.

25. De Ségur served as the dynamic president of the Association of St. Francis de Sales from 1857 to 1881, working incessantly for its growth and development. Religiously indifferent in his youth, de Ségur experienced a conversion during a retreat using the meditations in the *Introduction to the Devout Life* as a guide. During his studies for the priesthood at the Seminary of Saint-Sulpice in Paris, he found the warmth and accessibility of Salesian spirituality as a balance to the austere abnegation of the French School. Ordained in 1847, he dedicated himself to the evangelization of the people of Paris, especially children, the poor, and imprisoned soldiers. Five years after ordination, he was appointed as auditor of the Roman Rota, but blindness forced him to resign in 1856 and return to his native Paris, with the honorary rank of archbishop. In his work with the Association of St. Francis de Sales, de Ségur was often in contact with Chappuis and Brisson, whom he regarded as preeminent among the diocesan directors of the Association, singling out "the intelligence and ingenious zeal" with which Brisson carried out this ministry (Beaudoin, 41; Pocetto 2014, 126). See Marthe de Hédouville, *Monseigneur de Ségur: Sa vie-son action 1820–1881* (Paris: Nouvelles Éditions Latines, 1957); Beaudoin, 39–40; Wright 2004, 129–33.

26. Mermillod served as auxiliary bishop/vicar apostolic (1864–83) and later bishop of Lausanne and Geneva (1883–91). He was elevated to cardinal in 1890. Besides being a major figure in the Salesian Pentecost, Mermillod played an important role in the development of Catholic social teaching that served as

the foundation for Pope Leo XIII's encyclical *Rerum Novarum*, On the Condition of Labor (1891).

27. Pocetto 2014, 123.

28. Beaudoin, 39; Pocetto 2014, 124.

29. Pocetto 2014, 124.

30. Beaudoin, 39–44.

31. Pocetto 2014, 124–25.

32. See, e.g., "Troyes," in *The Grove Encyclopedia of Northern Renaissance Art*, ed. Gordon Campbell, 3 vols. (New York: Oxford University Press, 2009), 3:417–18.

33. Colin Heywood, "Learning Democracy in France: Popular Politics in Troyes, c. 1830–1900," *The Historical Journal* 47, no. 4 (2004): 921–39, at 924.

34. Beaudoin, 44–45.

35. Beaudoin, 45–46; Pocetto 2014, 135.

36. Beaudoin, 40–49; Pocetto 2014, 126–29.

37. Marie-Aimée d'Esmauges, *To Forget Myself Entirely: Mother Frances de Sales, 1844–1914*, trans. Oblate Sisters of St. Francis de Sales (Childs, MD: Oblate Sisters of St. Francis de Sales, 1991), 19–30 (hereafter d'Esmauges).

38. Chappuis Biography, 395–402.

39. St. Robert Bellarmine (1542–1621) was one of the most renowned and prolific Jesuit theologians of the early modern era. After a distinguished career as a teacher and then rector of the Roman College, Bellarmine served as papal theologian and was later elevated to cardinal in 1599, in which capacity he was a member of several key curial congregations. For a brief time, he was also archbishop of Capua (1602–5).

40. Denis-Simon de Marquemont (1572–1626) was archbishop of Lyon (1612–26), being elevated to cardinal in January 1626.

41. Louis de la Rivière (1593–1670) wrote one of the first biographies of St. Francis de Sales: *La vie de l'Illustrissime et Reverendissime François de Sales* (Lyon, 1624), with subsequent editions in 1625, 1626, 1627, and 1631. A Franciscan Minim, de la Rivière had preached the Lenten sermons in Annecy in 1616 and knew Francis well.

42. On Mermillod, see n. 26 above.

43. Emmanuel-Jules Ravinet (1801–81), a priest of the Archdiocese of Paris, was ordained as bishop of Troyes in 1861, serving in that capacity until his retirement in 1875.

44. Séguin des Hons was ordained bishop of Troyes in 1826 and served in that capacity until his death seventeen years later. Also see n. 10 above.

Notes

45. All Aviat texts that follow were translated by Sr. Audrey Frances Moran, OSFS, whose generous collaboration is gratefully acknowledged.

46. Wright 2004, 60, 159.

47. *Résumé des Noviciats faits par N.T.H. Mère Françoise de Sales Aviat aux premières novices de l'Institut et rédigés de mémoire par l'une d'elles* (Perugia, 1916; reprint, 1966).

48. Preserved in the archives of the Motherhouse of the Oblate Sisters in Troyes.

49. The booklet is entitled *Collection of Thoughts Drawn from the Letters of Our Venerable Mother Frances de Sales Aviat.*

50. The original, preserved in the archives of the Motherhouse of the Oblate Sisters in Troyes, is carefully formatted, written in clear handwriting, and has a decorative border. The words are Mother Aviat's.

51. Beaudoin, 93.

52. See Brisson's "Notes to Show That the Institute of the Oblates of St. Francis de Sales Is Not a New Idea," in the archives of the Congregation of Bishops and Regulars in Rome (Beaudoin, 123n5).

53. Brisson, 4:124.

54. Brisson, 4:127.

55. Gibson 1989, 80–87, 98–99; Gough, 1–21.

56. Salesian/Oblate Chronology, 272.

57. Brisson, 3:16.

58. Gibson 1989, 98–99; Pocetto 2014, 140.

59. Brisson, 4:126.

60. *Résumé des Retraites Prêchées aux jeunes Ouvrières des Œuvres des Oblates de Saint François de Sales à Troyes de 1870 à 1901 par leur Fondateur Le Vénéré Père Louis Brisson* (Perugia: Imprimerie G. Squartinini, 1927), 118, cited by Pocetto 2014, 132n37. As Pocetto importantly points out, the word *apostle* had special significance for Brisson: it was closely associated with Brisson's conception of the church, as well as Mother Chappuis, whose mission was to be an apostle of the Salesian spirit (see Pocetto 2009). He believed that the Oblates continued the evangelizing mission of the apostles and of Christ himself and thus extended the Savior's love to all those whom they were called to evangelize.

61. Pocetto 2014, 130–32, 136. Brisson made this point in his catechism classes for the girls working in the factories in Troyes by explaining "that by our fundamental purpose of being created to know, love, and serve God, we are also called to make him known, loved, and served by others, particularly in one's own family. Those who do so, he calls 'apostles of the love of God'" (Pocetto

2014, 132). Likewise, Brisson understood reception of the Eucharist as "not intended merely for one's own personal devotion but [it] must make us more aware of others and their needs. It makes us 'become more charitable, generous…, makes us see God in others.'…[Thus,] we 'must take God wherever we go,'" as "apostles of the love of God" (Pocetto 2014, 136).

62. Brisson, 4:129.

63. Brisson, 4:123–33.

64. "Male anxiety" about the foundational role that women sometimes have in a male religious order or congregation is well documented: see, e.g., Christopher C. Wilson, "Masculinity Restored: The Visual Shaping of St. John of the Cross," *Archive for Reformation History* 98, no. 1 (2007): 134–66.

65. Pierre-Tobie Yenni (1774–1845) was bishop of the Diocese of Lausanne and Geneva (1815–45), with residence at Fribourg.

66. Chappuis Biography, 260.

67. Beaudoin, 343.

68. Chappuis Biography, 259–61.

69. Chappuis Biography, 396.

70. Chappuis Biography, 395.

71. Brisson, 1:120.

72. Brisson, 1:120.

73. In the pre–Vatican II liturgical calendar, the Feast of St. Francis de Sales was assigned to January 29; in the current calendar, it is celebrated on January 24.

74. Brisson, 3:10–14.

75. Auguste-Marie de Mayerhoffen, OSFS (1856–1918), was chaplain to the Second Monastery of the Visitation in Paris and ministered to Brisson at the hour of his death. See Beaudoin, 301.

76. During a visit to Annecy in April 1869, Brisson had an apparition of St. Jane de Chantal in the chapel of the Visitation Monastery. The saint communicated, among other things, how pleased she was by the founding of the Oblates since that had been the ardent desire of her life. See Beaudoin, 343–44.

77. See *Œuvres*, 657–59 (*Treatise on the Love of God*, book 6, ch. 15).

78. *St. Francis de Sales: A Testimony by St. Chantal*, newly edited in translation with an introduction by Elisabeth Stopp (Hyattsville, MD: Institute of Salesian Studies, 1967), 96 (hereafter *A Testimony by St. Chantal*). For further testimony on this topic, see "Letter of December 1623 from Jane Frances de Chantal to Dom Jean de Saint-François," in *A Testimony by St. Chantal*, 165–72, esp. 172 ; and Vincent de Paul, "Deposition at the Process of Beatification of

Francis de Sales (April 17, 1628)," in Saint Vincent de Paul, *Correspondance, Conferences, Documents,* ed. and trans. Marie Poole, DC, et al., 14 vols. (Hyde Park, NY: New City Press, 1985–2014) 13a: 91 (Article 38).

79. Chappuis Biography, 445. Brisson frequently attests to this conviction of Chappuis: see, e.g., Brisson, 1:19, 58, 192, 254; 2:39, 330; 3:96, 220, 352, 421, 490, 531; 4:63.

80. Brisson, 3:10.

81. Anthony R. Ceresko, OSFS, "St. Francis de Sales's *Spiritual Directory* for a New Century: Re-interpreting the 'Direction of Intention,'" in his *St. Francis de Sales and the Bible* (Bangalore: SFS Publications, 2005), 110–27, at 111–12 (originally published in *Indian Journal of Spirituality* 14 [2001]: 377–91) (hereafter Ceresko).

82. Wright 2004, 140–41; Pocetto 2009, 328–31.

83. Like the *Introduction to the Devout Life,* the *Spiritual Directory* stood at the head of a substantial body of early modern French devotional manuals and catechisms that aimed to teach their readers how to organize each hour of the day so as to benefit from the God-given opportunity to gain eternal beatitude. See Mette Birkedal Bruun, "Time Well Spent: Scheduling Private Devotion in Early Modern France," in *Managing Time: Literature and Devotion in Early Modern France,* ed. Richard Maber and Joanna Barker, Medieval and Early Modern French Studies 15 (New York: Peter Lang, 2017), 35–68.

84. Alexander T. Pocetto, OSFS, "The *Spiritual Directory* in the American Oblate Tradition," 7, unpublished paper available online at https://www.desales.edu/docs/default-source/salesian-center-docs/salesian---fr.-pocetto/spir-direct.pdf?sfvrsn=2d632761_2.

85. Ceresko, 114.

86. "The *Spiritual Directory,*" in *The Constitutions, the General Statues, and the Spiritual Directory of the Oblates of Saint Francis de Sales,* 191–229, at 192–93.

87. *Œuvres,* 142 (*Introduction to the Devout Life,* part 3, ch. 8).

88. Wright 2004, 33, 41; Joseph F. Chorpenning, OSFS, "*Lectio divina* and Francis de Sales's Picturing of the Interconnection of Human and Divine Hearts," in *Imago Exegetica: Visual Images as Exegetical Instruments, 1400–1700,* ed. Walter S. Melion et al., Intersections: Interdisciplinary Studies in Early Modern Culture 33 (Boston: Brill, 2014), 449–77, esp. 459, 462.

89. Chappuis Biography, 444.

90. Chappuis Biography, 445.

91. Brisson, 3:140–43.

92. Brisson's linking of Francis de Sales and Vincent de Paul (1581–1660) is not accidental since the Doctor of Divine Love had served as a spiritual and priestly mentor to the Apostle of Charity: see, e.g., José María Román, CM, *St. Vincent de Paul: A Biography*, trans. Sr. Joyce Howard, DC (London: Melisende, 1999), 149–56. During his 1618–19 sojourn in Paris, Francis de Sales was invited to give a series of conferences for priests, which were the inspiration for Vincent de Paul's later "Tuesday Conferences" that played an important role in the renewal of the clergy. See E.-J. Lajeunie, OP, *Saint Francis de Sales: The Man, the Thinker, His Influence*, trans. Rory O'Sullivan, OSFS, 2 vols. (Bangalore: SFS Publications, 1986–87), 2:417–18; André Ravier, SJ, *Francis de Sales: Sage & Saint*, trans. Joseph D. Bowler, OSFS (San Francisco: Ignatius Press, 1988), 227 (hereafter Ravier). For his part, Vincent sought to create a new type of priest, as would Chappuis and Brisson in their era: "When [Vincent] began to give the much-needed missions to the poor country people he made a discovery…which revealed to him that there was urgent need for a new type of priest. This new type of priest must not be content simply to contemplate Christ the Eternal Priest offering Himself to the Father, but rather one who carries the living Christ into the marketplace of the neglected people, especially the poor and the destitute" (James Cahalan, "St. Vincent and the Priesthood," *Colloque: Journal of the Irish Province of the Congregation of the Mission* 7 [Spring 1983]: 51–58, at 53).

93. The Roman Pontifical is the episcopal ritual containing the rites (formularies and rubrics) for sacraments and sacramentals celebrated by a bishop, especially the consecration of the holy oils and the sacraments of confirmation and holy orders.

94. The Jansenists held that the early church was the model of perfection, which was gradually eroded by what they considered the usurping and ever more domineering papacy. See Van Kley, 26–27.

95. *Œuvres*, 39 (*Introduction to the Devout Life*, part 1, ch. 4). However, Francis de Sales cautions confessors that they are not angels (Annecy edition, 23:282).

96. Perrot letter.

97. Pocetto, "The *Spiritual Directory* in the American Oblate Tradition," 3–4.

98. St. Francis de Sales, *On the Preacher and Preaching*, trans. with an introduction and notes by John K. Ryan (Chicago: Henry Regnery Company, 1964; repr. Stella Niagara, NY: DeSales Resource Center, 2020).

99. Pocetto 2014, 138.

100. Pocetto 2014, 129, 135, 138.
101. Gibson 1989, 23.
102. Gibson 1989, 221.
103. *A Testimony by St. Chantal*, 138 (Article 46).
104. Brisson, 5:268.
105. Pocetto 2009, 333.
106. Brisson, 5:106–7. This text has been translated by Alexander T. Pocetto, OSFS, who suggested it as a particularly apt example of Brisson's theology/spirituality of work, for which the author is deeply grateful.
107. "Holy Mother Church has, moreover, instituted sacramentals. These are sacred signs which bear a resemblance to the sacraments. They signify effects, particularly of a spiritual nature, which are obtained through the intercession of the Church. By them men are disposed to receive the chief effect of the sacraments, and various occasions in life are rendered holy" (*Catechism of the Catholic Church*, 2nd ed., no. 1667).
108. Pocetto 2009, 333.
109. Faced with a changed economic reality, the church's approach to the new circumstances was twofold: direct assistance and the formulation of ethical norms. As Matthew E. Bunson has indicated, "Direct assistance was provided through hospitals and schools, as epitomized in Italy by St. John Bosco and the Salesians and in France by Frédéric Ozanam and the Society of St. Vincent de Paul. There were as well the efforts of Christian industrialists, such as Léon Harmel in France, who lived with his own employees. Bishops around the world provided leadership, including Bishop (Cardinal from 1890) Mermillod of Geneva and Lausanne, Cardinal Manning of Westminster, Cardinal Gibbons of Baltimore, Bishop Ireland of Minneapolis, and Cardinal Moran of Sydney" ("Pope of the Worker," Dec. 1, 2007 at https://www.catholic.com/magazine/print-edition/pope-of-the-worker [retrieved September 28, 2018]). In tandem with these efforts, an original body of Catholic teaching was developed that sought to understand the new social problems and to formulate solutions based on the gospel. "In France, Villeneuve de Bargemont wrote an 1834 treatise on political and Christian life, while in Germany, Bishop Wilhelm E. von Ketteler of Mainz helped launch a Catholic social movement that expanded swiftly across Europe after 1870. [Pope] Leo [XIII] later called von Ketteler 'our great predecessor from whom I have learned.'...Finally, the Fribourg Union, founded in 1884 and headed by Mermillod, brought together various leaders in the nascent Catholic social movement" (Bunson).
110. Gibson 1989, 161; Pocetto 2014, 127.

111. Gough, 1. Also see Gibson 1989, 80–87.

112. Wright 2004, 182n15; Chorpenning, 456–59. In the post–Vatican II era, there has been a burgeoning literature on *lectio divina*, attesting to the growing interest in and popularity of this slow, meditative approach to the sacred text. One of the most influential contemporary promoters and practitioners of *lectio divina*—the Jesuit biblical scholar Cardinal Carlo Maria Martini—looked to Francis de Sales as a guide for this prayerful approach to Scripture. See Carlo Maria Martini, SJ, *The Gospel Way of Mary: A Journey of Trust and Surrender*, trans. Marsha Daigle-Williamson (Frederick, MD: The Word Among Us Press, 2011), 31–35.

113. Terence McGoldrick, "The Living Word: Francis de Sales, A Humanist Biblical Theologian of the Renaissance," in *Love Is the Perfection of the Mind: Salesian Studies Presented to Alexander T. Pocetto, OSFS, on the Occasion of His 90th Birthday*, ed. Joseph F. Chorpenning, OSFS, Thomas F. Dailey, OSFS, and Daniel P. Wisniewski, OSFS (Center Valley, PA: Salesian Center for Faith and Culture, 2017), 83–101, at 92. The description of Francis as the "the gospel speaking" is found in "Déposition de M. Vincent au procès de béatification de saint François de Sales, version française, 1628," in John Rybolt, CM, *Saint Vincent de Paul / Correspondence, Conferences, Documents*, Unpublished Documents, Part 1 (2020), 174–87, at 178 (https://via.library.depaul.edu/coste_en/3, accessed May 14, 2020). The word *parlant* can also be translated as "revealing" (as in, he revealed the gospel), as well as "speaking" or even "eloquent." I am grateful to Dr. Suzanne Tocyski for this observation.

114. Brisson, 4:209–11.

115. Jacques-Bénigne Bossuet (1627–1704), a French bishop and theologian, is renowned as one of the most brilliant preachers of all time. He was instructed in preaching by St. Vincent de Paul, specifically his "Little Method," which in turn was influenced by St. Francis de Sales's theory and practice of preaching. See Edward R. Udovic, CM, "'On the Eminent Dignity of the Poor in the Church': A Sermon by Jacques Bénigne Bossuet," *Vincentian Heritage Journal* 13/1 (1992): 37–58, esp. 43.

116. Chappuis's Bible was a two-volume folio edition, illustrated with engravings by Gustave Doré (1832–83), the most popular French designer of wood-engraved book illustration of the mid-nineteenth century. Today this Bible rests on the table beside the Good Mother's deathbed in her room in the Troyes Visitation Monastery, which has been preserved intact. For a photo of this room, see *ICSS* (International Commission for Salesian Studies) *Newsletter* 21 (March 2008): 6, fig. 9.

117. Fr. Cyrille Chevalier (1801–61), a priest of the Diocese of Troyes and professor of moral theology at the diocesan seminary, was the teacher and long-time friend of Brisson. Chevalier frequently visited the Troyes Visitation Monastery to confer with Chappuis.

118. Brisson, 7:245–50.

119. Annecy edition, 23:303.

120. On his arrival in Paris in 1618, Francis de Sales was hailed as "the greatest theologian of [his] time" (Ravier, 222). When his masterwork, *Treatise on the Love of God*, was published (1616), the Sorbonne and the Jesuits declared that this work placed Francis de Sales among the ranks of the four great doctors of the Western Church—Augustine (354–430), Jerome (ca. 345–420), Ambrose (ca. 339–97), and Gregory the Great (ca. 540–604). See M. Hamon, *Vie de Saint François de Sales*, 6th ed., 2 vols. (Paris–Lyon: Librairie Jacques Lecoffre, 1875), 2:180.

121. For an introduction to Thérèse's Little Way, see Ernest Larkin, OCarm, "The Little Way of St. Thérèse of Lisieux," *Review for Religious* 59, no. 5 (2000): 507–17.

122. Brisson, 6:315–16.

123. Brisson's *Life of the Venerable Mother Mary de Sales Chappuis* was first published in 1886. A second edition appeared in 1891.

124. Here Brisson likely has in mind the article "Une nouvelle école de spiritualité," by the Jesuit Henri Watrigant, SJ, published in *Études publiées par les Pères de la Compagnie de Jésus* 79 (June 5, 1899): 614–32. Subsequently, Watrigant expanded his article into a book, entitled *Deux méthodes de spiritualité: Étude critique* [Two methods of spirituality: A critical study] (Lille-Paris: Desclée de Brouwer, 1900).

125. Johann Georg Hagen (1847–1930) was an Austrian Jesuit priest and astronomer. In 1880, he immigrated to the United States, eventually becoming a naturalized citizen. In 1888, Hagen was appointed director of the Georgetown University Observatory, where he published a number of important articles and books in the fields of astronomy and mathematics. In 1906, Pope St. Pius X (1835–1914, r. 1903–14) appointed him as the first Jesuit director of the Vatican Observatory, in which position he served until his death in 1930. Hagen was also the spiritual director of Maria Elizabeth Hesselblad (1870–1957), who was baptized by him in 1902 and canonized a saint by Pope Francis in 2016. The crater Hagen, 55 km in diameter, on the far side of the moon, is named for him.

126. The *Annales Salésiennes* is a periodical founded by Brisson in 1888. It is currently published under the auspices of the Association Recherches et Études Salésiennes (RES).

127. Fr. Joseph Fragnières's assessment took the form of a sermon, preached in the church of the monastery of the Visitation in Fribourg on November 19, 1897, during the triduum celebrating the introduction of the Good Mother's cause for beatification, and published in 1898 as a brochure by the *Annales Salésiennes*. Watrigant's 1899 article was a reaction to the sermon by Fragnières, who had let slip into his praise of "the Way" remarks critical of St. Ignatius of Loyola's *Spiritual Exercises*, drawing Watrigant's ire. For an account and critical analysis of the controversy, see Roger Balducelli, OSFS, *The Cause of the Beatification of the Venerable Mother Mary de Sales Chappuis*, trans. Alexander T. Pocetto, OSFS (Rome: International Commission for Salesian Studies, 2000).

128. Jean-Marie Tissot, MSFS (1810–90), was a member of the first team of missionaries sent to India by the founder of the Missionaries of St. Francis de Sales, or Fransalians, Fr. Pierre-Marie Mermier (1790–1862). Tissot later served as the fourth superior general of the Fransalians, as well as the second vicar apostolic and first bishop of Visakhapatnam (1863–90).

129. See Salesian/Oblate Chronology, 271–72; *The Life of the Venerable Mother Mary de Sales Chappuis of the Order of the Visitation of Holy Mary, 1793–1875* (Brooklyn: Sisters of the Visitation, 1924), 84–89 (account of the opening of the tomb), 104–10 (English translation of the decree introducing the cause of beatification).

130. Sr. Madeleine-Thérèse Dechambre, OSFS, "History of the Cause of Blessed Louis Brisson," *ICSS Newsletter* 29 (Feb. 2013): 23–28 (available in print and electronically at http://www.franz-von-sales.de/icss_en/index.html).

131. d'Esmauges, 166–78.

5. CAROLINE CARRÉ DE MALBERG, HENRI CHAUMONT, AND THE SOCIETY OF THE DAUGHTERS OF ST. FRANCIS DE SALES

1. Msgr. Laveille, *L'Abbé Henri Chaumont, La Première Mère des Filles de Saint-François de Sales*, 3rd ed. (Paris: Au Siège de la Société, 1900), 153.

2. *OEA* III, *Introduction à la vie dévote*, Preface 6.

3. Gaëtan Bernoville, *Madame Carré de Malberg, Fondatrice de la Société des Filles de Saint François de Sales* (Paris: Eds. Bernard Grasset, 1951), 64.

4. Msgr. Laveille, Vicaire général de Meaux, *L'abbé Chaumont, fondateur de trois sociétés salésiennes (1838–1896)* (Tours: Maison Alfred Mame et fils/Paris: Pierre Téqui, 1919), 55.

5. Laveille, *L'Abbé Chaumont*, 59.

6. L'Abbé Henri Chaumont, *Directions spirituelles de Saint François de Sales* (Paris: Victor Palmé, 1872–79).

7. A MS (not cited here) entitled "Explication du règlement" is available at the Centre salésien in Paris.

8. The perfection of love.

9. Henri Chaumont, *Rule of Life*, MS copy in the hand of Mlle Stiltz, n.d. Centre salésien, Paris.

10. Laveille, *L'Abbé Chaumont*, 153.

11. L'Abbé Henri Chaumont, *La Première Mère des Filles de Saint-François de Sales*, 3rd ed. (Paris: Au Siège de la Société, 1900), 138.

12. Chaumont, *La Première Mère*, xviii.

13. Laveille, *L'Abbé Chaumont*, 199.

14. Estimates suggest some twenty ecclesiastics were executed. Barbara de Courson, "Martyrs of the Paris Commune," *The Catholic Encyclopedia*, vol. 4 (New York: Robert Appleton Company, 1908), accessed June 5, 2019, http://www.newadvent.org/cathen/04168a.htm.

15. Chaumont, *La Première Mère*, 136.

16. Laveille, *L'Abbé Chaumont*, 165.

17. M. le Chanoine Collin, in his 1916 introduction to Msgr. Laveille, *Madame Carré de Malberg (Vénérable Caroline-Barbe Colchen), Fondatrice de la Société des Filles de Saint-François-de-Sales (1828–1891)* (Paris: Editions Pierre Téqui, 1925), viii.

18. Chaumont to Caroline Carré and her sisters, August 17, 1872, Centre salésien, Paris.

19. Laveille, *Madame Carré*, 163–65.

20. Chaumont, *La Première Mère*, 155. For more on the centrality of the "gentle and easy yoke" of Jesus to Salesian spirituality, see Wendy Wright, "'That Is What It Is Made For': Image of the Heart in the Spirituality of Francis de Sales and Jane de Chantal," in *Spiritualities of the Heart*, ed. Annice Callahan (Mahwah, NJ: Paulist Press, 1990): 143–58; Thomas McHugh, "The Distinctive Salesian Virtues: Humility and Gentleness," *Salesian Studies* (October 1963): 45–74; and Thomas A. Donlan, "Order of the Visitation of Holy Mary: Witness to a

Catholicism of *Douceur*," in *Love Is the Perfection of the Mind: Salesian Studies Presented to Alexander T. Pocetto, OSFS, on the Occasion of His 90th Birthday*, ed. Joseph F. Chorpenning, OSFS, Thomas F. Dailey, OSFS, and Daniel P. Wisniewski, OSFS (Center Valley, PA: Salesian Center for Faith and Culture, 2017), 35–48.

21. Orphaned herself at the age of eighteen months, Baroness Jane Frances de Chantal was widowed at age twenty-eight when her husband was killed in a hunting accident. Her first two children were stillborn, her youngest daughter Charlotte died at age nine, and her son Celse-Bénigne predeceased Jane in 1627 at the age of thirty-one. Over several years of her religious life, Jane would also experience periods of darkness, internal anguish, and spiritual dryness. Finally, she was the last who remained alive of all the Sisters with whom she began the Visitation Order.

22. Chaumont to the Daughters, August 19, 1872, Centre salésien, Paris.

23. Carré to Chaumont, August 25, 1872, Centre salésien, Paris.

24. Caroline Carré's *Acte de Protestation* came earlier.

25. The original reads, "une extrême et forte suavité."

26. Chaumont to Carré, October 11, 1872, Centre salésien, Paris.

27. Carré to Mlle de Parieu, October 22, 1872, Centre salésien, Paris.

28. In his letter to Mme Carré dated August 17, 1872, l'Abbé Chaumont expresses the regret "of not being able to speak to you often enough nor broadly enough about Mary, our Divine Mother. The direction of souls," he goes on to say, "requires so many details, that St. Francis de Sales, who so loved the Holy Virgin, rarely found the time to talk about her as his heart desired." (Chaumont to Carré and her sisters, August 17, 1872, Centre salésien, Paris).

29. A reference to the upcoming renewal of hostilities between France and Germany.

30. Chaumont to the Daughters, March 16, 1873, Centre salésien, Paris.

31. The quotation is borrowed from Prosper Louis Pascal Guéranger, OSB, *L'année liturgique*, a treatise in 15 volumes written between 1841 and 1875.

32. Chaumont, "Etre Marie," MS in the hand of Sr. Marie Gertrude, 1884, Centre salésien, Paris.

33. The original French reads, "Il ne faut pas écouter la fausse raison ou la fausse justice."

34. Chaumont to Carré and the Daughters, November 7, 1873, Centre salésien, Paris.

35. Chaumont, *La Première Mère*, 346.

36. Carré, MS of retreat notes, December 1–8, 1874, Centre salésien, Paris.

37. Brenna Moore, *Sacred Dread: Raïssa Maritain, the Allure of Suffering, and the French Catholic Revival (1905–1944)* (Notre Dame, IN: University of Notre Dame Press, 2013), 5–6.

38. Chaumont, *La Première Mère*, 20.

39. Mme Carré's suffering due to her husband's treatment are recounted at length in *Meten. Beatifications*, 47–49, 203–6, and 264–65.

40. Mlle Stiltz also notes that Mme Carré used stinging nettles as a kind of scourge. *Meten. Beatificationis*, 223.

41. Testimony of Mlle Stiltz, *Meten. Beatificationis*, 113.

42. Testimony of Mlle Stiltz, *Meten. Beatificationis*, 136.

43. Carré to Chaumont, August 18, 1878, Centre salésien, Paris.

44. Laveille, *Madame Carré*, 142.

45. Laveille, *Madame Carré*, 270–71.

46. Bernoville, 261.

47. St. Francis de Sales was declared a doctor of the church by Pope Pius IX in 1877.

48. The English translation is *Lift up your hearts!*

49. Carré to the first Catechist-Missionaries, October 8, 1889, Centre salésien, Paris.

50. Chaumont, *Première Mère*, 468–69.

51. This work could not have been completed without the support of the Centre salésien in Paris, and particularly the generous assistance of archivist Marie Lagriffoul.

BIBLIOGRAPHIES

SEMINAL SALESIAN SOURCES

Oeuvres de Saint François de Sales. Édition complète par les soins des Religieuses de la Monastère de la Visitation. XXVI vols. Annecy: J. Nierat, 1892–1964.

Saint François de Sales. Oeuvres. Textes presentés et annotés par André Ravier. Bibliotheque de la Pléiade. Paris: Éditions Gallimard, 1969.

Sainte Jeanne de Chantal. *Correspondance.* Édition critique établie et annotée par Soeur Marie-Patricia Burns. VIII vols. Paris: Les Éditions du Cerf, 1986–93.

————. *Sa vie et ses oeuvres.* VI vols. Par les soins des Religieuses de la Monastère de la Visitation. Paris: Plon, 1874–79.

Vie et Oeuvres de Sainte Marguerite Marie Alacoque. Présentation du professeur Darricau. II vols. Paris: Éditions Saint Paul, 1990–91.

THE LONG NINETEENTH CENTURY IN FRANCE

Aston, Nigel. *Religion and Revolution in France 1780–1804.* Washington, DC: Catholic University of America Press, 2000.

Bouflet, Joachim, and Philippe Boutry. *Un signe dans le ciel: les apparitions de la Vierge.* Paris: Bernard Grasset, 1997.

Burson, Jeffrey D. "The Catholic Enlightenment in France from the *fin de siècle* Crisis of Consciousness to the Revolution, 1650–1789." In *A Companion to the Catholic Enlightenment in Europe*, edited by Ulrich L. Lerner and Michael Printy, 63–125. Boston: Brill, 2010.

Cranston, Ruth. *The Miracle of Lourdes.* New York: Image/Doubleday, 1988.

Gibson, Ralph. *A Social History of French Catholicism, 1789–1914.* London: Routledge, 1989.

Harrison, Carol E. *Romantic Catholics: France's Post-revolutionary Generation in Search of a Modern Faith*. Ithaca, NY: Cornell University Press, 2014.

Kselman, Thomas A. *Miracles and Prophecies in Nineteenth-Century France*. New Brunswick, NJ: Rutgers University Press, 1983.

Lehner, Ulrich L. *The Catholic Enlightenment: The Forgotten History of a Global Movement*. New York: Oxford University Press, 2016.

Perry, Nicholas, and Loreto Echeverria. *Under the Hell of Mary*. London: Routledge, 1988.

Ravitch, Norman. *The Catholic Church and the French Nation 1598–1989*. New York: Routledge, 1990.

PIERRE-MARIE MERMIER, JOSEPH-MARIE FAVRE, PIERRE-JOSEPH REY, AND THE MISSIONARIES OF ST. FRANCIS DE SALES OF ANNECY

Primary Sources

Pierre-Marie Mermier: Recueil de Textes, Série I, Le Fondateur. Collected and transcribed by Adrien Duval, MSFS. n.d.

Secondary Sources

Carron, Yves, MSFS. "Fr. Mermier and the Usefulness of a Body of Missioners in the Diocese of Annecy." Jubilee talk, La Puya, Annecy, France, October 22, 2013.

———. "Towards the Beatification of the Servant of God: Fr. Peter Marie Mermier—What Is Done So Far and What Is Yet to Be Done...." *Missionaries of St. Francis de Sales Global Mission Bulletin* 1, no. 1 (June 2020): 23–25.

Châtellier, Louis. *The Religion of the Poor: Rural Missions in Europe and the Formation of Modern Catholicism, c. 1500–1800*. Translated by Brian Pearce. New York: Cambridge University Press, 1997.

Chorpenning, Joseph F., OSFS. "Salesian Gentleness and Humility in Action: St. Francis de Sales's Missionary Apostolate in the Chablais." *ICSS* [= International Commission for Salesian Studies] *Newsletter* 17 (Jan.–Feb. 2006): 3–5, 12.

————. "What Is the 'Chablais Spirit?'" *ICSS Newsletter* 18 (July 2006): 1–9.

Delahaye, Blandine. "Le visage du prêtre selon François de Sales (1567–1622) à la lumière de sa *Correspondance*." In *L'image du prêtre dans la littérature classique (XVIIe–XVIIIe siècles): Actes du colloque organisé par le Centre "Michel Baude—Littérature et spiritualité" de l'Université de Metz, 20–21 novembre 1998*, edited by Danielle Pister, 25–46. Bern: Peter Lang, 2001.

Dormandy, John. *A History of Savoy: Gatekeeper of the Alps.* London: Fonthill, 2018.

Duval, Adrien, MSFS. "At the Service of the Mission: Pierre-Marie Mermier." Unpublished paper. Translated by Ivo Carneiro, MSFS. 1987. Available at https://d2y1pz2y630308.cloudfront.net/19852/documents/2018/7/A.3.%20Fr%20Mermier%20at%20the%20service%20of%20the%20Mission.pdf (accessed November 24, 2021).

————. *Monsieur Mermier 1790–1862: Founder of Two Religious Congregations.* Translated by Vincent Kerns, MSFS. Bangalore: SFS Publications, 1985.

————. *Un disciple de Saint François de Sales: Pierre-Marie Mermier, 1790–1862. Pionnier de la "Mission Pastorale" en Savoie.* Annecy: Gardet, 1982.

Fehleison, Jill R. "Appealing to the Senses: The Forty Hours Celebrations in the Duchy of Chablais, 1597–98." *Sixteenth Century Journal* 36, no. 2 (2005): 375–96.

————. *Boundaries of Faith: Catholics and Protestants in the Diocese of Geneva.* Kirksville, MO: Truman State University Press, 2010.

Hennequin, Jacques. "Aspects du sacerdoce selon François de Sales." In *L'image du prêtre dans la littérature classique (XVIIe–XVIIIe siècles): Actes du colloque organisé par le Centre "Michel Baude—Littérature et spiritualité" de l'Université de Metz, 20–21 novembre 1998*, edited by Danielle Pister, 47–52. Bern: Peter Lang, 2001.

Moget, Francis, MSFS. *The Missionaries of St. Francis de Sales of Annecy.* Bangalore: SFS Publications, 1985.

Régent-Susini, Anne. "Tears for Fears: Mission Preaching in Seventeenth-Century France—A Double Performance." In *Spoken Word and Social Practice: Orality in Europe (1400–1700)*, edited by Thomas V. Cohen and Lesley K. Twomey, 185–205. Boston: Brill, 2015.

"St. Francis de Sales, A Missionary Leader; Fr. Mermier in His 'I Want Mission Experience.'" Working Paper 2, General Chapter 2007, Missionaries of St. Francis de Sales.

Stopp, Elisabeth. "*Meditations on the Church* (1595–96)." In Elisabeth Stopp, *A Man to Heal Differences: Essays and Talks on St. Francis de Sales*, 51–74. Philadelphia: Saint Joseph's University Press, 1997. (Originally published in *Salesian Studies* 4, no. 4 [Autumn 1967]: 35–69.)

Wright, Wendy M. *Heart Speaks to Heart: The Salesian Tradition.* Traditions of Christian Spirituality Series. Maryknoll, NY: Orbis Books, 2004.

SALESIAN FAMILY OF DON BOSCO

Primary Sources

Bosco, Giovanni, Santo. *Fonti Salesiane: 1. Don Bosco e la sua opera. Raccolta antologica.* A cura di Francesco Motto, José Manuel Prellezo, e Aldo Giraudo. Istituto Storico Salesiano. Rome: Libreria Ateneo Salesiano (LAS), 2014.

English-Language Resources

Bosco, Giovanni, St. *Memoirs of the Oratory of Saint Francis de Sales: The Autobiography of Saint John Bosco.* Translated by Daniel Lyons, SDB. Notes and commentary by Eugenio Certa, SDB, Lawrence Castelvecchi, SDB, and Michael Mendl, SDB. New Rochelle, NY: Don Bosco Publications, 1989.

————. *Salesian Sources: 1. Don Bosco and His Work.* Salesian Historical Institute, Rome. Translated by the SDB International English Translation Team. Bengaluru: Kristu Jyoti Publications, 2017.

Studies

Aubry, Joseph, ed. *The Spiritual Writings of Saint John Bosco.* 2 volumes. Translated by Joseph Caselli. New Rochelle, NY: Don Bosco Publications, 1984.

Auffray, Augustin. *Saint John Bosco.* Translated by William Henry Mitchell. 2nd ed. Reprint. Macclesfield, UK: Salesiana Publications, 1964.

Braido, Pietro. *Don Bosco's Pedagogical Experience.* Rome: LAS, 1989.

Desramaut, Francis. *Don Bosco and the Spiritual Life.* Translated by Roger B. Luna. New Rochelle, NY: Salesiana, 1979.

Egan, Patrick, and Mario Midali, eds. *Don Bosco's Place in History*. Acts of the First International Congress of Don Bosco Studies. Salesian Pontifical University, Rome, January 16–20, 1989. Rome: LAS, 1993.

Lemoyne, Giovanni Battista, Angelo Amadei, and Eugenio Ceria. *The Biographical Memoirs of Saint John Bosco*. 18 vols. Translated by Diego Borgatello and John Drury. New Rochelle, NY: Salesiana Publishers, 1964–2003.

Lenti, Arthur J. *Don Bosco, His Pope and His Bishop: The Trials of a Founder*. Centro Studi Don Bosco, Studi Storici—15. Rome: LAS, 2006.

————. *Don Bosco History and Spirit*. Edited by Aldo Giraudo. 7 volumes. Rome: LAS, 2007–2010.

Morrison, John. *The Educational Philosophy of St. John Bosco*. New Rochelle, NY: Salesian Publications, 1979.

Stella, Pietro. *Don Bosco and the Death of Charles*. An appendix to *Don Bosco: Life and Work*. Translated by John Drury. New Rochelle, NY: Don Bosco Publications, 1985.

————. *Don Bosco: Life and Work*. Translated by John Drury. New Rochelle, NY: Don Bosco Publications, 1985.

————. *Don Bosco: Religious Outlook and Spirituality*. Second revised ed. Translated by John Drury. New Rochelle, NY: Salesiana Publishers, 1996.

————. *Don Bosco's Dreams: A Historico-Documentary Analysis of Selected Samples*. Translated by John Drury. New Rochelle, NY: Salesiana Publishers, 1996.

DAUGHTERS OF MARY HELP OF CHRISTIANS

Capetti, Giselda, ed. *Cronistoria: Chronicles of the Institute of the Daughters of Mary Help of Christians*. 5 vols. Translated by the FMA English-Translation Group. New Rochelle, NY: Don Bosco Publications, 1981.

Maccono, Fernando. *Saint Mary D. Mazzarello: Co-foundress and First Superior General of the Daughters of Mary Help of Christians*. Translated by Catherine Hurley. New Rochelle, NY: Don Bosco Publications, 1980.

Mazzarello, Maria Domenica, St. *I Will Never Forget You: Letters of Maria Domenica Mazzarello*. Edited by María Esther Posada, Anna Costa, and Piera Cavaglià. Translated by the FMA English-Translation

Group. Rome: Institute of the Daughters of Mary Help of Christians, 2000.

SALESIAN FAMILY

Raphael, Jayapalan, ed. *The Salesian Family of Don Bosco*. Elmwood Park, NJ: G&H Soho, 2020.

MARY DE SALES CHAPPUIS, LOUIS BRISSON, LÉONIE FRANCES DE SALES AVIAT, AND THE OBLATE SISTERS AND OBLATES OF ST. FRANCIS DE SALES

Primary Sources

[Aviat, Françoise de Sales]. *Résumé des Noviciats faits par N.T.H. Mère Aviat aux premières novices de l'Institut et rédigés de mémoire par l'une d'elles.* Perugia, 1916; repr., 1966.

Brisson, Louis, OSFS. *Chapîtres, Retraites, Instructions et Allocutions.* 7 vols. Tilburg, The Netherlands: Maison "Ave Maria," 1966–68.

———. *Chapters, Retreats, Instructions, and Sermons.* Translated by Joseph D. Bowler, OSFS. 7 vols. Center Valley, PA: Oblates of St. Francis de Sales/Allentown College of St. Francis de Sales, 1981–86.

———. Draft of letter of October 14, 1867, to Fr. Claude Perrot, OSB. Archives of the Oblate Generalate, Rome. Box 30, Einsiedeln Collection.

———. *The Life of the Venerable Mother Mary de Sales Chappuis.* Translated by Joseph D. Bowler, OSFS. Center Valley, PA: Oblates of St. Francis de Sales, 1986.

———. *Œuvres.* Edition millénaire. Texte intégrale établis par le P. Roger Balducelli, OSFS, avec la collaboration de P. Jean Gayet, OSFS, et des Sœurs Oblates de la Maison Mère, Troyes. Available at louisbrisson.org.

———. *Résumé des Retraites Prêchées aux jeunes Ouvrières des Œuvres des Oblates de Saint François de Sales à Troyes de 1870 à 1901 par leur Fondateur Le Vénéré Père Louis Brisson.* Perugia: Imprimerie G. Squartinini, 1927.

————. *Vie de la vénérée Mère Marie de Sales Chappuis*. Paris: chez M. l'Aumonier de la Visitation, 1891.

Chantal, Jane Frances de, St. *St. Francis de Sales: A Testimony by St. Chantal*. Newly edited in translation with an introduction by Elisabeth Stopp. Hyattsville, MD: Institute of Salesian Studies, 1967.

The Constitutions, General Statues, and Spiritual Directory of the Oblates of Saint Francis de Sales. American Centenary Edition. Wilmington, DE: De Sales Publishing, 1991.

John Paul II, Pope St. *Letter on the Fourth Centenary of the Episcopal Ordination of St. Francis de Sales*. November 23, 2002. Available at https://www.vatican.va/content/john-paul-ii/en/letters/2002/documents/hf_jp-ii_let_20021209_francesco-sales.html.

Magistri, Barthélémy. *Cérémonies et resjouissances faites en la ville d'Annessy sur la solennité de la béatification et l'élévation du corps sacré du bienheureux François de Sales, le 30. d'avril 1662*. Annecy, Pierre Delachinal: 1662.

Paul VI, Pope St. *Sabaudiae gemma* [Gem of Savoy]: *Apostolic Letter Commemorating the 400th Anniversary of the Birth of St. Francis de Sales, Doctor of the Church*. Translated by Neil Kilty, OSFS. Hyattsville, MD: Institute of Salesian Studies, 1967.

Paul, Vincent de. "Deposition at the Process of Beatification of Francis de Sales (April 17, 1628)." In St. Vincent de Paul, *Correspondance, Conferences, Documents*, edited and translated by Marie Poole, DC, et al, 13a: 80–139. 14 vols. Hyde Park, NY: New City Press, 1985–2014.

Sales, François de, St. *Œuvres*. Edited by André Ravier and Roger Devos. Bibliothèque de la Pléiade. Paris: Gallimard, 1969.

————. *Œuvres de saint François de Sales*. Édition complete. 27 vols. Annecy: J. Niérat et al., 1892–1964.

St. Francis de Sales. *On the Preacher and Preaching*. Translated with an introduction and notes by John K. Ryan. Chicago: Henry Regnery Company, 1964.

Secondary Sources

Balducelli, Roger, OSFS. *The Cause of the Beatification of the Venerable Mother Mary de Sales Chappuis*. Translated by Alexander T. Pocetto, OSFS. Rome: International Commission for Salesian Studies, 2000.

Beaudoin, Yvon, OMI. *Father Louis Brisson (1817–1908): A Documented Biography*. Translated by several De Sales Oblates. Edited by Alexander

T. Pocetto, OSFS, and Daniel P. Wisniewski, OSFS. Wilmington, DE: Oblates of St. Francis de Sales, 2008.

Bouchard, Françoise. *Father Louis Brisson: A Heart That Beats in Rhythm with God*. Paris: Salvator, 2011.

Burton, Katherine. *So Much So Soon: Father Brisson, Founder of the Oblates of St. Francis de Sales*. New York: Benziger, 1953.

Cahalan, James. "St. Vincent and the Priesthood." *Colloque: Journal of the Irish Province of the Congregation of the Mission* 7 (Spring 1983): 51–58.

Carey, Patrick W. *Confession: Catholics, Repentance & Forgiveness in America*. New York: Oxford University Press, 2018.

Ceresko, Anthony R., OSFS. "St. Francis de Sales's *Spiritual Directory* for a New Century: Re-interpreting the 'Direction of Intention.'" In Anthony R. Ceresko, OSFS, *St. Francis de Sales and the Bible*, 110–27. Bangalore: SFS Publications, 2006. (Originally published in *Indian Journal of Spirituality* 14 [2001]: 377–91.)

Chorpenning, Joseph F., OSFS. "The Dynamics of Divine Love: Francis de Sales's Picturing of the Biblical Mystery of the Visitation." In *Ut pictura amor: The Reflexive Imagery of Love in Artistic Theory and Practice, 1500–1700*, edited by Walter S. Melion, Joanna Woodall, and Michael Zell, 485–531. Intersections: Interdisciplinary Studies in Early Modern Culture 48. Boston: Brill, 2017.

———. "*Lectio divina* and Francis de Sales's Picturing of the Interconnection of Human and Divine Hearts." In *Imago Exegetica: Visual Images as Exegetical Instruments, 1400–1700*, ed. Walter S. Melion and Michel Weemans, 449–77. Intersections: Interdisciplinary Studies in Early Modern Culture 33. Boston: Brill, 2014.

Dechambre, Sr. Madeleine-Thérèse, OSFS. "History of the Cause of Blessed Louis Brisson." *ICSS Newsletter* 29 (February 2013): 23–28.

Donlan, Thomas A. *The Reform of Zeal: François de Sales and Militant French Catholicism*. St. Andrews Studies in French History and Culture. St. Andrews, UK: Centre for French History and Culture of the University of St. Andrews, 2018.

Dufour, Prosper, OSFS. *Les Oblats de Saint-François de Sales*. Paris: Librairie Letouzey et Ané, 1933.

———. *Le Très Révérend Père Louis Brisson, Fondateur des Oblates et Oblats de S. François de Sales (1817–1908)*. Paris: Desclée de Brouwer, 1936.

d'Esmauges, Marie-Aimée. *To Forget Myself Entirely: Mother Frances de Sales, 1844–1914.* Translated by Oblate Sisters of St. Francis de Sales. Childs, MD: Oblate Sisters of St. Francis de Sales, 1991.

Gibson, Ralph. "Hellfire and Damnation in Nineteenth-Century France." *Catholic Historical Review* 74, no. 3 (1988): 383–402.

———. *A Social History of French Catholicism 1789–1914.* New York: Routledge, 1989.

Gough, Austin. *Paris and Rome: The Gallican Church and the Ultramontane Campaign 1848–1853.* Oxford: Clarendon Press, 1986.

Guiderdoni, Agnès. "Exegetical Immersion: The Festivities on the Occasion of Francis de Sales's Canonisation (1665–1667)." In *Imago Exegetica: Visual Images as Exegetical Instruments, 1400–1700,* edited by Walter S. Melion and Michel Weemans, 855–84. Intersections: Interdisciplinary Studies in Early Modern Culture 33. Boston: Brill, 2014.

Hedouville, Marthe de. *Monseigneur de Ségur: Sa vie-son action 1820–1881.* Paris: Nouvelles Éditions Latines, 1957.

Heywood, Colin. "Learning Democracy in France: Popular Politics in Troyes, c. 1830–1900." *The Historical Journal* 47, no. 4 (2004): 921–39.

Koster, Dirk, OSFS. *Louis Brisson.* Noorden, Netherlands: Publisher Bert Post, 2008.

Kwatera, Michael, OSB. "Marian Feasts in the Roman, Troyes and Paris Missals and Breviaries and the Critique of Dom Prosper Guéranger." PhD dissertation, University of Notre Dame, 1993.

Lajeunie, E.-J., OP. *Saint Francis de Sales: The Man, the Thinker, His Influence.* Translated by Rory O'Sullivan, OSFS. 2 vols. Bangalore: SFS Publications, 1986–87.

Larkin, Ernest, OCarm. "The Little Way of St. Thérèse of Lisieux." *Review for Religious* 59, no. 5 (2000): 507–17.

Lehner, Ulrich. *The Catholic Enlightenment: The Forgotten History of a Global Movement.* New York: Oxford University Press, 2016.

The Life of the Venerable Mother Mary de Sales Chappuis of the Order of the Visitation of Holy Mary, 1793–1875. Brooklyn: Sisters of the Visitation, 1924.

McGoldrick, Terence. "The Living Word: Francis de Sales, a Humanist Biblical Theologian of the Renaissance." In *Love Is the Perfection of the Mind: Salesian Studies Presented to Alexander T. Pocetto, OSFS on the Occasion of His 90th Birthday,* edited by Joseph Chorpenning, OSFS, Thomas Dailey, OSFS, and Daniel Wisniewski, OSFS, 83–101. Center Valley, PA: Salesian Center for Faith and Culture, 2017.

O'Malley, John W., SJ. *Vatican I: The Council and the Making of the Ultramontane Church*. Cambridge, MA: Harvard University Press, 2018.

Pocetto, Alexander T., OSFS. "Blessed Louis Brisson (1817–1908), the Laity, and the Social Dimensions of the New Evangelization." *Salesianum* 76 (2014): 121–40.

———. "Mary de Sales Chappuis (1793–1875): Apostle of the Salesian Spirit." *Salesianum* 71 (2009): 321–40.

———. "The *Spiritual Directory* in the American Oblate Tradition." Unpublished paper available online at https://www.desales.edu/docs/default-source/salesian-center-docs/salesian---fr.-pocetto/spir-direct.pdf?sfvrsn=2d632761_2.

Quantin, Jean-Louis. *Le rigorisme chrétien*. Histoire de Christianisme. Paris: Cerf, 2001.

Ranum, Orest. *Paris in the Age of Absolutism: An Essay*. Revised and expanded ed. 1968. University Park: Pennsylvania State University Press, 2002.

Ravier, André, SJ. *Francis de Sales: Sage & Saint*. Translated by Joseph D. Bowler, OSFS. San Francisco: Ignatius Press, 1988.

Román, José María, CM. *St. Vincent de Paul: A Biography*. Translated by Sr. Joyce Howard. London: Melisende, 1999.

Van Kley, Dale K. *Reform Catholicism and the International Suppression of the Jesuits in Enlightenment Europe*. New Haven, CT: Yale University Press, 2018.

Wilson, Christopher C. "Masculinity Restored: The Visual Shaping of St. John of the Cross." *Archive for Reformation History* 98, no. 1 (2007): 134–66.

Wright, Wendy M. "The Doctor of Divine Love and Fear of the Lord." In *Saving Fear in Christian Spirituality*, edited by Ann W. Astell, 182–208. Notre Dame, IN: Notre Dame University Press, 2020.

———. *Heart Speaks to Heart: The Salesian Tradition*. Traditions of Christian Spirituality Series. Maryknoll, NY: Orbis Books, 2004.

DAUGHTERS OF ST. FRANCIS DE SALES

Primary Sources

Caroline Carré de Malberg to Henri Chaumont (August 25, 1872). From Centre salésien, Paris (accessed July 22, 2019).

————. To Mlle de Parieu (October 22, 1872). From Centre salésien, Paris (accessed July 22, 2019).

————. To Henri Chaumont (August 18, 1878) Centre salésien, Paris (accessed July 22, 2019).

————. To the first Catechist-Missionaries (October 8, 1889). Centre salésien, Paris (accessed July 22, 2019).

————. Retreat Notes, December 1–8, 1874. Manuscript. From Centre salésien, Paris (accessed July 22, 2019).

Chaumont, Henri, Abbé. "Être Marie" (*probation* by Henri Chaumont in the hand of Sr. Marie Gertude), 1884. Manuscript. From Centre salésien, Paris (accessed July 22, 2019).

————. To Caroline Carré and her companions (August 17, 1872). Centre salésien, Paris (accessed July 22, 2019).

————. To the Daughters of St. Francis de Sales (August 19, 1872). Centre salésien, Paris (accessed July 22, 2019).

————. To Caroline Carré de Malberg (October 11, 1872). Centre salésien, Paris (accessed July 22, 2019).

————. To the Daughters of St. Francis de Sales (March 16, 1873). Centre salésien, Paris (accessed July 22, 2019).

————. To Caroline Carré de Malberg and the Daughters of St. Francis de Sales (November 7, 1873). Centre salésien, Paris (accessed July 22, 2019).

————. *Règlement de vie*, copy in the hand of Mlle Stiltz, n.d. Manuscript. Centre salésien, Paris (accessed July 22, 2019).

Secondary Sources

Bernoville, Gaëtan. *Madame Carré de Malberg, Fondatrice de la Société des Filles de Saint François de Sales*. Paris: Ed. Grasset, 1951.

Chaumont, Henri, Abbé. *De la direction des Filles de Saint François de Sales*. Edition revue et complétée par le Directeur général de la Société des Filles de Saint François de Sales. Rome: Tipografia Ouggiani, 1932.

————. *Directions spirituelles de Saint François de Sales*. Paris: Victor Palmé, 1872–79.

————. *Lettres spirituelles de l'abbé H. Chaumont*. Ed. J. Paguelle de Follenay. Paris: Impr. de J. Mersch, 1900.

————. *Notes explicatives sur l'Introduction à la vie dévote, recueillies des instructions de l'abbé H. Chaumont*. Paris: Impr. de J. Mersch, 1902.

————. *La Première Mère de la Société des Filles de Saint-François de Sales, 3e édition*. Paris: Au Siège de la Société, 1900.

De Courson, Barbara. "Martyrs of the Paris Commune." In *The Catholic Encyclopedia*, vol. 4 (New York: Robert Appleton Company, 1908). http://www.newadvent.org/cathen/04168a.htm (accessed June 5, 2019).

Deffense, Aude. *Tout par amour: Caroline Carré de Malberg.* Bruyères-le-Châtel, France: Ed. Nouvelle Cité, 2017.

De Sales, François. *Introduction à la vie dévote. Oeuvres de Saint François de Sales* (OEA). Vol. III. OEA III. Annecy, France: J. Niérat et al. 1892–1964.

Donlan, Thomas A. "Order of the Visitation of Holy Mary: Witness to a Catholicism of *Douceur.*" In *Love Is the Perfection of the Mind: Salesian Studies Presented to Alexander T. Pocetto, O.S.F.S. on the Occasion of His 90th Birthday*, edited by Joseph F. Chorpenning, OSFS, Thomas F. Dailey, OSFS, and Daniel P. Wisniewski, OSFS, 35–48. Center Valley, PA: Salesian Center for Faith and Culture, 2017.

Guéranger, Prosper Louis Pascal, OSB. *L'année liturgique.* 15 vols. Poitiers: H. Oudin, 1841–75.

Laveille, Msgr. *Madame Carré de Malberg (Vénérable Caroline-Barbe Colchen), Fondatrice de la Société des Filles de Saint-François-de-Sales (1828–1891).* Introduction by M. le chanoine Collin (1916). Paris: Editions Pierre Téqui, 1925.

———. *L'abbé Henri Chaumont, fondateur de trois sociétés salésiennes (1838–1896).* Tours: Maison Alfred Mame et fils/Paris, Pierre Téqui, 1919.

McHugh, Thomas. "The Distinctive Salesian Virtues: Humility and Gentleness." *Salesian Studies* (October 1963): 45–74.

Meten. Beatificationis et Canonizationis Servae Dei Carolae Barbarae Colchen Carré de Malberg Fundatricia Societatis Filiarum S. Francisci Salesii, Positio super Introductione Causae. Rome: Ex Typographia Polyglotta, S. C. de Propaganda Fide, 1906.

Moore, Brenna. *Sacred Dread: Raïssa Maritain, the Allure of Suffering, and the French Catholic Revival (1905–1944).* Notre Dame, IN: University of Notre Dame Press, 2013.

Moulinet, Daniel. *Henri Chaumont: A Priest Living the Spirit of Jesus in the Heart of the World.* Translated by Suzanne Gasster-Carrière. Scotts Valley, CA: CreateSpace Independent Publishing Platform, 2016.

Wright, Wendy. "'That Is What It Is Made For': Image of the Heart in the Spirituality of Francis de Sales and Jane de Chantal." In *Spiritualities of the Heart*, edited by Annice Callahan, 143–58. Mahwah, NJ: Paulist Press, 1990.

INDEX

Help of Christians and, 4,
119–20; Daughters of St.
Francis de Sales and, 8;
departure from seminary,
71–72; education of, 62–67;
farm work and school of,
67–69; Festive Oratory of St.
Francis de Sales and, 4;
immigrant apprentices and,
82–83; madness of, suspi-
cions of, 89–90; Maria
Mazzarello to, 121–22;
ministry of, first assigned,
77; Oratory of St. Francis de
Sales founding and, 4, 96;
ordinations of, 72–77;
priesthood of, 72–77;
Pugnetti and, 69–70; *Salesian
Bulletin* publication and, 131;
Troyes Pentecost and, 8; at
Turin seminary, 75–76;
Union of Salesian
Cooperators and, 4, 130;
Valimberti and, 69–70; years
before birth of, 55–56; youth
and, abandoned, 80–81,
95–96. See also *Life of
Dominic Savio* (Don Bosco);
Memoirs of the Oratory (Don
Bosco)
Bosco, Margherita Occhiena,
57, 93
Bossuet, Jacques-Bénigne, 18, 170
Brisson, Louis: apparition of Jesus
and, 154–56; approachabil-
ity/accessibility of priests
and, 166–68; Association of
St. Francis de Sales and,
138–39; Chappuis and, 6, 8,
138–39; Chapter Instruction

of December 19, 1894 and,
161–65; Chapter Instruction
of January 25, 1893 and,
157–59; Chaumont and, 8;
death of, 174–75; de Sales
and, view of, 137; Don Bosco
and, 8; God's call and, 138;
Gospel and, reimprinting,
168–72; legacy of, 144; *Life of
the Venerable Mother Mary
de Sales Chappuis* and,
140–44, 154–56, 172–73;
Oblate Retreat of 1882 and,
169–72; Oblate Retreat of
1888 and, 166–68; Oblate
Sisters of St. Francis de Sales
and, 7–8, 135, 147–49;
priesthood of, 148–49;
priests and, 148; science and,
skill/interest in, 138; *Spiritual
Directory* and, 165; women
factory workers and, 139–40

Cafasso, Giuseppe, 4, 73, 76–77,
81, 90
Cagliero, Giovanni, 98, 117, 120,
122–25
Cagliero, John, 95–96
Calling Down Curses Ceremony,
41
Calosso, Fr., 68–69, 74
Calvinism/Calvinists, 138–39
Canuet, Lucie, 141–43
Carmelites, 145
Carmen de Patagones sisters,
128–29
Carré, Caroline de Malberg (née
Colchen): beatification of,
213; beatification proceed-
ings of, 205–6; birth of, 177;

Chaumont and, 5, 178;
Chaumont letters to, 185–87,
190–91, 202–4, 208–9;
children's deaths and, 178,
206; Daughters of St. Francis
de Sales and, founding of, 5,
176, 178, 191–94; death of,
212; everyday duties and,
177; Holy Spirit and, devotion to, 178; letter to First
Catechist-Missionaries,
210–11; letter to Mlle de
Parieu, 192–94; letters to
Chaumont, 189–90, 206–7;
marriage of, 5, 177–78, 205;
mortifications imposed on
self and, physical, 205–6;
notes recorded at 1874
retreat and, 204–5; offshoots
of Daughters of St. Francis de
Sales and, 210; in Paris, 177;
Salesian Pentecost and, 1;
spiritual intervention on
behalf of women and, 210;
spiritual merits of, 212–13;
suffering of, 189–90, 206
Carré, Paul, 5, 177, 205–6
Catholic Church: *ancien régime*
and, 25; centralization of,
17–18; clergy and, 29;
de-Christianization of
France and, 25–29, 35, 168;
Enlightenment and, 21–22;
Enlightenment changes in,
21–22; faith and, resurgence/
renewal of, 27–33; in France,
17–18, 21–24, 27–33, 137; in
long nineteenth century, 1, 3;
modernization and, response

to advent of, 29, 31; revival/
renewal of, 5, 12, 15–16, 33
Catholic Readings, 99
Caussade, Jean-Pierre de, 18–19
Celebration of the Cross
Ceremony, 40
Chablais mission, 37, 44–45
Chappuis, Mary de Sales ("Good
Mother"): announcement of
work and, 153; biography of,
140–44; birth of, 136; Brisson
and, 6, 8, 138–39; Chaumont
and, 8; communications of,
153; death of, 174; de Sales's
writings and, 136; education
of, 136; entreaties of, to
Brisson, 153–54; faith in
mission and, 154; God's call
and, 150–53; names for, 135;
notebook of, 151–52; Oblate
Retreat of 1885 and, 150;
Oblate Sisters of St. Francis
de Sales and, 7–8, 135–36,
147–48; Order of the
Visitation of Holy Mary and,
135–36; reforming efforts of,
first, 138; Salesian Pentecost
and, 6; at Second Visitation
Monastery, 149; *Spiritual
Directory and,* 159, 165; at
Troyes diocese, 152–53; the
Way and, 172–74; Yenni and,
150–51
Charitable Works of Immaculate
Mary (Œuvre de Marie-
Immaculée), 210
Charity: Chaumont and, 185–87;
Daughters of Mary
Immaculate and, 119;
Daughters of St. Francis de